STRATEGIC HUMAN RESOURCE MANAGEMENT

SECOND EDITION

MICHAEL ARMSTRONG

STRATEGIC HUMAN RESOURCE MANAGEMENT

A GUIDE TO ACTION

KOGAN
PAGE

First published in 2000
Reprinted 2001

Kogan Page Limited
120 Pentonville Road
London N1 9JN

British Library Cataloguing in Publication Data

A CIP record for this book is available from the British Library.

ISBN 0 7494 3331 0

Typeset by Jean Cussons Typesetting, Diss, Norfolk
Printed and bound in Great Britain by Clays Ltd, St Ives plc

Contents

Introduction

The concept of strategic human resource management (SHRM) has captured the imagination of practitioners, academics and consultants in this field although, as Legge (1995) and Gratton *et al* (1999) have noted, there is often a gap between the rhetoric of SHRM and the reality. High-sounding HR strategies may be articulated but they do not necessarily seem to work in practice. It is easy to decide to do something – it is harder to do it.

The aim of this book is to fill this gap – to provide a guide to action, not only in formulating HR strategies but also in the process of implementing them. However, the theory of SHRM provides a useful background against which action can be taken, and Part 1 of this book therefore examines the concepts of human resource management, strategy and strategic human resource management. But it is theory-in-use that matters, and the rest of the book is therefore a guide to action.

Part 2 explores the practicalities of formulating and implementing HR strategies, how they work and what the HR function contributes. Parts 3 and 4 examine organizational and functional strategies from a practical point of view.

Part 1

The basis of strategic human resource management

1

The concept of human resource management

The concept of human resource management (HRM) has attracted a lot of attention from academics and practitioners alike since it first emerged in the mid-1980s. The former often suspect both the practicality and morality of HRM. The latter have often absorbed some if not all of the HRM philosophy and attempted to put it into effect with varying degrees of success for various good and bad reasons. For example:

- they genuinely believe that this is the right approach to managing people;
- it accords with what is happening to organizations in the form of the need to be competitive, to add value and to be managed efficiently; or
- simply this is a new idea that has been packaged attractively by writers or consultants.

Whether or not they adopt an HRM approach, the practitioners are increasingly calling themselves HR directors, managers, consultants, etc. The term, whether you like it or not, has entered the management vocabulary as a replacement for 'personnel management'.

The concept of strategic HRM is based on the important part of the HRM philosophy that emphasizes the strategic nature of HRM and the need to integrate HR strategy with the business strategy. This notion is not as straightforward as it is sometimes presented, and this chapter covers not only what HRM *is* (or is supposed to be) but also the issues that surround it, such as its morality and practicality. The substance of HRM and these issues are dealt with under the following headings:

- definition of HRM;
- hard and soft versions of HRM;
- aims of HRM;
- the development of the HRM concept;
- characteristics of HRM;
- reservations about HRM;
- HRM and personnel management;
- reactions to HRM;
- key HRM activities;
- key requirements of HRM;
- conclusions.

HRM DEFINED

HRM can be defined as a strategic and coherent approach to the management of an organization's most valued assets – the people working there who individually and collectively contribute to the achievement of its objectives. A distinction has been made by Storey (1989) between the 'hard' and 'soft' versions of HRM.

VERSIONS OF HRM

Hard HRM

The hard approach to HRM emphasizes the quantitative, calculative and business-strategic aspects of managing the headcount resource in as 'rational' a way as for any other economic factor. It adopts a business-oriented philosophy that emphasizes the need to manage people in ways that will obtain added value from them and thus achieve competitive advantage. It regards people as human capital from which a return can be obtained by investing judicially in their development. Fombrun *et al* (1984) quite explicitly presented workers as another key resource for managers to exploit. As Guest (1999) comments:

> The drive to adopt HRM is… based on the business case of a need to respond to an external threat from increasing competition. It is a philosophy that appeals to managements who are striving to increase competitive advantage and appreciate that to do this they must invest in human resources as well as new technology.

He also commented that HRM 'reflects a long-standing capitalist tradition in which the worker is regarded as a commodity'.

The emphasis is therefore on:

- the interests of management;
- adopting a strategic approach that is closely integrated with business strategy;
- obtaining added value from people by the processes of human resource development and performance management;
- the need for a strong corporate culture expressed in mission and value statements and reinforced by communications, training and performance management processes.

Soft HRM

The soft model of HRM traces its roots to the human relations school, emphasizing communication, motivation and leadership. As described by Storey (1989) it involves 'treating employees as valued assets, a source of competitive advantage through their commitment, adaptability and high quality (of skills, performance and so on)'. It therefore views employees, in the words of Guest (1999), as means rather than objects. The soft approach to HRM emphasizes the need to gain the commitment – the 'hearts and minds' – of employees through involvement, communications and other methods of developing a high-commitment, high-trust organization. Attention is also drawn to the key role of organizational culture.

The focus is on 'mutuality' – a belief that the interests of management and employees can, indeed should, coincide. It is a therefore a unitarist approach. In the words of Gennard and Judge (1997), organizations are assumed to be 'harmonious and integrated, all employees sharing the organizational goals and working as members of one team'.

It has, however, been observed by Truss (1999) that 'even if the rhetoric of HRM is soft, the reality is often hard, with the interests of the organization prevailing over those of the individual'. Research carried out by Gratton et al (1999) found out that in the eight organizations they studied, there was a mixture of hard and soft HRM approaches. This suggested to the researchers that the distinction between hard and soft HRM was not as precise as some commentators have implied.

AIMS OF HRM

The overall purpose of HRM is to ensure that the organization is able to achieve success through people. As Ulrich and Lake (1990) have remarked: 'HRM systems can be the source of organizational capabilities that allow firms to learn and capitalize on new opportunities'.

Specifically, HRM aims to:

■ enable the organization to obtain and retain the skilled, committed and well-motivated workforce it needs;

■ enhance and develop the inherent capacities of people – their contributions, potential and employability – by providing learning and continuous development opportunities;

■ develop high-performance work systems that include 'rigorous recruitment and selection procedures, performance-contingent incentive compensation systems, and management development and training activities linked to the needs of the business' (Becker *et al*, 1997);

■ develop high-commitment management practices that recognize that employees are valued stakeholders in the organization and help to develop a climate of cooperation and mutual trust;

■ create a climate in which productive and harmonious relationships can be maintained through partnerships between management and employees;

■ develop an environment in which teamwork and flexibility can flourish;

■ help the organization to balance and adapt to the needs of its stakeholders (owners, government bodies or trustees, management, employees, customers, suppliers and the public at large);

■ ensure that people are valued and rewarded for what they do and achieve;

■ manage a diverse workforce, taking into account individual and group differences in employment needs, work style and aspirations;

■ ensure that equal opportunities are available to all;

■ adopt an ethical approach to managing employees that is based on concern for people, fairness and transparency;

■ maintain and improve the physical and mental well-being of employees.

These aims are ambitious and could be regarded as mere rhetoric. The research conducted by Gratton *et al* (1999) found that there was generally a wide gap between rhetoric and reality. Managements may start off with good intentions to do some or all of these things but the realization of them – 'theory in use' – is often very difficult. This arises because of contextual and process problems: other business priorities, short-termism, lack of support from line managers, an inadequate infrastructure of supporting processes, lack of resources, resistance to change and a climate in which employees do not trust management, whatever they say.

THE DEVELOPMENT OF THE HRM CONCEPT

The background

Some aspects of the basic philosophy of 'soft HRM' can be traced back to the writings of McGregor (1960) who, as mentioned by Truss (1999), even used the terminology 'hard' and 'soft' to characterize forms of management control. McGregor's theory X essentially describes the 'control' model of management as described by Walton (1985), while McGregor's theory Y emphasizes the importance of integrating the needs of the organization and those of the individual – the principle of mutual commitment, again expressed by Walton.

The full concept of HRM emerged in the mid-1980s against the background of the popularist writers on management who flourished in that decade. These included Pascale and Athos (1981) and Peters and Waterman (1982) who produced lists of the attributes that they claimed characterized successful companies. These popular 'school of excellence' writers may have exerted some influence on management thinking about the need for strong cultures and commitment (two features of the HRM philosophy) but, as Guest (1993) has commented, they were right enough to be dangerously wrong.

The concept of HRM has gone through three stages:

1. The initial concepts developed by American writers in the 1980s.
2. The take-up of these comments by British writers in the late 1980s and earlier 1990s who were often sceptical about the reality beyond the rhetoric and dubious about its morality.
3. The assimilation of HRM into traditional personnel management.

The two initial concepts of HRM have been christened by Boxall (1992) as the 'matching model' and the 'Harvard framework'.

The matching model of HRM

One of the first explicit statements of the HRM concept was made by the Michigan School (Fombrun *et al*, 1984). They held that HR systems and the organization structure should be managed in a way that is congruent with organizational strategy (hence the name 'matching model'). They further explained that there is a human resource cycle (an adaptation of which is illustrated in Figure 1.1) which consists of four generic processes or functions that are performed in all organizations. These are:

1. *Selection* – matching available human resources to jobs.
2. *Appraisal* – (performance management).
3. *Rewards* – 'the reward system is one of the most under-utilized and mishandled managerial tools for driving organizational performance'. It must reward short- as well as long-term achievements, bearing in mind that 'business must perform in the present to succeed in the future'.
4. *Development* – developing high-quality employees.

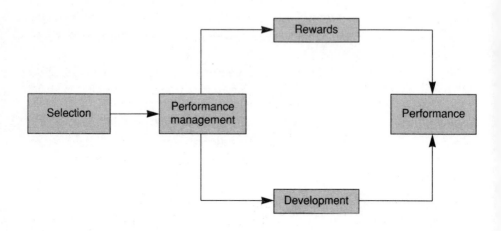

Figure 1.1 The Human Resource Cycle (adapted from Fombrun *et al*, 1984)

Fombrun *et al* suggest that the HR function should be linked to the line organization by providing the business with good HR databases, by ensuring that senior managers give HR issues as much attention as they give to other functions, and by measuring the contribution of the HR function at the strategic, managerial and operational levels.

The Harvard framework

The other founding fathers of HRM were the Harvard School of Beer *et al* (1984) who developed what Boxall (1992) calls the 'Harvard framework'. This framework is based on the belief that the problems of historical personnel management can only be solved

> when general managers develop a viewpoint of how they wish to see employees involved in and developed by the enterprise, and of what HRM policies and practices may achieve those goals. Without either a central philosophy or a strategic vision – which can be provided *only* by general managers – HRM is likely to remain a set of independent activities, each guided by its own practice tradition.

Beer and his colleagues believed that 'Today, many pressures are demanding a broader, more comprehensive and more strategic perspective with regard to the organization's human resources'. These pressures have created a need for 'a longer-term perspective in managing people and consideration of people as potential assets rather than merely a variable cost'. They were the first to underline the tenet that HRM belongs to line managers.

They also stated that: 'Human resource management involves all management decisions and action that affect the nature of the relationship between the organization and its employees – its human resources'.

The Harvard school suggested that HRM had two characteristic features: 1) line managers accept more responsibility for ensuring the alignment of competitive strategy and personnel policies; and 2) the personnel function has the mission of setting policies that govern how personnel activities are developed and implemented in ways that make them more mutually reinforcing.

The Harvard framework as modelled by Beer *et al* is shown in Figure 1.2.

According to Boxall (1992) the advantages of this model are that it:

- incorporates recognition of a range of stakeholder interests;
- recognizes the importance of 'trade-offs', either explicitly or implicitly, between the interests of owners and those of employees, as well as between various interest groups;
- widens the context of HRM to include 'employee influence', the organization of work and the associated question of supervisory style;
- acknowledges a broad range of contextual influences on management's choice of strategy, suggesting a meshing of both product-market and socio-cultural logics;
- emphasizes strategic choice – it is not driven by situational or environmental determinism.

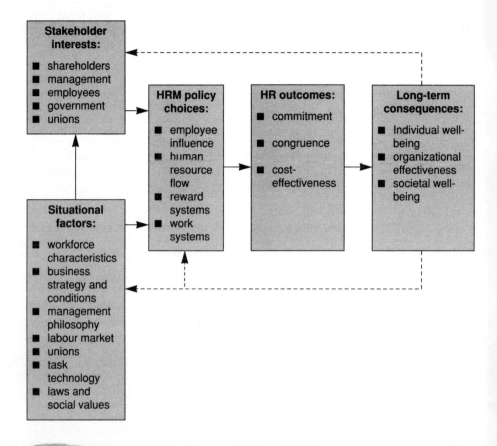

Figure 1.2 The Harvard Framework for Human Resource Management (source: Beer *et al*, 1984)

The Harvard model has exerted considerable influence over the theory and practice of HRM, particularly in its emphasis on the fact that HRM is the concern of management in general rather than the personnel function in particular.

Walton (1985), also of Harvard, expanded the concept by emphasizing the importance of commitment and mutuality:

> The new HRM model is composed of policies that promote mutuality – mutual goals, mutual influence, mutual respect, mutual rewards, mutual responsibility. The theory is that policies of mutuality will elicit commitment, which in turn will yield both better economic performance and greater human development.

This commitment model of human resource management is associated with the concept of soft HRM referred to earlier.

Developments in the concept of HRM

A number of academic commentators in the UK have developed the original American concept of HRM, as described below.

David Guest

Guest (1987, 1989a, 1989b, 1991) has taken the Harvard model and expanded it by defining four policy goals that he believes can be used as testable propositions:

1. *Strategic integration* – the ability of the organization to integrate HRM issues into its strategic plans, ensure that the various aspects of HRM cohere, and provide for line managers to incorporate an HRM perspective into their decision making.
2. *High commitment* – behavioural commitment to pursue agreed goals, and attitudinal commitment reflected in a strong identification with the enterprise.
3. *High quality* – this refers to all aspects of managerial behaviour that bear directly on the quality of goods and services provided, including the management of employees and investment in high-quality employees.
4. *Flexibility* – functional flexibility and the existence of an adaptable organization structure with the capacity to manage innovation.

Guest believes that the driving force behind HRM is:

> the pursuit of competitive advantage in the market place through provision of high-quality goods and services, through competitive pricing linked to high productivity and through the capacity swiftly to innovate and manage change in response to changes in the market place or to breakthroughs in research and development.

He considers that HRM values are *unitarist* to the extent that they assume no underlying and inevitable differences of interest between management and workers, and *individualistic* in that they emphasize the individual–organization linkage in preference to operating through group and representative systems.

Guest has also asserted that HRM has been 'talked up' and its impact has been on attitudes rather than behaviour.

Karen Legge

Legge (1989) considers that the common themes of the typical definitions of HRM are that:

> Human-resource policies should be integrated with strategic business planning and used to reinforce an appropriate (or change an inappropriate) organizational culture, that human resources are valuable and a source of competitive advantage, that they may be tapped most effectively by mutually consistent policies that promote commitment and which, as a consequence, foster a willingness in employees to act flexibly in the interests of the 'adaptive organization's' pursuit of excellence.

In 1998, Legge defined the 'hard' model of HRM as a process emphasizing 'the close integration of human resource policies with business strategy which regards employees as a resource to be managed in the same rational way as any other resource being exploited for maximum return'. In contrast, the soft version of HRM sees employees as 'valued assets and as a source of competitive advantage through their commitment, adaptability and high level of skills and performance'. She regards the three key features of HRM as first, various forms of flexibility, second, teambuilding, empowerment and involvement, and third, cultural management.

Chris Hendry and Andrew Pettigrew

Hendry and Pettigrew (1990) play down the prescriptive element of the Harvard model and extend the analytical elements. As pointed out by Boxall (1992), such an approach rightly avoids labelling HRM as a single form and advances more slowly by proceeding more analytically. Hendry and Pettigrew argue that 'better descriptions of structures and strategy-making in complex organizations, and of frameworks for understanding them, are an essential underpinning for HRM'.

Hendry and Pettigrew believe that as a movement, HRM expressed a mission, to achieve a turnaround in industry: 'HRM was thus in a real sense heavily normative from the outset: it provided a diagnosis and proposed solutions.' They also suggested that: 'What HRM did at this point was to provide a label to wrap around some of the observable changes, while providing a focus for challenging deficiencies – in attitudes, scope, coherence, and direction – of existing personnel management'.

John Purcell

Purcell (1993) thinks that 'the adoption of HRM is both a product of and a cause of a significant concentration of power in the hands of management', while the widespread use 'of the language of HRM, if not its practice, is a combination of its intuitive appeal to managers and, more importantly, a response to the turbulence of product and financial markets'. He asserts that HRM is about the rediscovery of management prerogative.

He considers that HRM policies and practices, when applied within a firm as a break from the past, are often associated with words such as commitment, competence, empowerment, flexibility, culture, performance, assessment, reward, teamwork, involvement, cooperation, harmonization, quality and learning. But 'the danger of descriptions of HRM as modern best-management practice is that they stereotype the past and idealize the future'.

Keith Sisson

Sisson (1990) suggests that there are four main features increasingly associated with HRM:

1. A stress on the integration of personnel policies both with one another and with business planning more generally.
2. The locus of responsibility for personnel management no longer resides with (or is 'relegated to') specialist managers.
3. The focus shifts from manager–trade union relations to management–employee relations, from collectivism to individualism.
4. There is a stress on commitment and the exercise of initiative, with managers now donning the role of 'enabler', 'empowerer' and 'facilitator'.

John Storey

Storey (1989) believes that HRM can be regarded as a 'set of interrelated policies with an ideological and philosophical underpinning'. He suggests four aspects that constitute the *meaningful* version of HRM:

1. a particular constellation of beliefs and assumptions;
2. a strategic thrust informing decisions about people management;
3. the central involvement of line managers;
4. reliance upon a set of 'levers' to shape the employment relationship – these are different from those used under proceduralist and joint regulative regimes typical of classical industrial relations systems.

He has written that: 'In stereotyped form it [HRM] appears capable of making good each of the main shortcomings of personnel management'. The HR function becomes recognized as a central business concern, and training and development assumes a higher profile: 'Its performance and delivery are integrated into line management: the aim shifts from merely securing compliance to the more ambitious one of winning commitment'.

The concept locates HRM policy formulation firmly at the strategic level and insists that a characteristic of HRM is its internally coherent approach.

Assimilation of HRM

Personnel managers are increasingly being called 'human resource managers'. This may often mean that it is only the name that has changed, but by a process of osmosis, much of the philosophy of HRM seems to be spreading into the day-to-day thinking and practice of personnel professionals. The debate that raged during the second phase of development referred to above no longer seems relevant to these practitioners. They simply get on with doing it; often imperfectly because of organizational constraints, but based on the observations I have made in research carried out over the last few years in over 100 British organizations, many are trying hard.

CHARACTERISTICS OF HRM

The combined contributions of the writers mentioned above and others suggest that the characteristic features of HRM as a new paradigm for managing people are that:

- it stresses the importance of gaining commitment to the organization's mission and values – it is 'commitment-oriented';
- it emphasizes the need for strategic fit – the integration of business and HR strategies;

- it is a top-management driven activity;
- the performance and delivery of HRM is a line management responsibility;
- it contributes in measurable ways to the creation and maintenance of competitive advantage, and the focus is on adding value, especially for shareholders;
- it involves the adoption of a comprehensive and coherent approach to the provision of mutually supporting employment policies and practices, ie the development of integrated HR policies and practices (configuration or bundling);
- importance is attached to strong cultures and values;
- it is performance-oriented, emphasizing the need for ever-higher levels of achievement to meet new challenges;
- employee relations are unitarist rather than pluralist, individual rather than collective;
- organizing principles are organic and decentralized with flexible roles, a focus on process (how things are done, especially across traditional organizational boundaries), and more concern for teamwork – flexibility and teambuilding are important;
- there is strong emphasis on the delivery of quality to customers and the achievement of high levels of customer satisfaction;
- rewards are differentiated according to performance, competence, contribution or skill.

Of these characteristics, perhaps the most important ones are the emphasis of HRM on gaining commitment and strategic fit.

RESERVATIONS ABOUT HRM

On the face of it, HRM has much to offer, at least to management. But strong reservations have been expressed about it by a number of academics and by a practitioner, Alan Fowler (1987). These reservations can be summed up as follows:

- HRM does not pass muster either as a reputable theory or as an alternative and better form of personnel management.
- HRM is, in Guest's (1991) words, an 'optimistic but ambiguous concept'; it is all hype and hope.

- Even if HRM does exist as a distinct process, which many doubt, it is full of contradictions, manipulative and, according to the Cardiff school (Blyton and Turnbull, 1992), downright pernicious.
- The 'prized goals' of HRM remain unproven at best, and unfulfilled at worst (Mabey *et al*, 1998).

HRM as a theory

Noon (1992) has commented that HRM has serious deficiencies as a theory:

> It is built with concepts and propositions, but the associated variables and hypotheses are not made explicit. It is too comprehensive.... If HRM is labelled a 'theory' it raises expectations about its ability to describe and predict.

HRM is simplistic

As Fowler (1987) has written:

> The HRM message to top management tends to be beguilingly simple. Don't bother too much about the content or techniques of personnel management, it says. Just manage the context. Get out from behind your desk, bypass the hierarchy, and go and talk to people. That way you will unlock an enormous potential for improved performance.

HRM as rhetoric

The HRM rhetoric presents it as an all-or-nothing process that is ideal for all organizations, despite the evidence that different business environments require different approaches. This produces the gap between rhetoric and reality referred to (frequently) by Gratton *et al* (1999).

HRM is over-ambitious and impractical

HRM can be accused of promising more than it can deliver. As Mabey *et al* (1998) comment, 'the heralded outcomes [of HRM] are almost without exception unrealistically high'. They imply that management has either been conned by consultants offering quick-fix solutions or is indulging in rhetoric influenced by 'extra-organizational values' such as excellence, flexibility, quality and customer focus.

To put the concept of HRM into practice involves strategic integration, developing a coherent and consistent set of employment policies, and gaining commitment. This requires high levels of determination and competence at all levels of management and a strong and effective HR function staffed by business-oriented people. It may be difficult to meet these criteria, especially when the proposed HRM culture conflicts with the established corporate culture and traditional managerial attitudes and behaviour.

Some commentators claim that the development of integrated HR strategies, a central feature of HRM, is difficult if not impossible in companies that lack any real sense of strategic direction. Business strategies, they say, where they *are* formulated, tend to be dominated by product-market imperatives, leading to product and systems developments. To support these, priority is given, understandably enough, to obtaining financial resources and maintaining a sound financial base. Human resource considerations often come off a poor second.

HRM and industrial relations

As Fowler (1987) has stated:

> At the heart of the concept is the complete identification of employees with the aims and values of the business – employee involvement but on the company's terms. Power in the HRM system remains very firmly in the hands of the employer. Is it really possible to claim full mutuality when at the end of the day the employer can decide unilaterally to close the company or sell it to someone else?

Contradictions in HRM

Legge (1989) believes that the concept of HRM contains the following internal contradictions:

- the complementarity and consistency of 'mutuality' policies designed to generate commitment, flexibility, quality, etc;
- problems over commitment: as Guest (1987) asked, 'commitment to what?';
- HRM appears torn between preaching the virtues of individualism (concentration on the individual) and collectivism (teamwork, etc);
- there is a potential tension between the development of a strong corporate culture and employees' ability to respond flexibly and adaptively.

The morality of HRM

In spite of all their protestations to the contrary, the advocates of HRM could be seen to be introducing alternative and more insidious forms of 'control by compliance' when they emphasize the need for employees to be committed to do what the organization wants them to do. As Legge (1989) pointed out:

> In its emphasis on 'strong culture', in theory HRM is able to achieve a cohesive workforce, but without the attendant dilemma of creating potentially dysfunctional solidarity. For a 'strong culture' is aimed at uniting employees through a shared set of managerially sanctioned values ('quality', 'service', 'innovation', etc) that assume an identification of employee and employer interests. Such co-optation – through cultural management of course – reinforces the intention that autonomy will be exercised 'responsibly', ie in management's interests.

Legge (1998) summed up her reservations about the morality of HRM as follows:

> Sadly, in a world of intensified competition and scarce resources, it seems inevitable that, as employees are used as means to an end, there will be some who will lose out. They may even be in the majority. For these people, the soft version of HRM may be an irrelevancy, while the hard version is likely to be an uncomfortable experience.

She contends that managements only go in for HRM out of self-interest, regarding employees as a means to an end.

HRM is accused by many academics of being manipulative. As Willmott (1993) remarks, HRM operates as a form of insidious control. It preaches mutuality but the reality is that behind the rhetoric it exploits workers. It is, they say, a wolf in sheep's clothing (Keenoy, 1990a). They note that chief executives with a mission for HRM tend to adapt the principle of 'what is good for General Motors is good for America' to that of 'what is good for the business must be good for everyone in it'. In other words, like an apple a day, HRM is good for you. Such executives could be right, but not always, and the forces of internal persuasion and propaganda may have to be deployed to get people to accept values with which they may not be in accord and which in any case may be against their interests.

Essentially, the accusation is that HRM treats employees as means to an end. However, it could be argued that if organizations exist to achieve ends, which they clearly do, and if those ends can only be achieved through people, which is clearly the case, the concern of managements for commitment and performance from those people is not unnatural and is not solely attributable to HRM – it existed in the good old days of personnel management before HRM was invented. What matters is *how* managements treat people as ends and *what* managements provide in return. And the philosophy of HRM can provide positive guidance on approaches to managing people in, for example, the concept of mutual commitment.

Inconsistencies in the comments on HRM

As Guest (1999) has suggested, there are two contradictory concerns about HRM. The first, as formulated by Legge (1995, 1998) is that while management rhetoric may express concern for workers, the reality is harsher. Keenoy (1997) complains that: 'The real puzzle about HRMism is how, in the face of such apparently overwhelming critical "refutation", it has secured such influence and institutional presence'.

Other writers, however, simply claim that HRM does not work. Scott (1994), for example, finds that both management and workers are captives of their history and find it very difficult to let go of their traditional adversarial orientations.

But these contentions are contradictory. As Guest (1989b) remarks:

> It is difficult to treat HRM as a major threat (though what it is a threat to is not always made explicit) deserving of serious critical analysis while at the same time claiming that it is not practised or is ineffective.

HRM AND PERSONNEL MANAGEMENT

Guest (1989b) asks: 'HRM and personnel management. Can you tell the difference?' Armstrong (1987) provides an answer (written before the question was put):

> HRM is regarded by some personnel managers as just a set of initials or old wine in new bottles. It could indeed be no more and no less than another name for personnel management, but as usually perceived, at least it has the virtue of emphasising treating people as a key resource, the management of which is the direct concern of top management as part of the strategic planning processes of the enterprise. Although there is nothing new in the idea, insufficient attention has been paid to it in many organizations. The new bottle or label can help to overcome that deficiency.

Torrington (1989) argued that: 'Personnel management has grown through assimilating a number of additional emphases to produce an ever-richer combination of expertise. HRM is no revolution but a further dimension to a multi-faceted role'.

Similarities

It can be argued that the similarities between personnel management and HRM are as follows:

■ Personnel management strategies, like HRM strategies, flow from the business strategy.
■ Personnel management, like HRM, recognizes that line managers are responsible for managing people. The personnel function provides the necessary advice and support services to enable managers to carry out their responsibilities.
■ The values of personnel management and at least the 'soft' version of HRM are identical with regard to 'respect for the individual', balancing organizational and individual needs, and developing people to achieve their maximum level of competence both for their own satisfaction and to facilitate the achievement of organizational objectives.
■ Both personnel management and HRM recognize that one of their most essential processes is that of matching people to ever-changing organizational requirements – placing and developing the right people in and for the right jobs.
■ The same range of selection, competence analysis, performance management, training, management development and reward management techniques are used both in HRM and personnel management.
■ Personnel management, like the 'soft' version of HRM, attaches importance to the processes of communication and participation within an employee relations system.

Differences

The differences between personnel management and HRM can be seen as a matter of emphasis and approach rather than one of substance. Or, as Hendry and Pettigrew (1990) put it, HRM can be perceived as a 'perspective on personnel management and not personnel management itself.'

From her review of the literature, Legge (1989) has identified three features that seem to distinguish HRM and personnel management:

1. Personnel management is an activity aimed primarily at non-managers whereas HRM is less clearly focused but is certainly more concerned with managerial staff.
2. HRM is much more of an integrated line management activity whereas personnel management seeks to influence line management.
3. HRM emphasizes the importance of senior management being involved in the management of culture whereas personnel management has always been rather suspicious of organization development and related unitarist, social-psychologically-oriented ideas.

The strategic nature of HRM is another difference commented on by a number of people who, in effect, dismiss the idea that traditional personnel management was ever really involved in the strategic areas of business. Hendry and Pettigrew (1990), for example, believe that the strategic character of HRM is distinctive.

Perhaps the most significant difference is that the concept of HRM is based on a management and business-oriented philosophy. It is claimed to be a central, senior management-driven strategic activity that is developed, owned and delivered by management as a whole to promote the interests of the organization that they serve. It purports to be an holistic approach concerned with the total interests of the organization – the interests of the members of the organization are recognized but subordinated to those of the enterprise. Hence the importance attached to strategic integration and strong cultures, which flow from top management's vision and leadership, and which require people who will be committed to the strategy, who will be adaptable to change, and who will fit the culture. By implication, as Guest (1991) says: 'HRM is too important to be left to personnel managers'.

HRM could be described as an approach to rather than as an alternative to traditional personnel management. When comparing HRM and personnel management, more similarities emerge than differences. However, concepts such as strategic integration, culture management, commitment, total quality, and investing in human capital, together with a unitary philosophy (the interests of management and employees coincide), are essential parts of the HRM model. And this model fits the way in which organizations have to do business and manage their resources in the environments in which they now exist. This is why, in spite of the reservations expressed about the concept by academics, the term HR is increasingly being used in businesses as an alternative to personnel management. This is because more and more people feel that it is in tune with the realities of organizational life.

REACTIONS TO HRM

Much of the hostility to HRM expressed by a number of academics centres on the belief that it is hostile to the interests of workers, ie that it is managerialist. Research conducted by Guest and Conway (1997) covering a stratified random sample of 1000 workers established that a notably high level of HRM was found to be in place. This contradicts the view that management has tended to 'talk up' the adoption of HRM practices. The HRM characteristics covered by the survey included the opportunity to express grievances and raise personal concerns on such matters as opportunities for training and development, communications about business issues, single status, effective systems for dealing with bullying and harassment at work, making jobs interesting and varied, promotion from within, involvement programmes, no compulsory redundancies, performance-related pay, profit sharing and the use of attitude surveys.

The reports of workers on outcomes showed that a higher number of HR practices was associated with higher ratings of fairness, trust and management's delivery of their promises. Those experiencing more HR activities also felt more secure in and more satisfied with their jobs. Motivation was significantly higher for those working in organizations where more HR practices were in place. In summary, as commented by Guest (1999), it appears that workers like their experience of HRM. These findings appear to contradict the 'radical critique' view produced by academics such as Mabey *et al* (1998) that HRM has been ineffectual, pernicious (ie managerialist) or both. Some of those who adopt this stance tend to dismiss favourable reports from workers about HRM because they have, in effect, been brainwashed by management. But there is no evidence to support this view.

However, Gratton *et al* (1999) are convinced on the basis of their research that there is:

> a disjunction between rhetoric and reality in the area of human resource management between HRM theory and HRM practice, between what the HR function says it is doing and that practice as perceived by employees, and between what senior management believes to be the role of the HR function, and the role it actually plays.

In their conclusions they refer to the 'hyperbole and rhetoric of human resource management'. The incessant use of the word 'rhetoric' by these and other academics suggests that they have a deeply held and cynical belief that managements never mean what they say, or if they do mean it, don't do anything about it.

KEY HRM ACTIVITIES

The key activities of HRM carried out by both line managers and HR professionals are as follows.

Organization

Organization design – developing an organization that caters for all the activities required, groups them together in a way that encourages integration and cooperation, operates flexibly in response to change, and provides for effective communication and decision making.

Job design – deciding on the content of jobs, their duties and responsibilities, and the relationships that exist between job holders and other people in the organization.

Organizational development – stimulating, planning and implementing programmes designed to improve the effectiveness with which the organization functions and adapts to change.

The employment relationship

Improving the quality of the employment relationship by creating a climate of trust, developing a more positive psychological contract.

Resourcing

Human resource planning – assessing future people requirements in terms both of numbers and of levels of skill and competence and formulating and implementing plans to meet those requirements.

Recruitment and selection – obtaining the number and type of people the organization needs.

Performance management

Getting better results from the organization, teams and individuals by measuring and managing performance within agreed frameworks of objectives and competence requirements; assessing and improving performance; identifying and satisfying learning and development needs.

Human resource development

Organizational and individual learning – systematically developing the business as a learning organization; providing employees with learning opportunities to develop their capabilities, provide for career growth and enhance employability.

Management development – providing learning and development opportunities that will increase the capacity of managers to make a significant contribution to achieving organizational goals.

Career management – planning and developing the careers of people with potential.

Reward management

Pay systems – developing pay structures and systems that are equitable, fair and transparent

Paying for contribution – relating rewards to effort, results, competence and skill.

Non-financial rewards – providing employees with non-financial rewards such as recognition, increased responsibility and the opportunity to achieve and grow.

Employee relations

Industrial relations – managing and maintaining formal and informal relationships with trade unions and their members.

Employee involvement and participation – giving them a voice, sharing information with employees and consulting them on matters of mutual interest.

Communications – creating and transmitting information of interest to employees.

KEY REQUIREMENTS OF HRM

These activities must emphasize and be aligned to the following key requirements:

- supporting the achievement of organizational strategies and goals;
- ensuring that added value is obtained from all HR activities;
- underpinning cultural change programmes;

■ releasing and developing the inherent capacities of people;
■ developing processes that maximize people's contributions;
■ enabling those with potential to obtain an organizational and management perspective early in their careers;
■ embedding continuous learning and development for everyone throughout the enterprise as an accepted feature of working life;
■ designing, implementing and managing systems to ensure access to relevant experience;
■ providing specific skills training;
■ recruiting, developing and training people with the right combination of specialist know-how and the broader skills and attitudes needed to match the changing demands of the business;
■ managing an increasingly diverse workforce with different career patterns, career aspirations and loyalties;
■ managing employee (and wider workforce) relations, collective and individual, and retaining commitment through times of change;
■ designing, implementing and managing reward and performance management systems that align and motivate people, individually and in teams, towards business priorities and results;
■ maintaining and improving the physical and mental well-being of the workforce by providing appropriate working conditions and health and safety initiatives.

CONCLUSIONS

It is probably true that there is no such thing as a universal model of HRM. It is certainly true that when comparing the concepts of HRM and personnel management all that happens is the production of distinctions without differences. As Guest (1989a) has written: 'The HRM model is just one among a variety of forms of personnel management, and for some companies it may not be the most viable'.

It is equally true that HRM is something that managements tend to believe in and it could therefore be regarded as simply a notion of how people can best be managed *in the interests of the organization*. If this is the case, then concepts such as strategic integration, culture management, commitment and total quality management, and a unitary philosophy (the interests of management and employees coincide) fit in well with the HRM model. Certainly, these notions have entered into the vocabulary of managers and support the idea that something which could be broadly described as 'strategic HRM' (although they may not use this phrase) will help them to improve organizational performance in the longer term, although their expectations of what HRM can achieve by the use of various simplistic mechanisms, such as performance-related pay, may be unrealistic, as Mabey *et al* (1998) and Gratton *et al* (1999) have demonstrated.

There can be no doubt that there is something, whether you like it or not, which can be described as an HRM philosophy. But it can be put into practice by people who are described as 'personnel directors' just as well as those who have been re-titled 'human resource directors'. HRM can be seen as an approach to managing people which is shared between line managers and personnel specialists and which, among other things, emphasizes the strategic nature of personnel management as a process that exists to enable the organization to achieve its objectives and, importantly, provide for the needs of its stakeholders.

Perhaps one of the most important defining characteristics of HRM is its strategic focus. This takes place within the framework of the business strategy as described in Chapter 2. The nature of strategic HRM is examined in Chapter 3.

2

The concept of strategy

Strategy was originally a military term, defined in the *Oxford English Dictionary* as: 'The art of a commander-in-chief; the art of projecting and directing the larger military movements and operations of a campaign'. This may not seem to have much relevance to strategy in business, public sector or voluntary organizations, but at least it conveys the message that strategy is an art and that the ultimate responsibility for it lies with the head of the organization.

It was Drucker who as long ago as 1955 pointed out in *The Practice of Management* the importance of strategic decisions, which he defined as 'all decisions on business objectives and on the means to reach them'. However, the concept of business strategy was not fully developed until three outstanding pioneers, Kenneth Andrews, Igor Ansoff and Alfred Chandler Jr made their mark. They were followed by Michael Porter, Henry Mintzberg, Hamel and Prahalad and many more who further developed the concepts and adapted them to contemporary conditions.

STRATEGY DEFINED

Strategy has been defined in various ways by the many writers on the subject, for example:

Strategy is the determination of the basic long-term goals and objectives of an enterprise, and the adoption of courses of action and the allocation of resources necessary for carrying out these goals. (Chandler, 1962)

Strategy is a set of fundamental or critical choices about the ends and means of a business. (Child, 1972)

Strategy is concerned with the long-term direction and scope of an organization. It is also crucially concerned with how the organization positions itself with regard to the environment and in particular to its competitors... It is concerned with establishing competitive advantage, ideally sustainable over time, not by technical manoeuvring, but by taking an overall long-term perspective. (Faulkner and Johnson, 1992)

The direction and scope of an organization over the longer term ideally, which matches its resources to its changing environment, and in particular, to its markets, customers and clients to meet stakeholder expectations. (Johnson and Scholes,1993)

Business strategy is concerned with the match between the internal capabilities of the company and its external environment. (Kay, 1999)

A strategy, whether it is an HR strategy or any other kind of management strategy, must have two key elements: there must be strategic objectives (ie things the strategy is supposed to achieve), and there must be a plan of action (ie the means by which it is proposed that the objectives will be met). (Richardson and Thompson, 1999)

To sum up, strategy may be defined as a statement of what the organization wants to become, where it wants to go and, broadly, how it means to get there. In its crudest form, strategy in a commercial enterprise answers the questions: 'What business are we in?' and, 'How are we going to make money out of it?'. Strategy determines the direction in which the enterprise is going in relation to its environment in order to achieve sustainable competitive advantage. The emphasis is on focused actions that differentiate the firm from its competitors (Purcell, 1999). It is a declaration of intent that defines means to achieve ends, and is concerned with the long-term allocation of significant company resources and with matching those resources and capabilities to the external environment. Strategy is a perspective on the way in which critical issues or success factors can be addressed, and strategic decisions aim to make a major and long-term impact on the behaviour and success of the organization.

KEY CONCEPTS OF STRATEGY

The three key concepts of strategy are competitive advantage, distinctive capabilities and strategic fit.

Competitive advantage

The concept of competitive advantage was formulated by Porter (1985). Competitive advantage, Porter asserts, arises out of a firm creating value for its customers. To achieve it, firms select markets in which they can excel and present a moving target to their competitors by continually improving their position.

Porter emphasized the importance of *differentiation*, which consists of offering a product or service 'that is perceived industry-wide as being unique', and *focus* – serving a particular buyer group or product market 'more effectively or efficiently than competitors who compete more broadly'.

He then developed his well-known framework of three generic strategies that organizations can use to gain competitive advantage. These are:

1. *innovation* – being the unique producer;
2. *quality* – delivering high-quality goods and services to customers;
3. *cost leadership* – the planned result of policies aimed at 'managing away expense'.

A distinction has been made by Barney (1991) between the competitive advantage that a firm presently enjoys but others will be able to copy, and sustained competitive advantage, which competitors cannot imitate. This leads to the important concept of distinctive capabilities.

Distinctive capabilities

As Kay (1999) comments: 'The opportunities for companies to sustain... competitive advantage is determined by their capabilities'. A distinctive capability or competence can be described as an important feature that in Quinn's (1980) phrase, 'confers superiority on the organization'. Kay extends this definition by emphasizing that there is a difference between distinctive capabilities and reproducible capabilities. Distinctive capabilities are those characteristics that cannot be replicated by competitors, or can only be imitated with great difficulty. Reproducible capabilities can be bought or created by any company with reasonable management skills, diligence and financial resources. Most technical capabilities are reproducible.

Prahalad and Hamel (1990) argue that competitive advantage stems in the long term from a firm building 'core competences' which are superior to its rivals and from learning faster and applying its learning more effectively than its competitors. The latter point provides the rationale for the concept of 'knowledge management', discussed in Chapter 14.

Distinctive capabilities, or core competences, describe what the organization is specially or uniquely capable of doing. They are what the company does particularly well in comparison with its competitors. Key capabilities can exist in such areas as technology, innovation, marketing, delivering quality, and making good use of human and financial resources. If a company is aware of what its distinctive capabilities are, it can concentrate on using and developing them without diverting effort into less rewarding activities.

Four criteria have been proposed by Barney (1991) for deciding whether a resource can be regarded as a distinctive capability or competency:

1. Value creation for the customer.
2. Rarity compared to the competition.
3. Non-imitability.
4. Non-substitutability.

The concept of distinctive capability forms the foundation of the resource-based approach to strategy as described later in this chapter.

Strategic fit

The concept of strategic fit states that to maximize competitive advantage a firm must match its capabilities and resources to the opportunities available in the external environment. As Hofer and Schendel (1986) conclude:

> A critical aspect of top management's work today involves matching organizational competences (internal resources and skills) with the opportunities and risks created by environmental change in ways that will be both effective and efficient over the time such resources will be deployed.

THE FUNDAMENTALS OF STRATEGY

Fundamentally, strategy is about defining intentions (*strategic intent*) and allocating or matching resources to opportunities (*resource-based strategy*) thus

achieving *strategic fit* between them. The effective development and implementation of strategy depends on the *strategic capability* of the organization, which
will include the ability not only to formulate strategic goals but also to develop
and implement strategic plans through the process of *strategic management.*

Strategic intent

In its simplest form, strategy could be described as an expression of the intentions of the organization – what it means to do and how; as Wickens (1987) put
it, the business means to 'get from here to there'. As defined by Hamel and
Prahalad (1989), strategic intent refers to the expression of the leadership position the organization wants to attain and establishes a clear criterion on how
progress towards its achievement will be measured. Strategic intent could be a
very broad statement of vision or mission and/or it could more specifically
spell out the goals and objectives to be attained over the longer term.

The strategic intent sequence has been defined by Miller and Dess (1996) as:

1. a broad *vision* of what the organization should be;
2. the organization's *mission*;
3. specific *goals* which are operationalized as:
4. strategic *objectives.*

Resource-based strategy

The resource-based view of strategy is that the strategic capability of a firm
depends on its resource capability. Resource-based strategy theorists such as
Barney (1991) argue that sustained competitive advantage stems from the
acquisition and effective use of bundles of distinctive resources that competitors cannot imitate.

As Boxall (1996) comments: 'Competitive success does not come simply
from making choices in the present; it stems from building up distinctive capabilities over significant periods of time'. Teece *et al* (1997) define 'dynamic
capabilities' as 'the capacity of a firm to renew, augment and adapt its core
competencies over time'.

Strategic capability

Strategic capability is a concept that refers to the ability of an organization to
develop and implement strategies that will achieve sustained competitive

advantage. It is therefore about the capacity to select the most appropriate vision, to define realistic intentions, to match resources to opportunities and to prepare and implement strategic plans.

Strategic capability has been defined by Harrison (1997) as:

> A capability that is based on a profound understanding of the competitive environment, the resource base and potential of the organization, and the values that engender commitment from stakeholders to organizational goals. It provides the strategic vision, the rich and sustained knowledge development, the integrity of common purpose, and the durable coherent direction and scope to the activities of the firm that are needed to secure long-term survival and advancement.

THE FORMULATION OF STRATEGY

The formulation of corporate strategy can be defined as a process for developing a sense of direction. It has often been described as a logical, step-by-step affair, the outcome of which is a formal written statement that provides a definitive guide to the organization's long-term intentions. Many people still believe and act as if this were the case, but it is a misrepresentation of reality. This is not to dismiss completely the ideal of adopting a systematic approach as described below – it has its uses as a means of providing an analytical framework for strategic decision-making and a reference point for monitoring the implementation of strategy. But in practice, and for reasons also explained below, the formulation of strategy can never be as rational and linear a process as some writers describe it or as some managers attempt to make it.

The systematic approach to formulating strategy

In theory, the process of formulating strategy consists of the following steps:

1. Define the mission.
2. Set objectives.
3. Conduct internal and external environmental scans to assess internal strengths and weaknesses and external opportunities and threats (a SWOT analysis).
4. Analyse existing strategies to determine their relevance in the light of the internal and external appraisal. This may include gap analysis, which will establish the extent to which environmental factors might lead to gaps between what could be achieved if no changes were made

and what needs to be achieved. The analysis would also cover resource capability, answering the question: 'Have we sufficient human or financial resources available now, or which can readily be made available in the future, to enable us to achieve our objectives?'.

5. Define in the light of this analysis the distinctive capabilities of the organization.
6. Define the key strategic issues emerging from the previous analysis. These will be concerned with such matters as product-market scope, enhancing shareholder value and resource capability.
7. Determine corporate and functional strategies for achieving goals and competitive advantage, taking into account the key strategic issues. These may include business strategies for growth or diversification, or broad generic strategies for innovation, quality or cost leadership; or they could take the form of specific corporate/functional strategies concerned with product-market scope, technological development or human resource development.
8. Prepare integrated strategic plans for implementing strategies.
9. Implement the strategies.
10. Monitor implementation and revise existing strategies or develop new strategies as necessary.

This model of the process of strategy formulation should allow scope for iteration and feedback, and the activities incorporated in the model are all appropriate in any process of strategy formulation. But the model is essentially linear and deterministic – each step logically follows the earlier one and is conditioned entirely by the preceding sequence of events; and this is not what happens in real life.

The reality of strategy formulation

It has been said that 'strategy is everything not well defined or understood' (Bower, 1982). This may be going too far, but in reality, strategy formulation can best be described as 'problem solving in unstructured situations' (Digman, 1990) and strategies will always be formed under conditions of partial ignorance.

The difficulty is that strategies are often based on the questionable assumption that the future will resemble the past. Some years ago, Heller (1972) had a go at the cult of long-range planning: 'What goes wrong,' he wrote, 'is that sensible anticipation gets converted into foolish numbers: and their validity always hinges on large loose assumptions'.

More recently, Faulkner and Johnson (1992) have said of long-term planning that it:

> was inclined to take a definitive view of the future, and to extrapolate trend lines for the key business variables in order to arrive at this view. Economic turbulence was insufficiently considered, and the reality that much strategy is formulated and implemented in the act of managing the enterprise was ignored. Precise forecasts ending with derived financials were constructed, the only weakness of which was that the future almost invariably turned out differently.

Strategy formulation is not necessarily a rational and continuous process, as was pointed out by Mintzberg (1987). He believes that, rather than being consciously and systematically developed, strategy reorientation happens in what he calls brief 'quantum loops'. A strategy, according to Mintzberg, can be deliberate – it can realize the intentions of senior management, for example to attack and conquer a new market, but this is not always the case. In theory, he says, strategy is a systematic process: first we think, then we act; we formulate, then we implement. But we also 'act in order to think'. In practice, 'a realized strategy can emerge in response to an evolving situation' and the strategic planner is often 'a pattern organizer, a learner if you like, who manages a process in which strategies and visions can emerge as well as be deliberately conceived'.

Mintzberg was even more scathing about the weaknesses of strategic planning in his 1994 article in the *Harvard Business Review* on 'The rise and fall of strategic planning'. He contends that 'the failure of systematic planning is the failure of systems to do better than, or nearly as well as, human beings'. He went on to say that:

> Far from providing strategies, planning could not proceed without their prior existence... real strategists get their hands dirty digging for ideas, and real strategies are built from the nuggets they discover. ...sometimes strategies must be left as broad visions, not precisely articulated, to adapt to a changing environment.

Other writers have joined in this chorus of disapproval, for example:

> Business strategy, far from being a straightforward, rational phenomenon, is in fact interpreted by managers according to their own frame of reference, their particular motivations and information. (Pettigrew and Whipp, 1991)

> Although excellent for some purposes, the formal planning approach emphasizes 'measurable quantitative forces' at the expense of the 'qualitative, organizational and power-behavioural factors that so often determine strategic success'... Large

organizations typically construct their strategies with processes which are 'frag-mented, evolutionary, and largely intuitive'. (Quinn, 1980)

The most effective decision-makers are usually creative, intuitive people 'employing an adaptive, flexible process'. Moreover, since most strategic decisions are event-driven rather than pre-programmed, they are unplanned. (Digman, 1990)

Goold and Campbell (1986) also emphasize the variety and ambiguity of influ-ences that shape strategy:

Informed understandings work alongside more formal processes and analyses. The headquarters agenda becomes entwined with the business unit agenda, and both are interpreted in the light of personal interests. The sequence of events from deci-sion to action can often be reversed, so that 'decisions' get made retrospectively to justify actions that have already taken place.

Mintzberg (1978, 1987, 1994) summarizes the non-deterministic view of strategy admirably. He perceives strategy as a 'pattern in a stream of activities' and highlights the importance of the interactive process between key players. He has emphasized the concept of 'emergent strategies', a key aspect of which is the production of something that is new to the organization, even if this is not developed as logically as the traditional corporate planners believed to be appropriate.

Kay (1999) also refers to the evolutionary nature of strategy. He comments that there is often little 'intentionality' in firms and that it was frequently the market rather than the visionary executive which chose the strategic match that was most effective. Quinn (1980) has produced the concept of 'logical incrementalism' which suggests that strategy evolves in several steps rather than being conceived as a whole.

A fourfold typology of strategy has been produced by Whittington (1993):

1. *Classical* – strategy formulation as a rational process of deliberate calcu-lation. The process of strategy formulation is seen as being separate from the process of implementation.
2. *Evolutionary* – strategy formulation as an evolutionary process that is a product of market forces in which the most efficient and productive organizations win through.
3. *Processual* – strategy formulation as an incremental process that evolves through discussion and disagreement. It may be impossible to specify what the strategy is until after the event.

4. *Systemic* – strategy is shaped by the social system in which it is embedded. Choices are constrained by the cultural and institutional interests of a broader society rather than the limitations of those attempting to formulate corporate strategy.

STRATEGIC MANAGEMENT

The concepts of strategy and its main characteristics are operationalized by strategic management. This can be regarded as a continuing process that in theory consists of a sequence of activities: strategy formulation, strategic planning, implementation, review, and updating, but in practice, as noted above, it is seldom applied so logically. Strategic management has been defined as follows:

> Strategic management is the set of decisions and actions resulting in the formulation and implementation of strategies designed to achieve the objectives of an organization. (Pearce and Robinson, 1988)

> Strategic management is concerned with policy decisions affecting the entire organization, the overall objective being to position the organization to deal effectively with its environment. (Gunnigle and Moore, 1994)

Strategic management means that managers are looking ahead at what they need to achieve in the middle or relatively distant future. Although, as Fombrun *et al* (1984) put it, they are aware of the fact that businesses, like managers, must perform well in the present to succeed in the future, they are concerned with the broader issues they are facing and the general directions in which they must go to deal with these issues and achieve longer-term objectives. They do not take a narrow or restricted view.

Strategic management deals with both ends and means. As an end, it describes a vision of what something will look like in a few years' time. As a means, it shows how it is expected that the vision will be realized. Strategic management is therefore visionary management, concerned with creating and conceptualizing ideas of where the organization should be going. But it is also empirical management that decides how in practice it is going to get there.

The focus is on identifying the organization's mission and strategies, but attention is also given to the resource base required to make it succeed. It is always necessary to remember that strategy is the means to create value. Managers who think strategically will have a broad and long-term view of where they are going. But they will also be aware that they are responsible firstly, for planning how to allocate resources to opportunities that contribute to the implementation of strategy, and secondly, for managing these opportunities in ways which will significantly add value to the results achieved by the firm.

Burns (1992), cited by Walton (1999), described strategic management as being primarily concerned with:

- the full scope of an organization's activities, including corporate objectives and organizational boundaries;
- matching the activities of an organization to the environment in which it operates;
- ensuring that the internal structures, practices and procedures enable the organization to achieve its objectives;
- matching the activities of an organization to its resource capability, assessing the extent to which sufficient resources can be provided to take advantage of opportunities or to avoid threats in the organization's environment;
- the acquisition, divestment and reallocation of resources;
- translating the complex and dynamic set of external and internal variables that an organization faces, into a structured set of clear future objectives that can then be implemented on a day-to-day basis.

Kanter (1984) sees the purpose of strategic management as being to 'elicit the present actions for the future' and become 'action vehicles – integrating and institutionalizing mechanisms for change'. She goes on to say:

> Strong leaders articulate direction and save the organization from change by drift... They see a vision of the future that allows them to see more clearly what steps to take, building on present capacities and strengths.

But beyond this rhetoric lies the reality of managers attempting to behave strategically in conditions of uncertainty, change and turbulence, even chaos. The strategic management approach is as difficult as it is desirable, and this has to be borne in mind when consideration is given to the concept of strategic HRM as described in Chapter 3.

3

The concept of strategic HRM

The concept of strategic HRM is discussed in this chapter under the following headings:

- definition;
- the meaning of strategic HRM;
- aims of strategic HRM;
- models of strategic HRM – the business-oriented and strategic fit models;
- strategic HRM and HR strategies;
- strategic fit;
- strategic fit and flexibility.

STRATEGIC HRM DEFINED

Strategic human resource management has been defined as:

All those activities affecting the behaviour of individuals in their efforts to formulate and implement the strategic needs of the business. (Schuler, 1992)

The pattern of planned human resource deployments and activities intended to
enable the firm to achieve its goals. (Wright and McMahan, 1992)

Strategic HRM is an approach to making decisions on the intentions and plans
of the organization concerning the employment relationship and its recruitment, training, development, performance management, reward, and employee relations policies and practices. It is an essential component of the
organization's corporate or business strategy.

Strategic HRM is concerned with the relationship between human resource
management and strategic management in the firm. Strategic HRM refers to
the overall direction the organization wishes to pursue in achieving its objectives through people. It is argued that, because human capital is a major source
of competitive advantage, and in the last analysis it is people who implement
the strategic plan, top management must take these key considerations fully
into account in developing corporate strategies. Strategic HRM is an integral
part of those strategies.

Strategic HRM addresses broad organizational concerns relating to changes
in structure and culture, organizational effectiveness and performance,
matching resources to future requirements, the development of distinctive
capabilities, and the management of change. It is concerned with both human
capital requirements and the development of process capabilities, ie the ability
to get things done effectively. Overall, it will consider any major people issues
that affect or are affected by the strategic plan of the organization. As Boxall
(1996) remarks: 'The critical concerns of HRM such as choice of executive leadership and formation of positive patterns of labour relations, are strategic in
any firm'.

THE MEANING OF STRATEGIC HRM

According to Hendry and Pettigrew (1986), strategic HRM has four meanings:

1. The use of planning.
2. A coherent approach to the design and management of personnel
   systems based on an employment policy and manpower strategy and
   often underpinned by a 'philosophy'.
3. Matching HRM activities and policies to some explicit business strategy.
4. Seeing the people of the organization as a 'strategic resource' for the
   achievement of 'competitive advantage'.

The main features of strategic HRM as defined by Dyer and Holder (1988) are:

- *Organizational level* – because strategies involve decisions about key goals, major policies and the allocation of resources, they tend to be formulated at the top.
- *Focus* – strategies are business-driven and focus on organizational effectiveness; thus in this perspective people are viewed primarily as resources to be managed toward the achievement of strategic business goals.
- *Framework* – strategies by their very nature provide unifying frameworks that are at once broad, contingency-based and integrative. They incorporate a full complement of HR goals and activities designed specifically to fit extant environments and to be mutually reinforcing or synergistic.
- *Roles* – as the foregoing suggests, strategy-making generally is the responsibility of line managers, with personnel playing a supportive role.

Origins of the concept

The concept of strategic HRM was first formulated by Fombrun *et al* (1984) who wrote that three core elements are necessary for firms to function effectively:

1. Mission and strategy.
2. Organization structure.
3. Human resource management.

They defined strategy as a process through which the basic mission and objectives of the organization are set, and a process through which the organization uses its resources to achieve its objectives.

They also made a distinction between the three levels of managerial work:

- *strategic level* – policy formulation and overall goal-setting;
- *managerial level* – concerned with the availability and allocation of resources to carry out the strategic plan;
- *operational level* – day-to-day management.

But their most important conclusion was that HR systems and organizational structures should be managed in a way that is congruent with organizational strategy. In other words, they emphasized the importance of strategic fit.

AIMS OF STRATEGIC HRM

The fundamental aim of strategic HRM is to generate strategic capability by ensuring that the organization has the skilled, committed and well-motivated employees it needs to achieve sustained competitive advantage. Its objective is to provide a sense of direction in an often turbulent environment so that the business needs of the organization and the individual and collective needs of its employees can be met by the development and implementation of coherent and practical HR policies and programmes. As Dyer and Holder (1988) remark, strategic HRM should provide 'unifying frameworks which are at once broad, contingency based and integrative'.

The rationale for strategic HRM rests on the perceived advantage of having an agreed and understood basis for developing approaches to managing people in the longer term. It has also been suggested, by Lengnick-Hall and Lengnick-Hall (1990), that underlying this rationale in a business is the concept of achieving competitive advantage through HRM:

> Competitive advantage is the essence of competitive strategy. It encompasses those capabilities, resources, relationships and decisions that permit an organization to capitalize on opportunities in the marketplace and to avoid threats to its desired position.

Increasingly, they claim, it is being acknowledged that the management of people is one of the key links to generating a competitive edge.

This rationale accepts the fact that the degree to which the concept of strategic HRM can be applied within organizations, and its form and content, will vary widely. It is recognized that organizations can be so preoccupied with survival and managing the here and now that, unwisely perhaps, they will not have an articulated corporate or business strategy. In these circumstances, which are typical of many organizations in the UK where 'short-termism' has prevailed, strategic HRM will not happen. A strategic approach to HR issues will only take place in an environment in which there is a strategic approach to corporate or business issues. In many organizations, the HR function will be carrying out a primarily administrative and service role and will not be at all concerned with strategic matters.

MODELS OF STRATEGIC HRM

The business-oriented model

Wright and Snell (1998) have suggested that, in a business, strategic HRM deals with 'those HR activities used to support the firm's competitive strategy'. Another business-oriented definition was provided by Miller (1989):

> Strategic human resource management encompasses those decisions and actions which concern the management of employees *at all levels* in the business and which are directed towards creating and sustaining *competitive advantage*.

The strategic fit model

Walker (1992) defines strategic HRM as 'the means of aligning the management of human resources with the strategic content of the business'. This is based on the concept of strategic fit as described in Chapter 2. In HRM terms, strategic fit means developing HR strategies that are integrated with the business strategy and support its achievement (vertical integration or fit), and also with the use of an integrated approach to the development of HR practices such as resourcing, employee development, reward and employee relations, so that they complement one another (horizontal integration or fit). This is tied to the concept of 'bundling', which is discussed later in this chapter. As defined by Dyer and Reeves (1995), human resource strategies are 'internally consistent bundles of human resource practices'.

STRATEGIC HRM AND HR STRATEGIES

The terms 'strategic HRM' and 'HR strategy' are often used interchangeably, but a distinction can be made between them.

Strategic HRM can be regarded as a general approach to the strategic management of human resources in accordance with the intentions of the organization on the future direction it wants to take. It is concerned with longer-term people issues as part of the strategic management processes of the organization. What emerges from this process is a stream of decisions over time that forms the pattern adopted by the organization for managing its human resources and defines the areas in which specific HR strategies need to be developed. It will deal with macro-concerns about structure, values, culture, quality, commitment, performance, competence and management development.

HR strategies will focus on the specific intentions of the organization as to what needs to be done and what needs to be changed. The issues with which these strategies may be concerned include ensuring that the organization has the people it needs, training, motivation, reward, flexibility, teamworking and stable employee relations. These are the issues that facilitate the successful achievement of the corporate strategy.

According to this analysis, strategic HRM decisions are built into the strategic plan while HR strategy decisions are derived from it. But the process of formulating such strategies should not be seen as a passive one. The strategic HRM concept requires that their thrust and purpose should be determined while developing the overall strategy, and this could well be an iterative process.

To sum up, it could be said that the relationship between strategic HRM and HR strategies is comparable with the relationship between strategic management and corporate or business strategies. Both 'strategic HRM' and 'strategic management' are terms describing an approach that may be adopted by top management and focuses on longer-term issues and setting the overall direction. HR and corporate/business strategies can be outcomes of this approach, which specify in more detail the intentions of the organization concerning key issues and particular functions or activities.

However, this distinction should not be pursued too rigorously. The concept of strategic HRM embraces both the overall approach and the manifestations of that approach in the form of specific HR strategies.

STRATEGIC FIT

The notion of strategic fit or integration, sometimes described as 'the matching model', is central to the concept of strategic HRM. Strategic integration is necessary to provide congruence between business and human resource strategy so that the latter supports the accomplishment of the former and, indeed, helps to define it. The aim is to provide strategic fit and consistency between the policy goals of human resource management and the business.

This point was originally made by Fombrun *et al* (1984) who stated that:

> Just as firms will be faced with inefficiencies when they try to implement new strategies with outmoded structures, so they will also face problems of implementation when they attempt to effect new strategies with inappropriate HR systems. The critical management task is to align the formal structure and the HR systems so that they drive the strategic objectives of the organization.

Guest (1989b) has suggested that strategic human resource management is largely about integration. This is one of his key policy goals, as listed in Chapter 1, which is to ensure that HRM 'is fully integrated into strategic planning so that HRM policies cohere both across policy areas and across hierarchies and HRM practices are used by line managers as part of their everyday work'.

Walker (1992) has pointed out that HR strategies are functional strategies like financial, marketing, production or IT strategies. In many organizations long-range functional planning is a mandated element of the long-range business planning process.

HR strategies are different, however, in the sense that they are intertwined with all other strategies. The management of people is not a distinct function but the means by which all business strategies are implemented. HR planning should be an integral part of all other strategy formulations. Where it is separate, it needs to be closely aligned.

Five types of fit have been identified by Guest (1997):

1. Fit as strategic interaction – linking HR practices to the external context.
2. Fit as contingency – approaches which ensure that internal practices should respond to particular external factors such as the nature of the market.
3. Fit as an ideal set of practices – the view that there are 'best practices' which all firms can advantageously adopt.
4. Fit as gestalt – an approach which emphasizes the importance of finding an appropriate combination of practices.
5. Fit as 'bundles' – the search for distinct configurations or 'bundles' of complementary practices in order to determine which is likely to be most effective.

Fit as an ideal set of practices (the 'best practice' approach), fit to the circumstances of the firm (the 'best fit' approach) and fit as bundles (the 'configurational' approach) are three possible approaches to strategic HRM. However, most discussions on the concept of fit or matching concentrate on external and internal fit, as described below.

External fit

External fit means that HR strategies are congruent with business strategies, match the firm's stage of development, take account of organizational dynamics, and are in line with the characteristics of the organization. These can be classified as contingency models (Marchington and Wilkinson, 1996). Where the fit refers to the link between the business strategy and HR strategy, it may be called 'vertical integration'.

Congruence with business strategies

The whole concept of strategic HRM is predicated on the belief that HR strategies should be integrated with corporate or business strategies. Miller (1989) believes that for this state of affairs to exist it is necessary to ensure that management initiatives in the field of HRM are *consistent* – consistent with those decisions taken in other functional areas of the business, and consistent with an analysis of the product-market situation. The key is to make operational the concept of 'fit' – the fit of human resource management with the strategic thrust of the organization The development of operational linkages is an important characteristic of strategic HRM. Tyson and Witcher (1994) consider that 'human resource strategies can only be studied in the context of corporate and business strategies'.

Congruence with business strategies may mean aligning HR strategies to the strategic orientation of the firm. Different orientations establish the need for different types of people and require changes in approaches to investing in the firm's human capital. The most familiar classification of strategic orientation is that of Porter (1985) who distinguished three generic approaches: innovation, quality and cost leadership.

Matching life-cycle stages

Matching the stage of the firm's development means aligning HR strategy to the business strategies appropriate at each stage of the life-cycle of the business, namely start-up, maturity, decline or degeneration, regeneration or transformation. Clearly the business strategies and therefore the HR strategies will differ, say between a firm opening up on a green-field site and one that is forced to embark on a comprehensive transformation programme.

Dynamics

The dynamics of organizational change should exert a marked influence on HR strategies. A transformational programme in any part of the life-cycle will indicate what specific organizational development and culture management strategies the organization should adopt. Managing the transition between the present state and a future state will mean the development of change strategies and, possibly, new strategic approaches to the employment relationship. HR strategies may have to be developed that support business initiatives in such areas as total quality, customer care, organizational restructuring, process re-engineering, product/market development, and the introduction of new technology or production systems, such as computer integrated manufacturing or just-in-time production.

Organizational characteristics

An alternative way of determining HR strategy requirements is to relate them to the overall characteristics of the organization. The most familiar classification is that produced by Miles and Snow (1978) who distinguish between:

- 'defenders' who seek stability and believe in strict control;
- 'prospectors' who seek new opportunities, focus on continuous development and believe in flexibility;
- 'analysers' who seek to incorporate the benefits of both defender and prospectors.

Problems of achieving vertical integration

Vertical integration (strategic fit between business and HR strategies) may be desirable but it is not easy to achieve, for the reasons discussed below.

Diversity of strategic processes, levels and styles

The different levels at which strategy is formulated and the different styles adopted by organizations may make it difficult to develop a coherent view of what sort of HR strategies will fit the overall strategies and what type of HR contributions are required during the process of formulation.

It has been argued by Miller (1987) that to achieve competitive advantage, each business unit in a diversified corporation should tailor its HRM policy to its own product-market conditions, irrespective of the HRM policies being pursued elsewhere in the corporation. If this is the case, there may be coherence within a unit but not across the whole organization, and it may be difficult to focus HR strategies on corporate needs. In a 'financial control' type of corporation, as defined by Goold and Campbell (1986), ie one in which the centre is mainly concerned with financial results that they control against targets, there may be no pressure for the creation of a corporate culture and HR strategies to support it at the centre. But need this matter? The centre may exercise financial control while the strategic business units (SBUs) are allowed to go their own way so far as strategic HRM is concerned, as long as they deliver the financial results expected of them. And there is no reason why the SBUs should not decide independently that the best way to achieve those results is to pursue their own version of strategic HRM.

The only time a serious problem is likely to emerge is if units have to be merged. Admittedly, synergy may have to be sacrificed and the organization might not reap the benefits of a corporate management development and career-planning strategy. But that choice has been made by those who are in command of such organizations and if it is their loss, it is only they who can do anything about it.

The complexity of the strategy formulation process

As Hendry and Pettigrew (1986) maintain, strategy formulation and implementation is a complex, interactive process heavily influenced by a variety of contextual and historical factors. In these circumstances, as Guest (1991) has asked, how can there be a straightforward flow from the business strategy to the HR strategy? It has been pointed out by Truss (1999), that the assumption of some matching models of strategic HRM is that there is a simple linear relationship between business strategy and human resource strategy. But this assumption:

> fails to acknowledge the complexities both between and within notions of strategy and human resource management [and] is based on a rational model of organizations and individuals which takes no account of the significance of power, politics and culture.

The evolutionary nature of business strategy

This phenomenon, and the incremental nature of strategy-making, may make it difficult to pin down the HR issues that are likely to be relevant. Hendry and Pettigrew (1990) suggest that there are limits to the extent to which rational HR strategies can be drawn up if the process of business strategic planning is itself irrational. Even if Mintzberg's (1978) description of strategy as a *pattern* in a stream of decisions over time is accepted, it may be difficult to 'fit' HR strategy into the process in any well-defined way. HR strategies would therefore have to be equally evolutionary and just as difficult to pin down to a set of definitive statements. If this is the case, why bother to seek the 'holy grail' of strategic fit, which implies a certain rigidity that is not in keeping with the realities of organizational life and the chaotic conditions in which organizations have to exist?

The absence of articulated business strategies

If, because of its evolutionary nature, the business strategy has not been clearly articulated, this would add to the problems of clarifying the business strategic issues that human resource strategies should address. But it should be noted that 'articulation' in this context means that the business strategies are fully understood by those concerned. It does *not* mean that they have to be written down, although this may help to create understanding.

The qualitative nature of HR issues

Business strategies tend, or at least aim, to be expressed in the common currency of figures and hard data on portfolio management, growth, competitive position, market share, profitability, etc. HR strategies may deal with quantifiable issues such as resourcing and skill acquisition but are equally likely to refer to qualitative factors such as commitment, motivation, good employee relations and high employment standards. The relationship between the pursuit of policies in these areas and individual and organizational performance may be difficult to establish.

Integration with what?

The concept of strategic HRM implies that HR strategies must be totally integrated with corporate/business strategies in the sense that they both flow from and contribute to such strategies. But as Brewster (1993) argues, HR strategy will be subjected to considerable environmental pressure, for example, in Europe, legislation about involvement. These may mean that HR strategies cannot be entirely governed by the corporate/business strategy.

The question also needs to be asked: 'To what extent should HR strategy take into account the interests of all the stakeholders in the organization, employees in general as well as owners and management?'. In Storey's (1989) terms, 'soft strategic HRM' will place greater emphasis on the human relations aspect of people management, stressing security of employment, continuous development, communication, involvement and the quality of working life. 'Hard strategic HRM' on the other hand will emphasize the yield to be obtained by investing in human resources in the interests of the business. As Lengnick-Hall and Lengnick-Hall (1990) comment:

There is now a growing realization that the overriding concern should be the yield from employees. Yield concentrates on the intricate web of costs and benefits that result from investing in and focusing human resource activities toward a certain set of activities and away from other behaviours and attitudes. Yield recognizes both trade-offs and choices. Yield depends on shared responsibilities and collaboration across functional units and hierarchical levels.

Ideally, strategic integration should attempt to achieve a proper balance between the hard and soft elements. The emphasis may be on achieving corporate or business objectives but this should be a process of planning with people in mind (Quinn Mills, 1983), taking into account the needs and aspirations of all the members of the organization.

An analytical model for vertical integration

To promote understanding of possible approaches to achieving vertical integration against the background of the problems referred to above, Walker (1992) has put forward a useful analytical model for assessing the degree of fit or integration. He suggests that the following three types of processes are used in developing and implementing HR strategy:

1. *The integrated process* – in this approach, HR strategy is an integral part of the business strategy, along with all the other functional strategies. In strategy review discussions, HR issues are addressed as well as financial, product-market and operational ones. However, the focus is not on 'downstream' matters such as staffing, individual performance or development but rather on people-related business issues, resource allocation, the implications of internal and external change and the associated goals, strategies and action plans.
2. *The aligned process* – in this approach, HR strategy is developed together with the business strategy. They may be presented and discussed together but they are distinct outcomes of parallel processes. By developing and considering them together, 'there is some likelihood that they will influence each other and be adopted as a cohesive or at least an adhesive whole!'.
3. *The separate process* – in this, the most common approach, a distinct HR plan is developed. It is both prepared and considered separately from the overall business plan. It may be formulated concurrently with strategic planning, before (and an input to), or following (to examine its implications). The environmental assessment is wholly independent. It

focuses on human resource issues and, so far as possible, looks for the 'business-relativeness' of the information obtained. Since the assessment is outside the strategic planning process, consideration of business strategy depends on a review of the current and past business strategies. The value of the HR strategy is therefore governed by the sufficiency (or insufficiency) of the business-related data. This approach perpetuates the notion of HR as a staff-driven, functionally specialist concern.

Internal fit

Internal fit or horizontal integration is accomplished by developing a coherent – a well-knit – range of interconnected and mutually reinforcing HR policies and practices. This may be achieved by the use of shared processes such as competence analysis, which provide a common frame of reference and performance management concerned with role definition, employee development and reward. Integration is also more likely to take place if shared values exist between line managers and HR specialist managers on how HR policies should be implemented.

Achieving integration is also about ensuring, when planning any innovation, that its implications on other aspects of HR policies and practice are fully considered and that further thought is given on how it could support those policies or practices.

Stevens (1995) made the following comments on the practicality of achieving coherence:

> People management practices and styles are sometimes very consciously coherent. Equally often, they are an amalgam of conscious decision, pragmatic development and compromise between 'what is' and 'what is to be desired'. Different approaches may be taken with different groups of employees. The consistency of policies for reward, training and development, job security and industrial relations may not be obvious to the outside observer; however, the apparent inconsistencies may be the result of subtle decisions made to fit in with the particular requirements of a particular organization at one point in time.

This is a good description of what actually happens. Conceptually, however, it can be argued that an appropriate measure of coherence is most likely to be attained if HR strategies, policies and processes are clearly based on a powerful and well-articulated vision of where the business is going and the part that should be played by its people in getting it there. This may be expressed as an overriding strategic imperative or driving force such as quality, performance, or the need to develop skills and competencies. Coherence and the integration of HR initiatives is most likely to be achieved if this declaration of intent initiates various processes and policies that are designed to link together and operate in concert to deliver certain defined results. This is the concept of 'bundling', as described below.

Bundling

'Bundling' is the development and implementation of several HR practices together so that they are interrelated and therefore complement and reinforce each other. The process is sometimes referred to as the use of 'complementarities' (MacDuffie, 1995) or as the adoption of a 'configurational mode' (Delery and Doty, 1996). MacDuffie (1995) explained the concept of bundling as follows:

> Implicit in the notion of a 'bundle' is the idea that practices within bundles are interrelated and internally consistent, and that 'more is better' with respect to the impact on performance, because of the overlapping and mutually reinforcing effect of multiple practices.

As Dyer and Reeves (1995) note: 'The logic in favour of bundling is straightforward... Since employee performance is a function of both ability and motivation, it makes sense to have practices aimed at enhancing both'. Thus there are several ways in which employees can acquire needed skills (such as careful selection and training) and multiple incentives to enhance motivation (different forms of financial and non-financial rewards). A study by Dyer and Reeves (1995) of various models listing HR practices for analysing the link between HRM and business performance found that the activities appearing in most of the models were involvement, careful selection, extensive training and contingent compensation.

On the basis of his research in flexible production manufacturing plants in the US, MacDuffie (1995) noted that flexible production gives employees a much more central role in the production system. They have to resolve problems as they appear on the line and this means that they have to possess both a conceptual grasp of the production process and the analytical skills to identify the root cause of problems. But the multiple skills and conceptual knowledge developed by the workforce in flexible production firms are of little use unless workers are motivated to contribute mental as well as physical effort. Such discretionary effort on problem solving will only be contributed if workers 'believe that their individual interests are aligned with those of the company, and that the company will make a reciprocal investment in their well-being'. This means that flexible production techniques have to be supported by bundles of high commitment human resource practices such as employment security, pay that is partly contingent on performance, and a reduction of status barriers between managers and workers. Company investment in building worker skills also contributes to this 'psychological contract of reciprocal commitment'. The research indicated that plants using flexible production systems that bundle human resource practices into a system that is integrated with production/business strategy, outperform plants using more traditional mass production systems in both productivity and quality.

Following research in 43 automobile processing plants in the US, Pil and MacDuffie (1996) established that when a high-involvement work practice is introduced in the presence of complementary HR practices, not only does the new work practice produce an incremental improvement in performance but so do the complementary practices.

The aim of bundling is to achieve coherence, which is one of the four 'meanings' of strategic HRM defined by Hendry and Pettigrew (1986). Coherence exists when a mutually reinforcing set of HR policies and practices has been developed to contribute to the achievement of the organization's strategies for matching resources to organizational needs, improving performance and quality and, in commercial enterprises, achieving competitive advantage.

In one sense, strategic HRM is holistic: it is concerned with the organization as a total entity and addresses what needs to be done across the organization as a whole in order to enable it to achieve its corporate strategic objectives. It is not interested in isolated programmes and techniques, or in the ad hoc development of HR programmes.

In their discussion of the four policy areas of HRM (employee influence, human resource management flow, reward systems and work systems) Beer *et al* (1984) suggested that this framework can stimulate managers to plan how to accomplish the major HRM tasks 'in a unified, coherent manner rather than in a disjointed approach based on some combination of past practice, accident and ad hoc response to outside pressures'.

Guest (1989b) includes in his set of propositions about HRM the point that strategic integration is about, *inter alia*, the ability of the organization to ensure that the various aspects of HRM cohere. One way of looking at the concept is to say that some measure of coherence will be achieved if there is an overriding strategic imperative or driving force such as quality, performance or the need to develop skills and competences, and if this initiates various processes and policies that are designed to link together and operate in concert to deliver certain defined results. For example, if the driving force were to improve performance, competence profiling techniques could be used to specify recruitment standards, identify learning and development needs and indicate the standards of behaviour or performance required. The competence frameworks could be used as the basis for human resource planning, in development centres. They could also be incorporated into performance management processes in which the aims are primarily developmental and competencies are used as criteria for reviewing behaviour and assessing learning and development needs. Job evaluation could be based on levels of competence, and competence-based pay systems could be introduced. This ideal would be difficult to achieve as a 'grand design' that can be put into immediate effect, and might have to be developed progressively.

Problems of achieving internal fit or horizontal integration

The research conducted by Gratton *et al* (1999) in eight British organizations established that there was little evidence of a comprehensive and successful attempt to achieve internal fit: 'In no case was there a clearly developed and articulated strategy that was translated into a mutually supportive set of human resource initiatives or practices'.

Problems of achieving internal fit may arise for the following reasons:

- the sheer complexity of the organization and its strategies, which might make it hard to achieve any coherence across a diverse range of activities and plans;
- senior managers who want quick fixes that lead to innovations that are isolated from complementary HR activities – the most common example of this is the introduction of performance-related pay without the existence of embedded performance management processes;
- incremental approaches to the development of HR practices, possibly arising from management pressures or the existence of financial constraints;
- difficulty in deciding which 'bundles' are likely to be most appropriate in the circumstances;
- lack of understanding amongst HR practitioners of the need actively to achieve integration;
- implementation difficulties, even where there is a 'grand design' and much rhetoric, but the reality is different – the links are difficult to maintain, line managers are indifferent or incapable of playing their part, and employees are suspicious or hostile to the newly linked initiatives.

Another overall problem that arises when attempting to achieve internal fit is the tension between the goals of fit and flexibility. Methods of overcoming the problems of developing HR strategies are discussed in Chapter 5.

STRATEGIC FIT AND FLEXIBILITY

At first sight, the goals of fit and flexibility may appear to be incompatible but, as argued by Wright and Snell (1998), the concepts are complementary:

> The strategic management challenge is to cope with change (requiring flexibility) by continually adapting to achieve between a firm and its external circumstances.... Fit exists at a point in time, flexibility is a characteristic that exists over a period of time.

This comment draws attention to the importance of the time element in strategic HRM. The formulation and implementation of strategy is an evolutionary process. Indeed, strategy may well be developed as it is being implemented because of the new demands arising from a changing environment. Gratton (1999) introduces a third temporal element in the development of strategy:

> Transformation capability depends in part on the ability to create and embed processes which link business strategy to the behaviour and performance of individuals and teams. These clusters of processes link vertically (to create alignment with short-term business needs), horizontally (to create cohesion), and temporally (to transform to meet future business needs).

The tension between fit and flexibility can be resolved, at least in part, by making the distinction between present fit and future flexibility, and by introducing the notion that the latter is a process that takes place over time. Another perspective was provided by Mintzberg (1994), cited by Wright and Snell (1998), who distinguishes 'strategic programming' from 'strategic thinking'. The former involves deciding on a series of action steps to achieve a strategic goal, formalizing those steps for implementation, and articulating the results expected from those steps. The latter entails taking information from numerous sources and integrating that information into a vision of what direction the business should take. Wright and Snell (1998) suggest that: 'Strategic programming seems quite consistent with an emphasis on achieving strategic fit, whereas strategic thinking is consistent with an emphasis on building flexibility and the integrative linkage'.

LIMITATIONS TO THE CONCEPT OF STRATEGIC HRM

The concept of strategic HRM appears to be based on beliefs about the rationality of the approaches used to develop strategy. The key 'matching model' of strategy assumes that the formulation of strategy is a rational and linear process whereas, according to Mintzberg (1987), it emerges over time in response to evolving situations. Truss (1999) comments that it underestimates the significance of politics, power and culture. Pfeffer and Cohen (1984) state that it is necessary to focus on 'organizational processes such as power and influence, institutionalization, conflict and contests for control' in order to understand how HRM functions in practice. And Wright and McMahon (1992) point out that:

> The implications of a power and politics perspective of HRM are numerous. First it changes the focus from viewing strategic HRM in mechanistic terms where all HRM practices are rationally determined and are perfectly supportive of organizational strategies. As anyone who has worked with organizations in the development of HR practices such as selection or appraisal systems has experienced, it is political rather than technical or strategic considerations that often strongly affect the development of the final product.

The notion of strategic HRM also seems to assume that there is a distinction between the three processes of formulating, planning and implementing strategy. In practice, because strategy tends to evolve in response to changing circumstances, these processes cannot really be separated. Strategies are formulated as they are used.

CONCLUSIONS

The fundamental concept of strategic HRM is based on the assumption that human resource strategy can contribute to the business strategy but is also justified by it. The validity of this concept depends on the extent to which it is believed that people are the basis for the achievement of competitive advantage and create added value, and should therefore be treated as a critical strategic resource. If these assumptions are accepted, then the validity of the concept of strategic HRM does depend on the extent to which it can be applied in practice and the outcomes of such applications. This means paying attention to the process of strategic HRM as discussed in Chapter 4, methods of formulating strategies as described in Chapter 5, and the particular aspects of HR strategy covered in Parts 2 and 3.

4

The process of strategic HRM

It is not too difficult to conceptualize strategic HRM as in Chapter 3; it is much harder to assess which factors organizations should take into account and what processes they can use when developing and implementing strategies. Account has to be taken of the problematic nature of the concept of HR strategy as a formal, well-articulated and linear process that flows logically from the business strategy. Tyson (1997) points out that:

- strategy has always been emergent and flexible – it is always 'about to be', it never exists at the present time;
- strategy is not only realized by formal statements but also comes about by actions and reactions;
- strategy is a description of a future-oriented action that is always directed towards change;
- the management process itself conditions the strategies that emerge.

In this chapter, issues affecting the process of strategic HRM are discussed in terms of:

- the various models that are available upon which HR strategies can be based;
- the concept of resource-based strategy as an underpinning approach to strategic HRM;
- the three main approaches to the development of HR strategies;
- approaches to the achievement of strategic fit.

MODELS FOR STRATEGIC HRM

There are a number of models that prescribe approaches for strategic HRM and there is an element of choice in which model or combination of models to adopt when developing HR strategies. (However, it should be remembered that the extent to which there is real choice will be contingent upon factors such as the business strategy, the resources available and the environment in which the firm operates.) The main models described below are:

- the high-commitment management model;
- the high-performance management model;
- the high-involvement model.

The high-commitment management model

One of the defining characteristics of HRM is its emphasis on the importance of enhancing mutual commitment (Walton, 1985). High-commitment management has been described by Wood (1996) as:

> A form of management which is aimed at eliciting a commitment so that behaviour is primarily self-regulated rather than controlled by sanctions and pressures external to the individual, and relations within the organization are based on high levels of trust.

The approaches to achieving high commitment as described by Beer *et al* (1984) and Walton (1985) are:

- the development of career ladders and emphasis on trainability and commitment as highly valued characteristics of employees at all levels in the organization;
- a high level of functional flexibility with the abandonment of potentially rigid job descriptions;
- the reduction of hierarchies and the ending of status differentials;

- a heavy reliance on team structure for disseminating information (team briefing), structuring work (teamworking) and problem solving (quality circles).

Wood and Albanese (1995) added to this list:

- job design as something management consciously does in order to provide jobs that have a considerable level of intrinsic satisfaction;
- a policy of no compulsory lay-offs or redundancies and permanent employment guarantees, with the possible use of temporary workers to cushion fluctuations in the demand for labour;
- new forms of assessment and payment systems and, more specifically, merit pay and profit sharing;
- a high involvement of employees in the management of quality.

High-performance management

High-performance management (called 'high-performance work systems or practices' in the US) aims to make an impact on the performance of the firm through its people in such areas as productivity, quality, levels of customer service, growth, profits and, ultimately, the delivery of increased shareholder value. High-performance management practices include rigorous recruitment and selection procedures, extensive and relevant training and management development activities, incentive pay systems and performance management processes.

The best-known definition of a high-performance work system was produced by the US Department of Labor (1993). The characteristics listed were:

- careful and extensive systems for recruitment, selection and training;
- formal systems for sharing information with the individuals who work in the organization;
- clear job design;
- high-level participation processes;
- monitoring of attitudes;
- performance appraisals;
- properly functioning grievance procedures;
- promotion and compensation schemes that provide for the recognition and financial rewarding of the high-performing members of the work-force.

There is some overlap between this concept and that of high-commitment management.

High-performance work design as described by Buchanan (1987), requires the following steps:

- management clearly defines what it needs in the form of new methods of working and the results expected from their introduction;
- management sets goals and standards for success;
- multi-skilling is encouraged – that is, job demarcation lines are eliminated as far as possible and encouragement and training are provided for employees to acquire new skills;
- equipment is selected that can be used flexibly and is laid out to allow freedom of movement and vision;
- self-managed teams or autonomous working groups are established;
- managers and team leaders adopt a supportive rather than an autocratic style (this is the most difficult part of the system to introduce);
- support systems are provided that help the teams to function effectively as operating units;
- the new system is introduced with great care by means of involvement and communication programmes;
- thorough training is carried out on the basis of an assessment of training needs;
- the payment system is specially designed with participation of employees, to fit their needs as well as those of management;
- payment may be related to team performance (team pay) but with skill-based pay for individuals;
- in some cases, a 'peer performance review' process may be used that involves team members assessing one another's performance as well as the performance of the team as a whole.

High-involvement management

This approach involves treating employees as partners in the enterprise, whose interests are respected and who have a voice in matters that concern them. It is concerned with communication and involvement. The aim is to create a climate in which a continuing dialogue between managers and the members of their teams takes place in order to define expectations and share information on the organization's mission, values and objectives. This establishes mutual understanding of what *is* to be achieved and a framework for managing and developing people to ensure that it *will* be achieved.

RESOURCE-BASED HR STRATEGY

A different perspective is provided by the concept of resource based HR strategy. This is founded on the belief that competitive advantage is obtained if a firm can obtain and develop human resources that enable it to learn faster and apply its learning more effectively than its rivals (Hamel and Prahalad, 1989). Barney (1995) defines human resources as follows: 'Human resources include all the experience, knowledge, judgement, risk-taking propensity and wisdom of individuals associated with the firm'. Kamoche (1996) suggests that: 'In the resource-based view, the firm is seen as a bundle of tangible and intangible resources and capabilities required for product/market competition'.

The aim of a resource-based approach is to improve resource capability – achieving strategic fit between resources and opportunities and obtaining added value from the effective deployment of resources. Resource-based theory provides a rationale for strategic HRM but does not attempt to prescribe certain solutions as do the other models referred to above.

In line with human capital theory, resource-based theory emphasizes that investment in people adds to their value to the firm. Resource-based strategy, as Barney (1991) indicates, can develop strategic capability. The strategic goal will be to 'create firms which are more intelligent and flexible than their competitors' (Boxall, 1996) by hiring and developing more talented staff and by extending their skills base. Resource-based strategy is therefore concerned with the enhancement of the human or intellectual capital of the firm. As Ulrich (1998) comments:

> Knowledge has become a direct competitive advantage for companies selling ideas and relationships. The challenge to organizations is to ensure that they have the capability to find, assimilate, compensate and retain the talented individuals they need.

A convincing rationale for resource-based strategy has been produced by Grant (1991):

> When the external environment is in a state of flux, the firm's own resources and capabilities may be a much more stable basis on which to define its identity. Hence, a definition of a business in terms of what it is capable of doing may offer a more durable basis for strategy than a definition based upon the needs (eg markets) which the business seeks to satisfy.

Unique talents among employees, including superior performance, productivity, flexibility, innovation and the ability to deliver high levels of personal customer service are ways in which people provide a critical ingredient in developing an organization's competitive position. People also provide the key to managing the pivotal interdependencies across functional activities and the important external relationships. It can be argued that one of the clear benefits arising from competitive advantage based on the effective management of people is that such an advantage is hard to imitate. An organization's HR strategies, policies and practices are a unique blend of processes, procedures, personalities, styles, capabilities and organizational culture. One of the keys to competitive advantage is the ability to differentiate what the business supplies to its customers from those supplied by its competitors. Such differentiation can be achieved by having HR strategies that ensure that the firm has higher quality people than its competitors, by developing and nurturing the intellectual capital possessed by the business and by functioning as a 'learning organization'.

A resource-based approach will address methods of increasing the firm's strategic capability by the development of managers and other staff who can think and plan strategically and who understand the key strategic issues. As Harrison (1997) notes:

> It is strategic capability that significantly determines the extent to which the organization achieves the best possible fit between the unique tangible and intangible assets that it possesses and the competitive position it occupies in its environment. It involves selecting resources and combinations of resources, most likely to generate the new strategic assets of the business.

The enhancement of strategic capability is an important part of the process of implementing a human resource management strategy, as described in Chapter 5.

APPROACHES TO THE DEVELOPMENT OF HR STRATEGIES

The three main approaches to the development of HR strategies were described by Delery and Doty (1996) as the 'universalistic', the 'contingency' and the 'configurational'. Richardson and Thompson (1999) re-described the first two approaches as 'best practice' and 'best fit', and retained the word 'configurational', meaning the use of 'bundles', as the third approach. Guest (1997) refers to 'fit' as an ideal set of practices, as contingency, and as 'bundles'.

The best practice approach

This approach is based on the belief that there is a set of best HRM practices and that adopting them will lead to superior organizational performance. Perhaps the best known set is Pfeffer's (1994) list of the seven HR practices of successful organizations. These are:

1. *Employment security* – this means that employees are not quickly made redundant for things such as economic downturns or the strategic mistakes of senior management over which they have no control. It is fundamental to the implementation of such high-performance management practices as selective hiring, extensive training, information sharing and delegation. Companies are unlikely to invest resources in the careful screening and training of new people if these people are not expected to stay long enough with the firm for it to recoup its investment. And if the policy is to avoid lay-offs, then the company will hire sparingly.

2. *Selective hiring* – this requires the organization to be clear about the critical skills and attributes it needs, to make a choice on the basis of those attributes that are difficult or impossible to change, and to train people in those behaviours and skills that are easily learned. They look for people with the right attitudes, values and cultural fit – attributes that are harder to train or change and that predict performance and likelihood to remain with the company.

3. *Self-managed teams* – these are a critical component of high-performance management systems. They a) substitute peer-based control for hierarchical control of work, b) by such substitution allow the removal of layers of hierarchy, and c) permit employees to pool their ideas in order to produce better and more creative solutions to work problems.

4. *High compensation contingent on performance* – this also figures in most high-performance work systems. Such compensation can be contingent on organizational performance, eg gainsharing or profit sharing, or it can be related to individual or team performance or individual skill.

5. *Training* – virtually all descriptions of high-performance work practices emphasize the importance of training to provide a skilled and motivated workforce that has the knowledge and capability to perform the requisite tasks.

6. *Reduction of status differentials* – the fundamental premise of high-performance work systems is that organizations perform at a higher level if they are able to tap the ideas, skill and effort of all their people. But this

will not happen if status differentials send signals that people are neither valuable nor valued.

7. *Sharing information* – this is an essential component of high-performance work systems, for two reasons. First, the sharing of information on the firm's financial performance and business strategies conveys to employees the fact that they are trusted. Second, even motivated and trained people cannot contribute to enhancing organizational performance if they don't have information on important dimensions of performance and, in addition, training in how to interpret and use that information.

The 'best practice' rubric has been attacked by a number of commentators. Cappelli and Crocker-Hefter (1996) comment that the notion of a single set of best practices has been over-stated:

> There are examples in virtually every industry of firms that have very distinctive management practices. We argue that these distinctive human resource practices help to create unique competencies that differentiate products and services and, in turn, drive competitiveness.... Distinctive human-resource practices shape the core competencies that determine how firms compete.

Purcell (1999) has also criticized the best practice or universalist view by pointing out the inconsistency between a belief in best practice and the resource-based view, which focuses on the intangible assets including HR, that allow the firm to do better than its competitors. He asks how can 'the universalism of best practice be squared with the view that only some resources and routines are important and valuable by being rare and imperfectly imitable?'. The danger, as Legge (1995) points out, is that of 'mechanistically matching strategy with HRM policies and practices'.

In accordance with contingency theory, it is difficult to accept that there is any such thing as universal best practice. What works well in one organization will not necessarily work well in another because it may not fit its strategy, culture, management style, technology or working practices. As Becker *et al* (1997) remark: 'Organizational high-performance work systems are highly idiosyncratic and must be tailored carefully to each firm's individual situation to achieve optimum results'.

Best fit

For the reasons given above, it is accepted by most commentators that 'best fit' is more important than 'best practice'. There can be no universal prescriptions for HRM policies and practices. It all depends. This is not to say that 'good practice', ie practice that does well in one environment, should be ignored. Benchmarking has its uses as a means of identifying areas for innovation or development that are practised to good effect elsewhere. But having learned about what works and, ideally, what does not work in comparable organizations, it is up to the firm to decide what may be relevant in general terms and what lessons can be learnt and adapted to fit its particular strategic and operational requirements. The starting point should be an analysis of the business needs of the firm within its context (culture, structure, technology and processes). This may indicate clearly what has to be done. Thereafter, it may be useful to pick and mix various 'best practice' ingredients and develop an approach that applies those that are appropriate in a way that is aligned to the identified business needs.

But there are problems with the best-fit approach, as pointed out by Purcell (1999) who, having rubbished the concept of best practice, proceeded to do the same for the notion of best fit:

> Meanwhile, the search for a contingency or matching model of HRM is also limited by the impossibility of modelling all the contingent variables, the difficulty of showing their interconnection, and the way in which changes in one variable have an impact on others.

In Purcell's view, organizations should be less concerned with best fit and best practice and much more sensitive to processes of organizational change so that they can 'avoid being trapped in the logic of rational choice'.

Bundling

As Richardson and Thompson (1999) comment: 'A strategy's success turns on combining "vertical" or external fit and "horizontal" or internal fit. This has consolidated the importance of "bundles" of HR practices'. They cite MacDuffie (1995), Arthur (1992) and Ichniowski et al (1997) as having explored the extent to which combinations of practices can be determined and whether organizational performance is related to the adoption of such 'bundles'. Their conclusion was that a firm with bundles of HR practices should have a higher level of performance, provided it also achieves high levels of fit with its competitive strategy.

In the opinion of MacDuffie (1995):

Implicit in the notion of a 'bundle' is the idea that practices within bundles are interrelated and internally consistent, and that 'more is better' with respect to the impact on performance, because of the overlapping and mutually reinforcing effect of multiple practices.

The problem with the bundling approach is that of deciding which is the best way to relate different practices together. There is no evidence that one bundle is generally better than another, although the use of performance management practices and competence frameworks are two ways that are typically adopted to provide for coherence across a range of HR activities.

APPROACHES TO ACHIEVING STRATEGIC FIT

Approaches to the achievement of strategic fit can be described by reference to the competitive strategy of the firm, organizational types, or the life-cycle of the firm.

The competitive strategy approach

This approach, as described by Schuler and Jackson (1987), identifies the different strategies for role behaviours and HR practices that can relate to the three competitive strategies listed by Porter (1985).

1. Innovation strategy

For firms pursuing a strategy of innovation the role behaviours include:

- a high degree of creative behaviour;
- a longer-term focus;
- a relatively high degree of cooperative, interdependent behaviour;
- greater degree of risk taking;
- a high tolerance of ambiguity and unpredictability.

The HR practices that characterize these firms include:

- jobs that require close interaction between people;
- jobs that allow people to develop skills that can be used in other positions in the firm;

- broader career paths that reinforce the development of a wider range of skills;
- performance appraisals that are more likely to reflect longer-term and group-based achievements.

2. Quality enhancement strategy

For firms pursuing a strategy of quality enhancement the role behaviours include:

- a high concern for quality;
- a high concern for process (how goods and services are made or delivered);
- low risk-taking activity;
- high levels of commitment.

The key HR practices include:

- relatively fixed and explicit job descriptions;
- relatively egalitarian treatment of employees and some guarantees of employment security;
- high levels of employee participation on work issues;
- extensive and continuous training.

3. Cost leadership strategy

For firms pursuing a strategy of cost leadership the role behaviours include:

- primary concern for results, especially output quantity;
- low risk-taking activity;
- a relatively short-term focus;
- modest concern for quality.

The key HR practices include:

- narrowly designed jobs and explicit job descriptions;
- short-term, results-oriented performance appraisals;
- little training;
- close monitoring of employee activities.

The organizational typology approach

The three types of organization strategies defined by Miles and Snow (1978) can provide a basis for analysing and assessing relevant HR strategies. The approaches to the use of these typologies for this purpose, as suggested by Marchington and Wilkinson (1996), are as follows.

In *defender* organizations, which seek stability, centralization, high-volume, low-cost production and strict control, HR strategy is based on few entry ports from outside, promotion from within, extensive training and a reward system that is focused on internal consistency.

In *prospector* organizations, which seek new opportunities, focus on continuous development and believe in flexibility, the HR strategy is based on buying in staff through the use of sophisticated recruitment and selection techniques. Training is targeted to meeting specific organizational requirements and the reward system is likely to be results-oriented.

In *analyser* organizations, which seek to incorporate the benefits of both defenders and prospectors, HR strategies are likely to be more diverse or mixed.

The life-cycle approach

As described by Storey and Sisson (1993), the four stages of an organization's life-cycle influence HR practices as follows:

1. *Start-up* – flexible working patterns, the recruitment of employees who are likely to be well-motivated and highly committed, competitive pay, little formality and, probably, no unions.
2. *Growth* – more progressive and sophisticated recruitment and selection, training and development, performance management processes and reward systems, focus on achieving high commitment and emphasis on developing stable employee relations.
3. *Maturity* – close attention to the control of labour costs and increasing productivity, harder to justify training, strained employee relations.
4. *Decline* – the emphasis shifts to rationalization and downsizing, long-standing practices may be abandoned or severely curtailed to cut costs, trade unions are threatened with de-recognition or, at best, a marginalized role.

Comments on these approaches

All these models identify links between business strategies and HR strategies and practices. They provide a basis for assessing what approaches may be appropriate in different circumstances. But they can only be used as guidelines; the relationship between strategy and practice is more complex and variable than they suggest. HR strategies will be influenced by a much greater range of considerations and a number of other factors will have to be taken into account, as discussed in Chapter 5.

Part 2

The practice of strategic human resource management

5

Formulating and implementing HR strategy

It may not be too hard to produce very broad statements of strategic intent but the development and articulation of specific long-term strategies may be much more difficult. In fact, it can be argued that in some circumstances it is hardly worth doing at all: for example, in start-up situations or when the organization is subject to sudden and harsh external pressures that can only be dealt with tactically.

The primary role of strategic HRM may be to promote a fit with the demands of a dynamic and competitive environment, but it is not easy. A strategic process of human-resource management may be desirable but there are no obvious ways of doing it successfully.

However, this chapter is based on the belief that, although there are many difficulties, a strategic approach is desirable in order to give a sense of direction and purpose and as a basis for the development of relevant and coherent HR policies and practices. As Dyer and Holder (1988) remark, strategic HRM should provide 'unifying frameworks which are at once broad, contingency based and integrative'.

The formulation and implementation of HRM strategies is discussed in this chapter under the following headings:

- fundamental process considerations – approaches to the development of HR strategies;
- strategic frameworks – the overriding strategic thrusts that will influence particular strategies;
- models for the development of HR strategies;
- approaches to addressing key business issues concerning fit, flexibility and the achievement of coherence;
- implementing HR strategies.

FUNDAMENTAL PROCESS CONSIDERATIONS

When considering approaches to the formulation of HR strategy it is necessary to underline the interactive (not unilinear) relationship between business strategy and HRM, as have Hendry and Pettigrew (1990). They emphasize the limits of excessively rationalistic models of strategic and HR planning. The point that HR strategies are not necessarily developed formally and systematically but may instead evolve and emerge has been made by Tyson (1997):

> The process by which strategies come to be realized is not only through formal HR policies or written directions: strategy realization can also come from actions by managers and others. Since actions provoke reactions (acceptance, confrontation, negotiation, etc) these reactions are also part of the strategy process.

Strategy formulation propositions

Boxall (1993) has drawn up the following propositions about the formulation of HR strategy from the literature:

- there is typically no single HR strategy in a firm, although research conducted by Armstrong and Long (1994) showed that a number of the firms we contacted *did* have an overall strategic approach within which there were specific HR strategies;
- business strategy may be an important influence on HR strategy but it is only one of several factors and the relationship is not unilinear;
- implicit (if not explicit) in the mix of factors that influence the shape of HR strategies is a set of historical compromises and trade-offs from stakeholders;
- management may seek to shift the historical pattern of HR strategy significantly in response to major contextual change, but not all managements will respond in the same way or equally effectively;

■ the strategy formation process is complex, and excessively rationalistic models that advocate formalistic linkages between strategic planning and HR planning are not particularly helpful to our understanding of it;
■ descriptions of the dimensions that underpin HR strategies are critical to the development of useful typologies but remain controversial, as no one set of constructs has established an intellectual superiority over the others.

It is also necessary to stress that coherent and integrated HR strategies are only likely to be developed if the top team understand and act upon the strategic imperatives associated with the employment, development and motivation of people. This will be achieved more effectively if there is an HR director who is playing an active and respected role as a business partner. A further consideration is that the effective implementation of HR strategies depends on the involvement, commitment and cooperation of line managers and staff generally. Finally, there is too often a wide gap between the rhetoric of strategic HRM and the reality of its impact, as Gratton *et al* (1999) emphasize. Good intentions can too easily be subverted by the harsh realities of organizational life. For example, strategic objectives such as increasing commitment by providing more security and offering training to increase employability may have to be abandoned or at least modified because of the short-term demands made on the business to increase shareholder value.

Many different routes may be followed when formulating HR strategies – there is no one right way. On the basis of their research in 30 well-known companies, Tyson and Witcher (1994) commented that: 'The different approaches to strategy formation reflect different ways to manage change and different ways to bring the people part of the business into line with business goals'.

In strategic HRM, process may be as important as content. Tyson and Witcher (1994) also noted from their research that:

> The process of formulating HR strategy was often as important as the content of the strategy ultimately agreed. It was argued that by working through strategic issues and highlighting points of tension, new ideas emerged and a consensus over goals was found.

Levels of strategic decision-making

Ideally, the formulation of HR strategies is conceived as a process that is closely aligned to the formulation of business strategies. HR strategy can influence as well as be influenced by business strategy. In reality, however, HR strategies are more likely to flow from business strategies that will be dominated by product/market and financial considerations. But there is still room for HR to make a useful, even essential contribution at the stage when business strategies are conceived, for example, by focusing on resource issues. This contribution may be more significant if strategy formulation is an emergent or evolutionary process – HR strategic issues will then be dealt with as they arise during the course of formulating and implementing the corporate strategy.

A distinction is made by Purcell (1989) and Purcell and Ahlstrand (1994) between:

- *'upstream' first-order decisions* which are concerned with the long-term direction of the enterprise or the scope of its activities;
- *'downstream' second-order decisions* which are concerned with internal operating procedures and how the firm is organized to achieve its goals;
- *'downstream' third-order decisions* which are concerned with choices on human resource structures and approaches and are strategic in the sense that they establish the basic parameters of employee relations management in the firm.

It can indeed be argued that HR strategies, like other functional strategies such as product development, manufacturing and the introduction of new technology, will be developed within the context of the overall business strategy, but this need not imply that HR strategies come third in the pecking order. Observations made by Armstrong and Long (1994) during research into the strategy formulation processes of 10 large UK organizations suggested that there were only two levels of strategy formulation. First, there is the corporate strategy relating to the vision and mission of the organization but often expressed in terms of marketing and financial objectives. Second, there are specific strategies within the corporate strategy concerning product-market development, acquisitions and divestments, human resources, finance, new technology, organization, and such overall aspects of management as quality, flexibility, productivity, innovation and cost reduction.

The development process

The process of developing HR strategies involves generating strategic HRM options and then making appropriate strategic choices. These choices should, so far as possible:

- relate to but also anticipate the needs of the business;
- be congruent with the present or desired culture of the organization;
- have the capacity to change the character and direction of the business;
- equip the organization to deal effectively with the external pressures and demands affecting it;
- focus on areas of critical need;
- answer fundamental questions such as: 'What is constraining us?', 'What is stopping us from delivering business results?';
- be founded on detailed analysis and study, not just wishful thinking;
- incorporate the experienced and collective judgement of top management;
- take account of the needs of line managers and employees generally as well as those of the organization and its other stakeholders;
- anticipate the problems of implementation that may arise if line managers are not committed to the strategy and/or lack the skills and time to play their part;
- anticipate any problems that may arise because of the hostility or indifference of employees or trade unions;
- ensure that the organization has the resources required to implement the strategy;
- provide for the acquisition and development of people with the skills needed to manage and sustain the organization in the future to meet organizational objectives;
- consist of components that fit with and support each other;
- be capable of being turned into actionable programmes.

STRATEGIC FRAMEWORKS

The formulation of coherent HR strategies is more likely if the overall approaches the organization intends to adopt to managing its human resources are understood. These can then serve as the framework within which specific strategies can evolve. The most common approaches are:

- the development of resource capability;
- high-commitment management;
- high-performance management;
- best practice.

Resource capability

The resource capability approach regards the firm as a bundle of tangible and intangible resources and capabilities required for product/market competition (Kamoche, 1996). Human resources are seen as a major source of competitive advantage.

As expressed by Kamoche, the basis of this approach to HR strategy is the acknowledgement of the 'stock of know-how' in the firm. The capability-based framework is concerned with the actions, processes and related behavioural efforts required to attain a competitive position. As Schuler and Jackson (1987) note:

> Within this framework, firms attempt to gain competitive advantage using human resources through developing distinctive capabilities (competencies) that arise from the nature of the firm's relationships with its suppliers, customers and employees.

Kamoche describes the resource capability view of the firm as one that 'builds on and provides a unifying framework for the field of strategic human resource management'.

A resource capability approach is concerned with the acquisition, development and retention of human or intellectual capital. It will focus on how added value can be obtained by treating people as strategic assets in the sense that they perform activities that create advantage in particular markets. This is in accord with the fundamental principle of economics that wealth is created when assets are moved from lower-value to higher-value uses.

The high-commitment management approach

As mentioned in Chapter 4, high-commitment management as originally described by Walton (1985) is based on the assumption that higher levels of performance from people, and a belief that the organization is worth working for, are more likely when employees are not tightly controlled. Instead, they should be given broader responsibilities, encouraged to contribute and helped to achieve satisfaction in their work.

This approach involves treating employees as partners in the enterprise, whose interests are respected, who have a voice on matters that concern them and whose opinions are sought and listened to. It is concerned with *communication* and *involvement*. It creates a climate in which a continuing dialogue between managers and the members of their teams takes place to define expectations and share information on the organization's mission, values and objectives. This establishes mutual understanding of what *is* to be achieved and a framework for managing and developing people to ensure that it *will* be achieved.

The high-performance management approach

As described in Chapter 4, high-performance management aims to raise the performance of the organization through its people. High-performance management practices involve the development of resourcing, employee development, performance management and reward processes that focus on the delivery of added value.

The best practice approach

This approach is based on the questionable assumption (see Chapter 4) that there is a set of best HRM practices and that adopting them will inevitably lead to superior organizational performance. Most commentators agree that best fit is more important than best practice, but when formulating HR strategies, many people continue to seek the 'holy grail' of a range of ideal approaches to HRM. But views will always differ on what constitutes best practice, as is illustrated in Table 5.1.

MODELS FOR DEVELOPING HR STRATEGIES

Essentially, the formulation of HR strategy requires answers to just three questions:

1.   Where are we now?
2.   Where do we want to be in one, two or three years' time?
3.   How are we going to get there?

But it is more complicated than that and the process could be modelled as shown in Figure 5.1.

A systematic approach

There is much to be said for adopting a systematic approach to formulating HR strategies that considers all the relevant business and environmental issues,

Table 5.1 Views on HR best practices
(source Marchington and Wilkinson, 1996)

Best practice	Storey (1992a)	Pfeffer (1994)	Wood (1995)	Huselid (1995)
Sophisticated selection	*	*	*	*
Flexibility/teamworking	*	*	*	
Internal promotion		*	*	
Employment security		*	*	
Employee involvement	*	*	*	*
Employee voice				*
Commitment	*	*	*	*
to learning	*	*	*	*
Performance-related reward	*	*	*	
Harmonization	*	*	*	
Employee ownership				

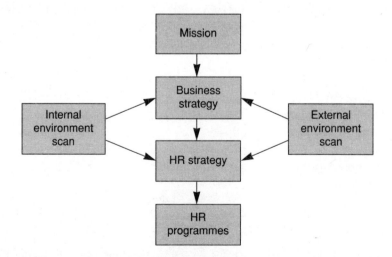

Figure 5.1 A sequential strategic HRM model

and a methodology for this purpose was developed by Dyer and Holder (1988) as follows:

1. *Assess feasibility* – from an HR point of view, feasibility depends on whether the numbers and types of key people required to make the proposal succeed can be obtained on a timely basis and at a reasonable cost, and whether the behavioural expectations assumed by the strategy are realistic (eg retention rates and productivity levels).
2. *Determine desirability* – examine the implications of strategy in terms of sacrosanct HR policies (eg a strategy of rapid retrenchment would have to be called into question by a company with a full employment policy).
3. *Determine goals* – these indicate the main issues to be worked on and they derive primarily from the content of the business strategy. For example, a strategy to become a lower-cost producer would require the reduction of labour costs. This in turn translates into two types of HR goals: higher performance standards (contribution) and reduced head counts (composition).
4. *Decide means of achieving goals* – the general rule is that the closer the external and internal fit, the better the strategy, consistent with the need to adapt flexibly to change. External fit refers to the degree of consistency between HR goals on the one hand and the exigencies of the underlying business strategy and relevant environmental conditions on the other. Internal fit measures the extent to which HR means follow from the HR goals and other relevant environmental conditions, as well as the degree of coherency or synergy among the various HR means.

In addition, the HR strategist should take pains to understand the levels at which business strategies are formed and the style adopted by the company in creating strategies and monitoring their implementation. It will then be easier to focus on those corporate or business unit issues that are likely to have HR implications.

The sequence of strategy formulation

A sequence of questions for formulating strategy is illustrated in Figure 5.2. In reality, of course, the process of developing HR strategies does not follow this sequence so neatly. The analysis may be incomplete or out-of-date as soon as it is made. The diagnosis may be superficial in the face of rapidly evolving factors that are difficult to pin down. The alternatives may not be easy to evaluate and iteration is required to optimize the solution. Action plans may look good on paper but are hard to put into practice, and it may be difficult to estimate costs and the need for other resources. But an attempt is worth making and this framework is useful when putting a strategy proposal together.

General issues affecting the formulation of HR strategies

Although systematic approaches such as those described above are desirable, it should be remembered that strategic HRM is more of an attitude of mind than a step-by-step process that takes you inexorably from a mission statement to implementation.

Strategic HR planning is usually a much less orderly affair than the models suggest. This is entirely understandable if it is borne in mind that strategic HRM is as much about the management of change in conditions of uncertainty as about the rigorous development and implementation of a logical plan.

Perhaps the best way to look at the reality of strategic HRM is to remember the statement made by Mintzberg *et al* (1988) that strategy formulation is about 'preferences, choices, and matches' rather than an exercise 'in applied logic'. It is also desirable to follow Mintzberg's analysis and treat HR strategy as a perspective rather than a rigorous procedure for mapping the future. Moore (1992) has suggested that Mintzberg has looked inside the organization, indeed inside the heads of the collective strategists, and come to the conclusion that, relative to the organization, strategy is analogous to the personality of an individual. As Mintzberg sees them, all strategies exist in the minds of those people they make an impact upon. What is important is that people in the organization share the same perspective 'through their intentions and/or by their actions'. This is what Mintzberg calls the 'collective mind', and reading that mind is essential if we are 'to understand how intentions... become shared, and how action comes to be exercised on a collective yet consistent basis'.

No one else has made this point so well as Mintzberg and what the research conducted by Armstrong and Long (1994) revealed is that strategic HRM *is* being practised in the Mintzbergian sense in the organizations they visited. In other words *intentions* are shared amongst the top team and this leads to actions being exercised on a *collective yet consistent basis*. In each case the shared intentions emerged as a result of strong leadership from the chief executive, with the other members of the top team acting *jointly* in pursuit of well-defined goals. These goals indicated quite clearly the critical success factors of competence, commitment, performance, contribution and quality that drive the HR strategy.

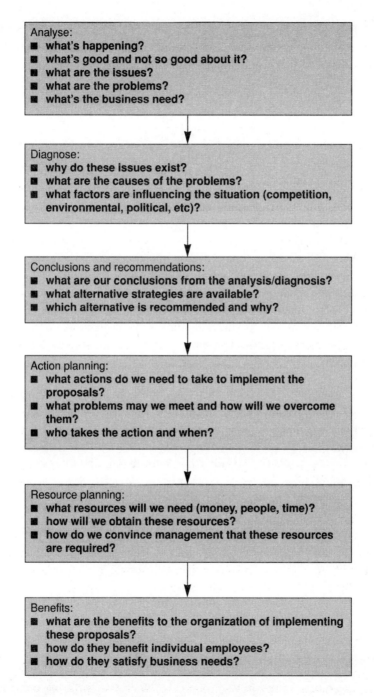

Figure 5.2 The sequence of HR strategy formulation

Against this background the specific issues that have to be addressed comprise: 1) the business issues facing the organization, 2) achieving integration and vertical fit, 3) approaches to achieving horizontal integration or fit – ie coherence through 'bundling', and 4) achieving flexibility.

KEY BUSINESS ISSUES

The key business issues that may impact on HR strategies include:

■ intentions concerning growth or retrenchment, acquisitions, mergers, divestments, diversification, product/market development;
■ proposals on increasing competitive advantage through innovation leading to product/service differentiation, productivity gains, improved quality/customer service, cost reduction (downsizing);
■ the felt need to develop a more positive, performance-oriented culture;
■ any other culture management imperatives associated with changes in the philosophies of the organization in such areas as gaining commitment, mutuality, communications, involvement, devolution and teamworking.

Business strategies in these areas may be influenced by HR factors although not excessively so. HR strategies are, after all, about making business strategies work. But the business strategy must take into account key HR opportunities and constraints.

Business strategy sets the agenda for HR strategy in the following areas:

■ HR mission;
■ values, culture and style;
■ organizational philosophy and approach to the management of people;
■ top management as a corporate resource;
■ resourcing;
■ skills acquisition and development;
■ high-commitment management;
■ high-performance management.

Achieving vertical integration and fit

Vertical integration comes in two forms: 1) integration with the culture of the organization, and 2) fit with the business strategy.

Culture integration

HR strategies need to be congruent with the existing culture of the organization or designed to produce cultural change in specified directions. This will be a necessary factor in the formulation stage but could be a vital factor when it comes to implementation. In effect, if what is proposed is in line with 'the way we do things around here', then it will be more readily accepted. However, in the more likely event that it changes 'the way we do things around here', then careful attention has to be given to the real problems that may occur in the process of trying to embed the new initiative in the organization.

It is therefore necessary to analyse the existing culture to provide information on how HR strategies will need to be shaped. The analysis may cover the following 12 points listed by Cooke and Lafferty (1989) in their organizational culture inventory:

1. *Humanistic-helpful* – organizations managed in a participative and person-centred way.
2. *Affiliative* – organizations that place a high priority on constructive relationships.
3. *Approval* – organizations in which conflicts are avoided and interpersonal relationships are pleasant, at least superficially.
4. *Conventional* – conservative, traditional and bureaucratically controlled organizations.
5. *Dependent* – hierarchically controlled and non-participative organizations.
6. *Avoidance* – organizations that fail to reward success but punish mistakes.
7. *Oppositional* – organizations in which confrontation prevails and negativism is rewarded.
8. *Power* – organizations structured on the basis of the authority inherent in members' positions.
9. *Competitive* – a culture in which winning is valued and members are rewarded for out-performing one another.
10. *Competence/perfectionist* – organizations in which perfectionism, persistence and hard work are valued.
11. *Achievement* – organizations that do things well and value members who set and accomplish challenging but realistic goals.
12. *Self-actualization* – organizations that value creativity, quality over quantity, and both task accomplishment and individual growth.

Achieving vertical fit – integrating business and HR strategies

When considering how to integrate business and HR strategies it should be remembered that business and HR issues influence each other and in turn influence corporate and business unit strategies. It is also necessary to note that in establishing these links, account must be taken of the fact that strategies for change have also to be integrated with changes in the external and internal environments. Fit may exist at a point in time but circumstances will change and fit no longer exists. An excessive pursuit of 'fit' with the status quo will inhibit the flexibility of approach that is essential in turbulent conditions. This is the 'temporal' factor in achieving fit identified by Gratton *et al* (1999). An additional factor that will make the achievement of good vertical fit difficult is that the business strategy may not be clearly defined – it could be in an emergent or evolutionary state. This would mean that there could be nothing with which to fit the HR strategy.

Making the link

However, an attempt can be made to understand the direction in which the organization is going, even if this is not expressed in a formal strategic plan. All businesses have strategies in the form of intentions although these may be ill-formed and subject to change. The ideal of achieving a link in rigorous terms may be difficult to attain. Cooke and Armstrong (1990) suggested that one approach might be to find a means of quantifying the additional resources required by HR overall and at the level of each element of HR strategy, and measuring and comparing the marginal return on investing in each element. But it is highly unlikely that this approach would be practicable.

The link must therefore be judgemental, but it could still be fairly rigorous. Conceptually, the approach would be to develop a matrix as illustrated in Table 5.2, which for each of the key elements of business strategy identifies the associated key elements of HR strategy.

Even if the approach cannot be as rigorous as this, the principle of considering each key area of business strategy and, reciprocally, the HR implications, provides a possible basis for integration.

An alternative framework for linking business and HR strategies is the competitive strategy approach as described in Chapter 4. This identifies the different HR strategies that can relate to the firm's competitive strategies, including those listed by Porter (1985). An illustration of how this might be expressed is given in Table 5.3.

Table 5.2 A conceptual approach to linking business and HR strategies

	Market development	Product development	New technology mergers	Acquisitions/ divestments
Organization				
Resourcing				
HRD				
Performance management				
Reward				
Employee relations				

Requirements for the achievement of vertical fit

As suggested by Wright and Snell (1998), seeking fit requires:

- knowledge of the skills and behaviour necessary to implement the strategy;
- knowledge of the HRM practices necessary to elicit those skills and behaviours;
- the ability to quickly implement the desired system of HRM practices.

Achieving horizontal fit and coherence

Horizontal fit is achieved when the various HR strategies cohere and are mutually supporting. This can be attained by the process of 'bundling', ie the use of complementary HR practices, also known as 'configuration'.

Bundling implies the adoption of an holistic approach to the development of HR strategies and practices. No single aspect of HR strategy should be considered in isolation. The links between one area and other complementary areas need to be established so that the ways in which they can provide mutual support to the achievement of the overall strategy can be ascertained. The synergy that can result from this process means that the impact of the whole

Table 5.3 Linking HR and competitive strategies

Competitive Strategy	HR Strategy		
	Resourcing	HR Development	Reward
Achieve competitive advantage through innovation	Recruit and retain high-quality people with innovative skills and a good track record in innovation	Develop strategic capability and provide encouragement and facilities for enhancing innovative skills	Provide financial incentives and rewards for successful innovations
Achieve competitive advantage through quality	Use sophisticated selection procedures to recruit people who are likely to deliver quality and high levels of customer service	Encourage the development of a learning organization and support total quality and customer care initiatives with focused training	Link rewards to quality performance and the achievement of high standards of customer service
Achieve competitive advantage through cost-leadership	Develop core/ periphery employment structures; recruit people who are likely to add value; if unavoidable, plan and manage downsizing humanely	Provide training designed to improve productivity; inaugurate just-in-time training that is closely linked to immediate business needs and can generate measurable improvements in cost-effectiveness	Review all reward practices to ensure that they provide value for money and do not lead to unnecessary expenditure
Achieve competitive advantage by employing people who are better than those employed by competitors	Use sophisticated recruitment and selection procedures based on a rigorous analysis of the special capabilities required by the organization	Develop organizational learning processes; encourage self-managed learning through the use of personal development plans as part of a performance management process	Develop performance management processes that enable both financial and non-financial rewards to be related to competence and skills; ensure that pay levels are competitive

bundle on organizational effectiveness can be greater than the sum of its parts. Thus, a job family pay structure (see Chapter 15) can be associated with competence frameworks and profiles and the definition of career paths as a basis for identifying and meeting development needs. The message provided by the pay structure that rewards follow from career progression is much more powerful if is linked to processes that enable people to develop their capabilities and potential.

How to bundle

The process of bundling is driven by the needs of the business. It involves six steps:

1. An analysis of what the needs of the business are.
2. An assessment of how HR strategy can help to meet them.
3. The identification of the capabilities and behaviours required of employees if they are to make a full contribution to the achievement of strategic goals.
4. A review of appropriate HR practices, followed by the grouping together (bundling) of them in ways that are likely to ensure that people with the required capabilities are attracted to and developed by the organization and which will encourage appropriate behaviours.
5. An analysis of how the items in the bundle can be linked together so that they become mutually reinforcing and therefore coherent. This may mean identifying integrating practices such as the use of competence-based processes and performance management.
6. The formulation of programmes for the development of these practices, paying particular attention to the links between them.

Approaches to selecting the right bundle, the use of integrative processes and the development of complementary practices are discussed below.

Selecting the right bundle

There have been a number of attempts at producing universally applicable lists of best practices which, it is assumed, will be effective in improving performance. A good example is the list of seven practices of successful organizations produced by Pfeffer (1994): employment security, selective hiring, self-managed teams, high performance-contingent pay, training, reduction of status differentials and sharing information.

However, there is no evidence that a particular bundle is superior to any other bundle in all circumstances. Delaney and Huselid (1996) failed to find any positive impact for specific combinations of practices as opposed to the total number of HR practices. As noted by Guest (1997), a number of researchers have shown that the more high-performance HRM practices that are used, the better the performance as indicated by productivity, labour turnover or financial indicators. These high-performance practices as defined by the US Department of Labor (1993) include:

- careful and extensive systems for recruitment, selection and training;
- formal systems for sharing information with the individuals who work in the organization;
- clear job design;
- high-level participation processes;
- monitoring of attitudes;
- performance appraisals;
- properly functioning grievance procedures;
- promotion and compensation schemes that provide for the recognition and reward of high-performing members of the workforce.

The choice of what is the best bundle for an organization from this shopping list and the others that have been published (see Table 5.1) will depend upon its business needs and strategy and its culture. In other words, a contingency (best fit) approach rather than a best practice approach is likely to be most appropriate. And whatever combination of practices is adopted it is still necessary to consider how to achieve coherence and mutual support by the use of integrative processes and by linking different practices together.

The use of integrative processes

The two main integrative processes are performance management and the use of competencies. The ways in which they can provide the 'glue' between different HR practices are illustrated in Figures 5.3 and 5.4.

Linking HR practices

Bundling is not just a pick-and-mix process. The aim should be first to establish overriding areas of HR practice that need to be applied generally and second, to examine particular practices to establish links or common ground between them so that they provide mutual support.

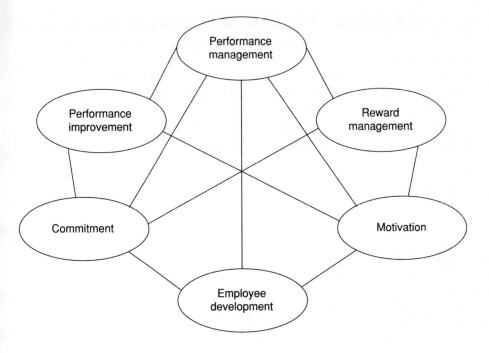

Figure 5.3 Performance management as an integrating force

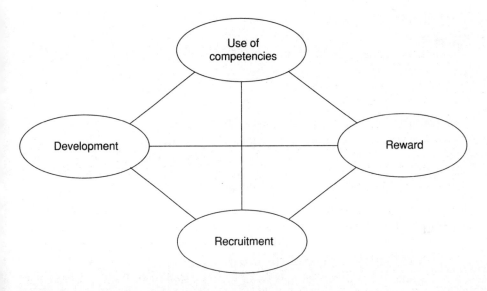

Figure 5.4 Use of competencies as an integrating force

The overriding areas of HR practice will be concerned with organization development, the management of change, creating a positive employment relationship, developing mutual commitment policies, communicating with employees, and giving employees a voice (involvement and participation). These should be taken into account generally and their relevance should be considered when introducing any practices concerned with resourcing, human resource development and reward management. It is necessary to take specific steps in the latter areas to achieve coherence.

Achieving coherence

To achieve coherence the following approaches are necessary:

- never consider any innovation in isolation;
- seek synergy – look for ways in which one practice can support another practice;
- identify common requirements that can be met by initiatives in different areas of HR practice, as long as they are deliberately linked – examples of how this may happen are given in Table 5.4.

Achieving flexibility

Strategic flexibility is about the ability of the firm to respond and adapt to changes in its competitive environment. Fit is concerned with aligning business and HR strategy. It has been argued that these concepts of flexibility and fit are incompatible: 'fit' implies a fixed relationship between the HR strategy and business strategy, but the latter has got to be flexible, so how can good fit be maintained? But Wright and Snell (1998) have suggested that the concepts of fit and flexibility are complementary – fit exists at a point in time while flexibility has to exist over a period of time. They call this 'dynamic fit' and have developed a fit/flexibility model of strategic HRM, as shown in Figure 5.5. The top half of the model depicts the fit component, that is, the means through which the firm seeks to fit HRM practices, employee skills and employee behaviours to the immediate competitive needs of the firm as dictated by the business strategy. The lower half of the model illustrates the flexibility component that focuses on developing the organizational capability to a variety of competitive needs other than those dictated by the current strategy.

Environmental differences will affect a fit/flexibility strategy. As indicated by Wright and Snell, in a stable predictable environment, the strategy could be

Table 5.4 Common elements in HR strategy areas

Overall HR Strategy	HR Strategy		
	Resourcing	HR Development	Reward
Improve performance	Competence-based recruiting; assessment centres	Competence-based training; development centres	Competence-related pay
Extend skills base	Identify skills development needs of recruits.	Skills analysis; focused training in identified needs; accreditation of skills	Skills-based pay
Provide for competence and career development	Develop competency frameworks and profiles; identify competence levels and potential through performance management processes	Use performance management and personal development plans as basis for defining and meeting learning needs; establish broad career development bands for mapping lateral development paths; identify career ladders in job families defined in competence terms	Develop broad-banded or job family structures defined in competence terms and which clearly indicate 'aiming points' (competence requirements in different roles within or outside job family; institute systems of career development pay for lateral progression through bands
Provide for employability	Develop a positive psychological contract based on an undertaking to identify and develop transferable skills; provide scope for job enlargement/ enrichment and opportunities to move into new roles	Identify skills development needs through personal development planning; institute programmes for developing transferable skills	Develop broad-banded/job family structures that identify competence levels for roles or job families and provide a basis for identifying learning needs

Table 5.4 (*contd*)

Increase commitment	Analyse characteristics of committed employees; use sophisticated selection methods to identify candidates who have these characteristics and are likely to be committed to the organization; define and communicate organizational core values	On the basis of the analysis of the characteristics of committed employees, provide learning experiences that enhance understanding and acceptance of organizational core values and encourage value-driven behaviour	Reinforce value-driven behaviour by providing rewards that are based on evidence that core values are being upheld
Increase motivation	Analyses characteristics of well-motivated employees and structure selection interviews to obtain evidence of how well-motivated candidates are likely to be	Provide learning opportunities that reinforce characteristics of well-motivated employees and offer non-financial rewards	Use performance management processes as a basis for providing non-financial rewards related to opportunities for development and growth

to develop people with a narrow range of skills (or not to develop multi-skilled people) and to elicit a narrow range of behaviour (eg tight job descriptions). In a dynamic unpredictable environment, however, organizations might develop organic HR systems that produce a human capital pool with people possessing a wide range of skills who can engage in a wide variety of behaviours. The need is to achieve resource flexibility by developing a variety of 'behavioural scripts' and encouraging employees to apply them in different situations, bearing in mind the increased amount of discretionary behaviour that may be appropriate. The main components of the flexibility strategy could be to:

- develop HR systems that can be adapted flexibly;
- develop a human capital pool with a broad range of skills;

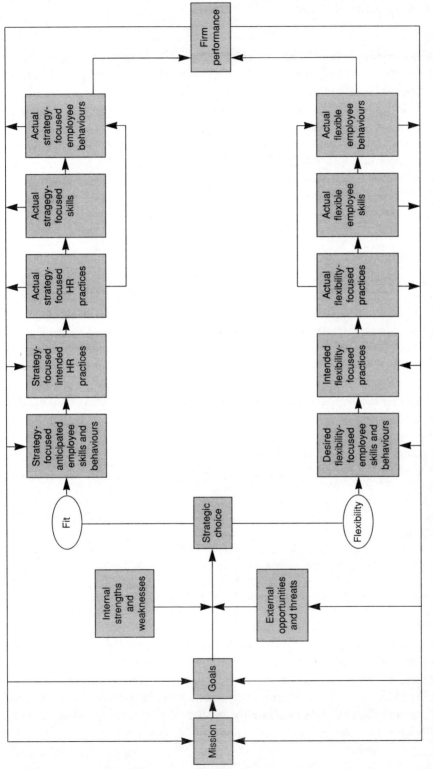

Figure 5.5 Fit and flexibility model (reproduced with permission from Wright and Snell, 1998)

- select people who have the ability to train and adapt;
- promote behavioural flexibility by, for example, training to extend 'behavioural repertoire';
- use performance management and reward systems that encourage flexible behaviour;
- bundle these with participative work systems that give employees opportunities to contribute their discretionary behaviours;
- consider other ways to extend organizational and role flexibility, as described in Chapter 13.

IMPLEMENTING HR STRATEGIES

Because strategies tend to be expressed as abstractions, they must be translated into programmes with clearly stated objectives and deliverables. But getting strategies into action is not easy. The term 'strategic HRM' has been devalued in some quarters, sometimes to mean no more than a few generalized ideas about HR policies, at other times to describe a short-term plan, for example, to increase the retention rate of graduates. It must be emphasized that HR strategies are not just programmes, policies, or plans concerning HR issues that the HR department happens to feel are important. Piecemeal initiatives do not constitute strategy.

The problem with strategic HRM as noted by Gratton *et al* (1999) is that too often there is a gap between the rhetoric of the strategy and the reality of what happens to it. As they put it:

> One principal strand that has run through this entire book is the disjunction between rhetoric and reality in the area of human resource management, between HRM theory and HRM practice, between what the HR function says it is doing and how that practice is perceived by employees, and between what senior management believes to be the role of the HR function, and the role it actually plays.

The factors identified by Gratton *et al* which contribute to creating this gap included:

- the tendency of employees in diverse organizations only to accept initiatives they perceive to be relevant to their own areas;
- the tendency of long-serving employees to cling to the status quo;
- complex or ambiguous initiatives may not be understood by employees or will be perceived differently by them, especially in large, diverse organizations;

- it is more difficult to gain acceptance of non-routine initiatives;
- employees will be hostile to initiatives if they are believed to be in conflict with the organization's identity, eg downsizing in a culture of 'job-for-life';
- the initiative is seen as a threat;
- inconsistencies between corporate strategies and values;
- the extent to which senior management is trusted;
- the perceived fairness of the initiative;
- the extent to which existing processes could help to embed the initiative;
- a bureaucratic culture that leads to inertia.

Barriers to the implementation of HR strategies

Each of the factors listed by Gratton *et al* can create barriers to the successful implementation of HR strategies. Other major barriers that can be met by HR strategists when attempting to implement strategic initiatives are:

- failure to understand the strategic needs of the business with the result that HR strategic initiatives are seen as irrelevant, even counter-productive;
- inadequate assessment of the environmental and cultural factors that affect the content of the strategies;
- the development of ill-conceived and irrelevant initiatives, possibly because they are current fads or because there has been an ill-digested analysis of best practice that does not fit the organization's requirements;
- the selection of one initiative in isolation without considering its implications on other areas of HR practice or trying to ensure that a coherent, holistic approach is adopted;
- failure to appreciate the practical problems of getting the initiative accepted by all concerned and of embedding it as part of the normal routines of the organization;
- inability to persuade top management actively to support the initiative;
- inability to achieve ownership among line managers;
- inability to gain the understanding and acceptance of employees;
- failure to take into account the need to have established supporting processes for the initiative (eg performance management to support performance pay);

- failure to recognize that the initiative will make new demands on the commitment and skills of the line managers who may have to play a major part in implementing it (for example, skills in setting objectives, providing feedback and helping to prepare and implement personal development plans in performance management processes);
- failure to ensure that the resources (finance, people and time) required to implement the initiative will be available; these include the HR resources needed to provide support to line managers, conduct training programmes and communicate with and involve employees;
- failure to monitor and evaluate the implementation of the strategy and to take swift remedial action if things are not going according to plan.

Overcoming the barriers

To overcome these barriers it is necessary to carry out the following steps:

1. *Conduct analysis* – the initial analysis should cover business needs, corporate culture and internal and external environmental factors. The framework could be a SWOT analysis of strengths, weaknesses, opportunities and threats facing the organization, or a PESTLE analysis (the political, economic, social, technological, legal and environmental contexts within which the organization operates). The checklist at the end of this chapter sets out a number of questions that should be answered at the analysis stage.
2. *Formulate strategy* – the formulation should set out the rationale for the strategy and spell out its aims, cost and benefits.
3. *Gain support* – particular care needs to be taken to obtain the support of top managers (for whom a business case must be prepared), line managers, employees generally and trade unions. This means communication of intentions and their rationale and the involvement of interested parties in the formulation of strategic plans.
4. *Assess barriers* – an assessment is required of potential barriers to implementation, especially those relating to indifference, hostility (resistance to change) and lack of resources. Unless and until a confident declaration can be made that the initiative will receive a reasonable degree of support (it could be too much to expect universal acclamation) and that the resources in terms of money, people, time and supporting processes will be available, it is better not to plunge too quickly into implementation.

5. *Prepare action plans* – these should spell out what is to be done, who does it and when it should be completed. A project plan is desirable, indicating the stages of the implementation programme, the resources required at each stage, and the stage and final completion dates. The action plan should indicate the consultation, involvement, communication and training programmes that will be required. It should also state how progress will be monitored and the criteria for measuring success against objectives.
6. *Project-manage implementation* – this should be conducted by reference to the action or project plan and involves monitoring progress and dealing with problems as they arise.
7. *Follow up and evaluate* – nothing can be taken for granted. It is essential to follow up and evaluate the results of the initiative. Follow-up can take place through interviews, focus groups and, desirably, attitude surveys. The evaluation should point the way to action in the form of amendments to the original proposals, the provision of supporting processes, additional support to line managers, intensified communication and training, or getting more resources.

Setting out the strategy

The following are the headings under which a strategy and the plans for implementing it could be set out:
1. *Basis*
   - business needs in terms of the key elements of the business strategy;
   - environmental factors and analysis (SWOT/PESTLE);
   - cultural factors – possible helps or hindrances to implementation.
2. *Content* – details of the proposed HR strategy.
3. *Rationale* – the business case for the strategy against the background of business needs and environmental/cultural factors.
4. *Implementation plan*
   - action programme;
   - responsibility for each stage;
   - resources required;
   - proposed arrangements for communication, consultation, involvement and training;
   - project-management arrangements.
5. *Costs and benefits analysis* – an assessment of the resource implications of the plan (costs, people and facilities) and the benefits that will accrue, for

the organization as a whole, for line managers and for individual employees. (So far as possible these benefits should be quantified in terms of value added.)

However, there is no standard model; it all depends on the circumstances of the organization. Here is how a large voluntary organization set out its approach to developing HR strategies.

HR Strategic Review

Background

A major strategic review has taken place and a new Chief Executive and other members of the senior management team have been appointed within the last two years. In essence, the review led to a business strategy which:

- redefined the purpose of the organization;
- emphasized that the core purpose will continue to be given absolute priority;
- set out the need to secure the future of activities outside its core purpose; and importantly,
- made proposals designed to shape and secure the financial future.

HR issues emerging from the strategic review

The key HR issues emerging from the strategic review are that:

- Effectively, it declares an intention to transform the organization.
- This involves major cultural changes, for example:
  - some change in the focus to activities other than the core activity;
  - a move away from a paternalistic, command-and-control organization;
  - introducing processes that enable the organization to operate more flexibly;
  - clarifying expectations, but simultaneously gaining commitment to managing and carrying out activities on the basis of increased self-regulation and decision-making at operational level rather than pressures or instructions from above;

- – more emphasis on managerial as distinct from technical skills for managers;
- – greater concentration on the financial requirement to balance income and expenditure while continuing to develop and improve service delivery.
- A significant change in the regional organization and the roles of the management team and regional controllers/managers is taking place; this means that new skills will have to be used, which some existing managers may not possess.
- From a human resource planning viewpoint, decisions will have to be made on the capabilities required in the future at managerial and other levels, and these may involve establishing policies for recruiting new managerial talent from outside the organization rather than relying on promotion from within.
- Difficult decisions may have to be made on retaining some existing managers in their posts who have not been successful in applying for new regional posts or who lack the required skills, and there may be a requirement to reduce staff numbers in the future.
- More positively, management development and career planning activities will need to be introduced, which reflect the changing culture and structure of the organization and the different roles managers and others will be expected to play.

The provision of the core HR services such as recruitment and training is not an issue.

Steps to address the issues

Steps have already been taken to address these issues, for example:

- major communication initiatives introduced by the Chief Executive;
- a review of the pay system, which will no doubt bear in mind the unsatisfactory experience of the organization in applying performance management/pay procedures a few years ago;
- decisions on the shape of the regional organization;
- an analysis and diagnosis has taken place on cultural issues, ie what the present culture is and what it should become.

Future strategy

Against this background, it is necessary to build on the steps already taken by:

- adopting a systematic approach to the achievement of culture change, bearing in mind that this can be a long haul because it involves changing behaviour and attitudes at all levels and is difficult if not impossible to attain simply by managerial dictation;
- developing an HR strategy which, as a declaration of intent, will provide a framework for the development of HR processes and procedures that address the issues referred to above; this involves:
  - strategic integration, matching HR policies and practices to the business strategy,
  - a coherent approach to the development of these processes so that HR activities are interrelated and mutually reinforcing,
  - a planned approach, but one that is not bureaucratic,
  - an emphasis on the needs to achieve flexibility, quality and cost-effectiveness in the delivery of HR services;
- focusing on the activities that will not only deal with the HR issues but will also help to achieve culture change, namely:
  - *resourcing:* deciding what sort of people are required and ensuring that they are available,
  - *human resource development:* identifying the skills required, auditing the skills available, taking steps to match skills to present and future business requirements and initiating processes for enhancing organizational and individual learning related to business needs,
  - *reward:* using reward processes to ensure that people are valued according to their contribution and to convey messages about the behaviour, capabilities and results expected of them,
  - *employee relations:* building on the steps already taken to communicate to employees and to involve them in decision-making processes on matters that concern them.

The HR strategy will have to establish priorities. Because the thrust of the strategic review initially makes most impact on managers, the priority may well be given to people at this level but without neglecting the needs of the rest of the staff.

HR strategic review model

A model for the strategic review is set out in Figure 5.6.

Figure 5.6 A model for the strategic review

STRATEGIC HM CHECKLIST

The questions to which answers are required when formulating HR strategies are:

1. What are the key components of the business strategy?
2. How can HR strategies support the achievement of the business strategy?
3. What are the strengths and weaknesses of the organization and the opportunities and threats it faces?
4. What are the implications of the political, economic, social, technological, legal and environmental contexts in which the organization operates?
5. To what extent is the organization in a stable or dynamic (turbulent) environment and how will this affect our strategies?
6. What is the nature of the corporate culture? Does it help or hinder the achievement of the organization's goals?

7. What needs to be done to define or redefine our values in such areas as quality, customer service, innovation, teamworking and the responsibility of the organization for its employees?

8. What do we need to do to increase commitment? How do we communicate our intentions and achievements to employees and what steps do we take to give them a voice – obtaining feedback from them and involving them in the affairs of the organization?

9. To what extent do we need to pursue a strategy of high-performance or high-commitment management, and what would be the main features of such a strategy?

10. How in general can we increase the resource capability of the organization?

11. To what extent do existing HR practices meet future business needs? What needs to be done about any gaps or inadequacies?

12. In the light of this gap analysis, what specific aspects of HRM (processes and practices) do we need to focus on when formulating strategy?

13. How can we best 'bundle' together the various HR practices?

14. How can we achieve coherence in developing the different HR practices?

15. How can we achieve the flexibility required to cope with change?

16. What kind of skills and behaviours do we need now and in the future?

17. Are performance levels high enough to meet demands for increased profitability, higher productivity, better quality and improved customer service?

18. Will the organization's structure and systems be able to cope with future challenges in their present form?

19. Are we making the best use of the skills and capabilities of our employees?

20. Are we investing enough in developing those skills and capabilities?

21. Are there any potential constraints in the form of skills shortages or employee relations problems?

22. Are our employment costs too high?

23. Is there likely to be any need for de-layering or downsizing?

The answers to these and similar questions define the areas in which HR strategies need to be developed. The important thing is to give an overall sense of purpose to HR activities by linking them explicitly to the needs of the business and its employees.

6

Strategic HRM in action

The examples of strategic HRM in action referred to in this chapter are mainly drawn from research conducted by Armstrong and Long (1994). The action issues are concerned with the formulation and content of HR strategy, the corporate perspective and approaches to integrating strategy. The chapter ends with a summary of the characteristic features of strategic HRM.

FORMULATING HR STRATEGY

Taking into account Tyson and Witcher's (1994) point that you can only study HR strategy in the context of business strategies, the processes of formulating both business and HR strategies as identified in research conducted by Armstrong and Long (1994) in a number of companies (some of which preferred to remain anonymous) are described below.

ABC Distribution

ABC Distribution distributes food products, mainly to major retailers. The critical success factors for the organization as spelt out by its Managing Director and the Finance Director are its ability to meet its profit targets and to grow the business substantially on a consistent basis by developing a reputation for providing added value services, developing business with existing customers, winning new customers, and acquisitions. The company has doubled in size in the last four years. Underpinning the development of the company are the needs to grow the infrastructure, to develop management and leadership and to extend quality and safety programmes.

Business strategy

The Managing Director agreed that, in a sense, their business strategy evolved in a semi-formal way, but this evolution took place 'by the key people understanding what the business was trying to do, and their part in it; then they went away and put their bits together; then we pulled all of it together'. He commented that:

> Our strategy is very simple and very broad... it can be put down in a few sentences. It's what lies around it that has to be developed.

He emphasized that:

> We sought to demonstrate to the rest of the business that we (the Board) were a team. Where a team hadn't existed before, a team was now running the company.

The Deputy Managing Director explained how he saw the formulation of the business strategy taking place:

> We put our strategy together within the framework of the financial targets we have to meet and our values for quality, integrity and management style.

In answer to the question: 'How does your organization develop its business strategies?' the Director of Finance said that:

> It started off as being very simple in that we had an objective to grow in excess of the rate of growth demanded by our parent company... However, that process has become less naive, more detailed and more structured as the business grows... I see planning as a process that goes on and on and on and becomes more complex and more refined.

He also made the following comment:

> Don't forget, not all strategies necessarily involve massive change... you can have a strategy to stay as you are.

The Director of Marketing emphasized the dynamic nature of strategy in a growing business operating in a highly competitive environment:

> We have a strategy document which is concerned with developing market share and growth and is being continuously updated... The update is driven by the Board... We have to make sure that we continue to refresh the strategy.

The Director of Personnel commented that:

> The longer-term strategy is developed basically by the Board getting together and working its way through... We also share that plan with the senior management team.

HR strategy

The Managing Director described their approach to developing the HR strategy as follows:

> Our HR strategy has to respond to our business needs... So we start with a business plan; we know we are going to grow at a certain rate. Then we do a skills audit and predict how many managers we are going to need. Out of this comes our HR development policy on skills training, leadership training and recruitment.

The Deputy Managing Director thought that the Personnel Director was basically responsible for developing their HR strategy:

> We all look at our business strategy and express a view on the people we need, but our HR director pulls it all together and interprets our ramblings into something coherent.

However, in answering a question on how HR strategies were developed, the Director of Finance admitted that:

> We probably have more HR policies than strategies because the strategies are there in a simple sense but not 100 per cent well articulated – for valid reasons; we are a growing business.

The Director of Personnel referred to the way in which strategic initiatives were developed:

> First the personnel people meet and we bounce ideas about and seek ideas. Then if we have a new initiative we put it to the Board for discussion.

Loamshire Council

Loamshire Council is a District Council that is generally recognized as being a very well run and capable local authority. It is particularly good at dealing with the environment and, as the Chief Executive said: 'We tend to care so passionately about our environment that we focus an almost disproportionate amount of our resources on environmental issues'. He further commented that the critical success factors for the authority were meeting the perceived needs of the community, creating customer satisfaction with the services provided and, importantly: 'an overall appreciation of the effectiveness of members of staff and the contribution they make towards the organization as a whole'.

Corporate strategy

The following comments were made by the Chief Executive on how corporate strategy was developed:

> We do not have a single document which says 'this is the Loamshire Council corporate strategy'. What we do have are three processes which run in parallel and together represent the corporate strategy. These comprise a *general strategy* for developing services, a *management strategy* which concentrates on the managerial processes, which we need to design to bring out the best in the organization, and the *key areas for achievement* document, which focuses on specific actions.
>
> Strategies are developed by a top-down, bottom-up process. The members of the Council, the policy makers, debate the strategic issues from which firm strategic proposals would develop. Individual members of staff are then given opportunities to contribute... A distinguishing feature of all our corporate strategy work has been the opportunity for widespread involvement in the process.
>
> It is incredibly important that within an organization there is somebody who has the personal responsibility for monitoring, evaluating and reviewing the effectiveness of that organization... That strategic management role lies at the heart of the Chief Executive's responsibility.

The Director of Planning commented as follows on the process of strategic planning:

> The reality is you choose directions and you move in particular directions, then all sorts of things happen that you can't possibly have conceived of, and you weave these into your strategy.

Strategy is rooted in the vision and the culture... Life's very complicated, there are no easy solutions, and you don't start at 'Go' when you throw a six and proceed from there. You pick up a very complex jigsaw and you work through it. But the vision helps.

On how the top team operates, the Director of Planning said that:

The things we bring to the team are personal characteristics as much as the management skills we all learn at various stages... the fact that we have a spectrum of personalities strengthens the team.

HR strategy

The Chief Executive stated that:

Human resource strategy has got to be owned by the top management body within an organization. Their commitment must be absolute, otherwise it simply won't be applied in practice. Everything flows from the corporate strategies we have set down. It's about having a very strong focus on the overall effectiveness of the organization, its direction and how it's performing.

There is commitment to, and belief in, and respect for individuals, and I think that these are very important factors in an organization.

When asked how HR strategies were developed, the Director of Personnel replied:

Initially what I did was to list all the activities in which we were currently involved in personnel and sent a questionnaire to all the directors stating, 'This is what we are doing' and asking, 'Do you want us to continue doing it? If so, do you want the same, or more, or less? Are we doing it well? Could we do it better? What are the things we are not doing that you think we ought to be doing?' The next thing I did was to have two open days in which I invited managers to come in and tell us what their perceptions of personnel were. And this confirmed our eagerness to get rid of duplication and delays in personnel matters. We were fast getting in the way and holding the whole process up. And that's where we got the agreement of the organization that empowerment should be our strategy.

On this strategy for empowerment, the Director of Technical Services remarked:

The positive aspects of the devolution of responsibility for personnel management is that it puts people management back where it should be.

Megastores

Megastores is one of the country's largest and most successful high-street retailers. It has a very powerful overriding commercial objective, to increase shareholder's value, and to do this by providing value-for-money products and delivering consistently high levels of customer service.

Business strategy

The Managing Director made the following observations about strategic management:

> Strategy is developing a route to better the business in the medium to long term. You cannot fully maximize the business opportunities unless you've got the proper management structure to create them.
>
> In business you have to look at the options available, make a decision and then drive that way.

The approach to strategy formulation was described by the Director of Finance as follows:

> Our strategy tends to be based on the resolution of issues. There is a base strategy and we continue to question whether that is the right thing to be going forward with.
>
> We have a strategic planning framework throughout the group. It's called value-based management (VBM), the fundamentals of which are to make sure that whatever you do, you must maximize shareholder value... It provides us with a basis for looking at what we are doing and the resources we require that we've never had before.

He also commented, however, that:

> We're highly profitable, but in turn we invest an awful lot in our people. We spend a lot of money on the training and development of people throughout the organization. It's probably one of our key differentiators.

The Director of Stores gave these perspectives on the strategic planning process:

> We have in place a formal business planning process in which we divide the planning into three levels. One is at business level where we identify issues that we deal with as a company, the second level is product-market planning, and the third level is local market planning.

Our business strategy is formed through value-based management, which is a discipline for pulling everything together and ensures that decisions are made on the basis of their real value to the business rather than someone's strength of personality or hunch. This in itself required the involvement of all the directors in a more formal business planning process. Three or four years ago we worked more individually and now we work more as a team.

There are elements of our business which are incredibly value creating. There are others which are incredibly value destroying. The trick is to identify the ones which *are* value creating and funnel resources to them.

There are a number of blocks that make up our business strategy. The first is our overall objective. Against this we spin off a number of elements we call major initiatives. These are coordinated by our Director of Corporate Planning, but it is the functional directors who are really charged with taking ownership of these objectives.

HR strategy

The comments made by the Managing Director and a number of other directors on the formulation of HR strategy are given below:

The biggest challenge will be to maintain [our] competitive advantage and to do that we need to maintain and continue to attract very high-calibre people. (Managing Director)

All we do in terms of training and manpower planning is directly linked to business improvement. (Managing Director)

The key differentiator on anything any company does is fundamentally the people, and I think that people tend to forget that they are the most important asset. Money is easy to get hold of, good people are not. (Managing Director)

The influence in terms of strategic direction must always be based on the key areas of marketing and operations. (Director of Finance)

We have to help the business achieve its objectives and the HR strategy has to be very much tailored towards those objectives. (Director of Personnel)

When questioned on his approach to the development of personnel strategies the Director of Personnel replied:

I start with the top line, the four or five things which are the strategic platform for the company. I get my managers together to look at the implications. We then pull it together so that it is all derived from the original strategic platforms and then work top-down and bottom-up to get the amalgam of what we can achieve. This then feeds into the final operating plan so we can agree budgets.

Pilkington Optronics Limited

Background

Pilkington Optronics is engaged in the business of precision engineering, including the development and manufacture of specialized optical, mechanical, electrical and electronic equipment primarily for defence purposes.

Two major factors have affected the company: first, the contraction in the defence industry and second, the change in government policy from cost-plus contracting to competitive tendering. This compelled the company to develop an entirely new business strategy and to carry out a comprehensive re-engineering process.

Critical success factors

The Managing Director stated unequivocally that:

> The things that are essential to an organization's success, any organization, not just this one, are the people. They are the common denominator throughout the organization.

The critical success factors for Pilkington Optronics were defined as follows:

> The one factor that drives us is technology know-how. This means we offer solutions, not products. That is really what we have to sell and it depends on people strength. (Managing Director)

> We have a vision of what we want to be and are advancing more quickly than the rest of the competition. CIM (computer integrated manufacture) is at the heart of it. We have tackled MRPII (manufacturing resource planning) as the first phase of CIM and this means that we are faster than our competitors and are more likely to deliver on time than them. (General Manager)

> We are characterized in the marketplace as a high-tech company with specific expertise in the field of optics and particularly electro-optics. We are known for the excellence of our technical solutions and the quality of our products. In the past we have been criticized for asking a premium price for high technology products. Part of the message we are now getting across is that we can battle it out on

value for money as well... People like working with us because they get straight answers to their questions including, 'We don't know' if we really don't know. So our basic competences are high technical quality and people with the skills needed to forge good relationships with customers. (Marketing Director)

Business strategy

Business strategy is stimulated and reviewed centrally by a business strategy group. The business is split into a number of sectors (three in Glasgow) and each sector submits its business plan to the strategy group. This is a simple three-page summary that describes the broad objectives of their business sector, discusses the key competitive factors affecting it and sets out specific short- to medium-term objectives, which are then translated into an operating plan. The plans look at a horizon of ten years but for practical purposes there is a rolling three-year budget. This means that besides looking at the immediate budget the two key questions asked are, as the General Manager put it: 'Where are you going to be in three years' time? What are you doing now to get better?' And this, he said, 'is a very demanding discipline'.

The Marketing Director explained the approach as follows:

> The key to the business planning process is that it has to be a linked story from the top to the bottom of the company and MRPII (manufacturing resourse planning) is part of the vehicle for doing that. Our Director of Strategic Planning works with the Technical Director to involve and guide the Board on the overall strategic direction of the company. This is communicated as the strategic vision. Working from that, my role is to work with the group directors to evolve strategies for each of the businesses we have chosen to be in. These are then reviewed and agreed by the executive and a strategic development group. One of the roles of that group is to check that our activities relate to and support the strategy established by the executive. If they do not, this may not be because they are wrong, and we may have to go back and review the strategy.

The formulation of business strategy is very much a team effort. As the Managing Director said:

> I tell all the top executive people, including the personnel and finance directors, that they are directors first and foremost and all must make a contribution to strategic planning.

The lead may be taken by the Managing Director and the strategic team, of which the Personnel Director is a member, but the heads of the business groups make a major and continuing contribution. The broad thrust of the strategy as a means of realizing the vision is quite clear, but it is in a constant state of evolution, reacting as necessary in response to changing situations but also proactively anticipating new opportunities.

Personnel strategies

The overall approach to the formulation of personnel strategies was summarized by the Managing Director as follows:

> The main thing we have to do is to ensure that we have the right core technologies and the right competences within the company to achieve the vision and strategy.

The General Manager commented that:

> Within the Board one of the things that is constantly reviewed is human resource strategy. We have the long-term view of the type of organization we believe we need as a technology company and we have evolutionary plans of how we are going to get there. In the early stages we had a very strong functional organization; our evolution process now involves the development of problem-solving teams which are set up at a high standard to encourage getting it right first time. In manufacturing we have mixed-discipline teams with a team leader and a much flatter structure than we used to have. We have two pilot projects where research and development engineers are part of the team on the shop floor with a common team leader. The eventual aim is for all engineering and manufacturing to be organized in this way. The next step is to develop product families in which business generation and sales are brought into the team as well. So the team leaders almost become general managers.

The Marketing Director pointed out that the personnel strategy 'was clearly established in the planning process and it had hard objectives in the same way as the business strategy'.

The Personnel Director explained that business strategy defines what has to be done to achieve success and that personnel strategy must complement it, bearing in mind that one of the critical success factors for the company is its ability to attract and retain the best people. Personnel strategy must help to ensure that Pilkington Optronics is a best practice company. This implies that:

> The personnel strategy must be in line with what is best in industry and this may mean visiting four or five different companies, looking at what they are doing and taking a bit from one and a bit from another and moulding them together to form the strategy.

Welland Water

Welland Water is a large water company operating, as pointed out by the Managing Director, 'in a monopolistic situation providing a service that is absolutely fundamental to life'. But he also stated that: 'we recognize that our organization must not abuse that situation and that we must implant in the company values that would be appropriate in a competitive environment'. He went on to say that:

> We can demonstrate that the services we are giving our customers are improving dramatically, year on year… We have an ongoing commitment to involve our customers – we were the first water company to actually prepare an annual report for them… We carry out frequent tracking research which shows that our customers' perceptions of us are improving, on occasions despite a contrary trend in the national water industry… But the critical success factor which allows all this to happen is the level of employee satisfaction and commitment we have, because without that, we can't achieve any of the other things. And we know about this because we get consultants to carry out periodical employee surveys which we discuss with everyone.

Business strategy

The Managing Director described the approach to formulating business strategy as follows:

> Our strategic approach is very simple. It is summarized in our vision statement: we aim to provide the level of services our customers demand at a level of charges that our customers would see as acceptable. Our business strategies are formed essentially from top-down setting of the parameters and then bottom-up preparation of business plans in which all our people are involved. They prepare all their own business plans which reflect the top-down constraints, and because they are preparing them that automatically buys their commitment to them.
>
> Our best ideas for policies and strategies come from the people who carry out the work. We don't have people locked into little rooms thinking: 'What's the next strategic move for the business?'.
>
> What you need are people who are in tune with what's happening throughout the organization; who are listening, talking, picking up all the ideas… What we try to do is to capture all that knowledge, all those initiatives, all that expertise, and reflect that in the way we take the business forward.
>
> I like to talk about getting values in place rather than constructing strategies.

The Finance Director explained the significance of the vision statement in developing business strategies:

> The company developed a vision statement which encompasses the key forward-looking strategy over a period of time but without time-scales having been set down. This has set the guidelines for future initiatives and any such initiative in the rolling five-year business plan is judged on whether it fits in with that vision.

HR strategy

The Managing Director made the point that:

> The only human resource strategy you really need is the tangible expression of values and the implementation of values... unless you get the human resource values right you can forget all the rest.

The Finance Director commented that:

> There's a lot of interaction, prior to and during the top board discussion, which tends to be concerned with culturally based issues and the way we manage people.

And the Director of Operations indicated that the organization developed its HR strategy:

> Through evolution; it's an aggregation of things that have come together, not necessarily in the right order.

The approach to developing HR strategy was described by the Head of Personnel as follows:

> In our original HR strategy we tried to encompass the emerging values and principles that we felt should determine how we should conduct our business in terms of people. HR strategies come from the ideas we share together and the problems and issues that managers are working on... It's very much a team effort, working with line colleagues in whatever they do... I use e-mail to flash ideas round to groups of managers and thus build up draft policy papers. E-mail is a very powerful device for getting ideas back rapidly.

Comments

In all the organizations referred to above:

- There is a well defined corporate or business strategy, although the extent to which it is formalized varies.
- HR strategy is seen as part of the business strategy.
- HR strategy or policy issues *appeared* to be of interest to all members of the board and, contrary to popular opinion, that includes the finance director.

THE CONTENT OF HR STRATEGIES

The rhetoric behind the concepts of human resource management, strategic management and strategic HRM has an inspiring ring about it, but does anything actually happen? And if so, what does it look like? Process is important, but content and action are also required. In the research conducted by Armstrong and Long (1994) it was assumed that the basis of any approach an organization used to develop and implement HR strategies would be the philosophy of influential members of the top team on managing people. The content and programmes of the organizations covered by the research were examined to identify what was contained in their HR strategies and how they were implementing them. This was done under two headings: first, the macro, corporate issues such as vision and mission, organization, performance, quality and customer care, commitment, and the introduction of new technology; second, the more specific HR strategy areas of resourcing, learning, development and training, reward and employee relations.

Philosophy on managing people

The philosophy on managing people is a broad strategic issue associated with management style and it is one that may never be articulated, and so often remains on a 'taken for granted' basis like other manifestations of corporate culture. The philosophy may lead to a 'hard HRM' or a 'soft HRM' approach or a combination of the two, as described in Chapter 1.

But to adapt a common if somewhat inadequate definition of corporate culture, strategic HRM is about 'the way things should be done around here in the future'. Questions can be asked about the traditional or underlying philosophy, the extent to which it is still relevant and the directions in which it might usefully change.

The philosophy of the Managing Director of Megastores on managing people was expressed as follows:

> There is immense strength and talent in any body of people numbering 50,000 and we are negligent if we don't tap that resource as far as we possibly can... The contribution of our managers to added value is immense because they are people managers... They are not managing systems, they are not managing machinery and they are not managing shops – you can't manage a shop, you manage people within a shop.
>
> I have always advocated the employment of the highest calibre of people we can find, and I think we've got that... We are in the vanguard of retailing. Our net profit to sales ratio is about the highest in the high street and in profit terms we are growing at a faster rate than the market. The biggest challenge will be to maintain that competitive advantage and to do that we need to maintain and continue to attract very high-calibre people.

The Operations Director of Merton Health Care Trust said: 'Ours is a success-oriented approach... what we aim to do is to create an environment in which people are successful'.

The Chief Executive of a manufacturing company expressed his philosophy as follows:

> The only way anything happens in any business, large or small, is through the people in the business. If you have got policies and processes in place which allow them to make their contribution in a more forceful and highly motivated way, then you are going to have a wonderfully run business. That's the difference. At one time the role of personnel was to get people to do what they were supposed to do; the future role of personnel is much more about stretching the limits of what people are actually capable of doing.

As the HR Director of the same company stated:

> Our strategy is to stimulate changes on a broad front aimed ultimately at achieving competitive advantage through the efforts of our people. In an industry of fast followers, those who learn quickest will be the winners.

The philosophy on managing people will depend upon the extent to which top management *really* believes in 'success through people'. Certainly the Group Chief Executive of the National Westminster Bank has recognized that HR is a key player in bringing about changes in attitude and behaviour, and as the Director of Human Resources said:

In strategic terms our fundamental reason for being in this position is that in a competitive world it is acknowledged that products do not differentiate you and it's easy to buy technology. What actually gives you the competitive edge is the people that serve the customers.

CORPORATE ISSUES

Vision and mission

In the broadest terms strategic HRM is concerned with the people implications of top management's vision of the future of the organization and the mission it is there to fulfil. HR strategies, like those of all the other functions, are there to support the realization of the vision and mission of the organization and the achievement of its goals.

At Lloyds TSB, the people strategy was devised to facilitate the achievement of the following three strategic goals underpinning the governing objective of maximizing shareholder value:

1. To be a leader in chosen markets.
2. To be the first choice for our customers.
3. To reduce the day-to-day costs of our business.

The HR mission to support these goals is to be a leading employer in retail services as measured from the following perspectives:

- productivity as judged by our shareholders;
- service as judged by our customers;
- satisfaction as judged by our employees;
- management practices as judged by external organizations.

The Personnel Director at Pilkington Optronics made the following comment about vision and strategy:

> The first thing is that the organization has to know where it is going. That is why it needs a vision. It has to know why it exists and who its customers are. This leads to the development of strategies which in turn lead to action plans. The plans follow three lanes: systems, processes and people.

Two of the other functional directors at Pilkington Optronics commented on the significance of vision and a sense of purpose or mission:

I would put it in a single word – vision. If you can create a vision and communicate it to people you can release a colossal current of energy... Communication and vision means education and training and I am one of the operational guys who believe that whatever you are currently spending on education and training, you start by doubling it.

What contributes most to success is a clear sense of purpose and definition of where you are trying to get to. Unless you have a top team with a clear and unified understanding of purpose and direction, it can be difficult to cascade it throughout the organization.

The Managing Director of Welland Water commented that:

We look at our vision for the company and we say: 'How do we maximize the contribution that our people can make to achieving that vision?'.

Organization

HR strategy may address such issues as:

- organizational capabilities;
- structure;
- teamworking;
- performance;
- quality and customer care.

Organizational capabilities

The organizational capabilities at Lloyds TSB that HR needed to address were change management, motivation and direction, knowledge management and resource management. The HR actions to support the business strategy in connection with these capabilities were concerned with change management, leadership and learning, maximizing performance, employee commitment and flexible resourcing.

Structure

The Managing Director of ABC Distribution said that:

I do not see any difference between the HR strategy and the business strategy on organization because we evolve our organization to reflect where the business is going.

As the Managing Director of Megastores said:

> You cannot fully maximize business opportunities unless you have the proper management structure to create them.

Teamworking

At Pilkington Optronics the background to the work on team building was the demolition of traditional hierarchies over the last two to three years. In manufacturing and engineering there are never more than three layers between team members and the director. In 80 per cent of the engineering teams there are now only two layers – the Team Manager and the Engineering Manager. It is believed that these changes have had far-reaching effects on flexibility and performance and have contributed significantly to the achievement of better coordination in manufacturing and engineering.

At Motorola a strategy for developing teamwork forms an important part of the HR strategy. As the HR Director explained, team development and training is an important contribution that the HR function makes to the business. The initial training emphasizes the concept of total customer satisfaction, which automatically includes internal as well as external customers. People are asked to discuss the projects they are working on and if they have problems, they are encouraged to get a team of people to work with them to push the project forward. When a group of people do get together they identify what additional skills they need, and training on team dynamics and team building is provided.

Performance

A performance strategy will be based on an analysis of the critical success factors and the performance levels reached in relation to them. Steps can then be agreed as to what needs to be done to improve performance by training, development, reorganization, the development of performance management processes, some form of business process re-engineering, or simply 'taking cost out of the business'. At Homebase, as indicated by Evans (1998), integrated performance management was an important component of the HR strategy.

This is how a cost-reduction strategy works in one of the key divisions of ABC Distribution, as described by the Managing Director:

> We know that over the next three years we have to take more than £10 million worth of cost out of the business. So our Personnel Director sits down with the business head of the division and they identify the areas we need to focus on. It could be productivity enhancement, it could be changing work practices, it could

be making sure that we have no anomalies round the depots in terms of payment, it could even be taking tea breaks out. A three-year strategy is agreed, targets are set and then they get on with it.

The approach at Loamshire Council was described by the Director of Personnel as follows:

We have a general strategy of performance measurement and management from which grew our performance appraisal system, which has worked extremely well... We spent a lot of time ensuring that people understood that this was a development process and it was about not just their competence, but also the ability of the organization to achieve what it wants to achieve.

The strategy for improving performance at Megastores involves the use of a performance management system that was introduced, as the Director of Personnel explained, 'Because we didn't have any mechanism through which we could run the business through the people'. He went on to say that, 'Line management own it totally. It's not a personnel system, it's a line management system for running the business'.

The Director of Personnel for Megastores also made the following comments on performance strategies:

We set out to understand the differences between successful and less successful performance within the organization and we call those our competency frameworks... By developing these frameworks we have educated the whole of our line management throughout the organization into how to think about their people in a much wider sense. Our key HR strategy question is: 'How do we actually get the people to deliver what the business requires?'.

The process of performance improvement could mean, as Pilkington Optronics' Marketing Director put it:

Going through a lot of effort to ensure that we have the correct level of performance in what we do and underpinning this with financial and commercial stability.

Pilkington Optronics has become one of the most quoted examples of successful performance improvement through business process re-engineering in the UK. The exercise took the form of a functional analysis process which, according to the Personnel Director, was carried out as shown in Figure 6.1. This could be described as business process re-engineering with people in mind.

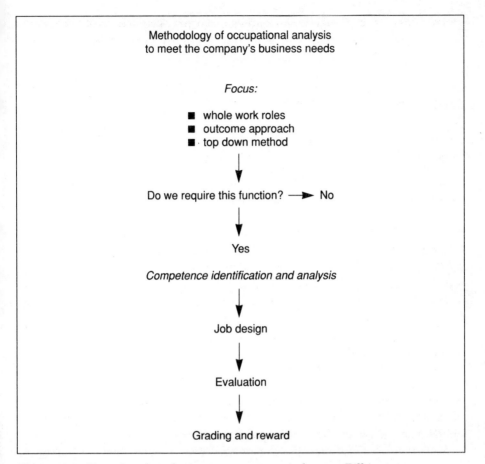

Figure 6.1 Functional analysis process, as carried out at Pilkington Optronics

At Welland Water, the Head of Personnel thought that:

> Performance improvement lies not so much in creating the hard issues at the bottom line but on creating an environment within which people will accept change and cooperate in different methods of working. And I believe our partnership approach does create such an environment, one in which we can manage change successfully and which encourages people to accept new responsibilities and acquire new skills.

The majority of the organizations covered by the research had installed performance management processes in which the emphasis was on performance improvement and development and not reward. The scheme in Midlands Manufacturing emphasized the new priorities of involvement, teamwork and self-development as well as more standard measures.

Quality and customer care

Quality, which in essence means customer satisfaction, is generally recognized today as the key to the achievement of competitive advantage. Innovation and cost reduction are still important, but they are to no avail if, ultimately, customers reject the product because it does not meet their expectations. Quality is achieved through people and, in accordance with a basic HRM principle, investment in people is a prerequisite for achieving high quality standards.

A strategy for total quality is a true HRM strategy in the sense that it is owned and delivered by management. It should therefore be built into their business strategy as it is, for example, at Pilkington Optronics and Motorola. The Chief Executive of Loamshire Council said that:

> We have a performance appraisal system and one area that we are particularly keen should be dealt with as part of that process is the contribution of the individual to our customer care standards.

The HR Director of Motorola describes it as a 'quality-driven' company, and at National Westminster Bank the focus is very much on service – on meeting the demands of customers for more sophisticated banking.

At Pilkington Optronics, the Personnel Director stated that, in pursuit of their goal of world-class performance, personnel strategy must help to ensure that they are a best practice company. An important aspect of this strategy, 'is to educate everyone to build quality into every job, aiming to convey to people that if you get it right first time they will be saving a lot of unnecessary work'.

ACHIEVING INTEGRATION

The integration of HR and business strategies is seen by some commentators as a main distinguishing feature of strategic HRM. Doubts have been cast by a number of commentators such as Storey (1993) on the extent to which such integration does take place, often on the grounds that integration is not an issue when there are no corporate strategies. This was not the case in any of the eight organizations covered by Armstrong and Long's research. In all but two of them the HR strategies, in Walker's (1992) terms, were fully integrated; in the remaining cases the strategies were 'aligned'.

As the Managing Director of ABC Distribution pointed out:

> Our HR strategy has to respond to our business strategy... The challenge for HR is to look at all the areas that they encompass and make sure they are integrated into the main plan.

But he admitted that:

> One of the problems this company used to have up to a few years ago was that HR strategy was seen as something completely separate from the corporate strategy. What we have tried to do in the past few years is to make them one and the same thing.

The Director of Personnel of ABC Distribution recognized that:

> The development of HR strategies should be shared more widely with the business controllers. If we don't do that we run the risk of not developing the consistent themes we need to have.

But the Director of Finance was positive that:

> In terms of performance improvement the business and HR strategies are very closely linked. Productivity is a major area and the HR implications of pursuing these policies is critical.

Another positive comment from a Finance Director (Bookworld) was to the effect that:

> I think more and more we should recognize that there are human resource issues in almost everything we do... Everything that happens in the company is to do with people and therefore it's almost inconceivable that HR shouldn't be involved with everything.

These, incidentally, were not the only positive contributions from Finance Directors. It was found by Armstrong and Long that, without exception, the eight finance directors were all fully aware of the significance of the HR perspective for their organizations, although they were obviously concerned with financial performance and budgets.

In Loamshire Council, the approach to integration as described by the Director of Personnel was simply to get the top team together and ask them:

'What are the real strategies that will help the organization and its functioning?'. The Director of Planning for the Authority commented on the important integrating role of the Director of Personnel as follows:

> In the old days, the personnel manager was not a member of the management team, and I got used to a culture where personnel advice was not really part of strategic direction. And any debate there may have been at the corporate level came out in the wash. It was not led by someone like our Director of Personnel. She is now on a par with the rest of us in terms of status and contribution and she brings the whole of the human resource angle into the debate.

And in reply to the question, 'How well are corporate and HR strategies integrated?', the Director of Technical Services for the Authority said:

> The short answer is that they are inextricably linked... you cannot do anything without having worked through the human resource implications and it's all about better performance by teams and individuals.

The approach of Megastores was described by the Director of Stores as follows:

> The starting point is the operating plan emerging from and contributing to the business plan. There is only a certain level of change we can cope with and what we have is a funnel of brilliant ideas and strategies, but they all end up in the stores. So we only commit to a plan we can deliver and we identify the levels of change that we can manage and calculate how much time the stores have to implement it. That is fed into the planning process so that it becomes realistic. The human resource strategy is integral to the process, it's not linked.

At Pilkington Optronics integration was not an issue. As explained by the Marketing Director:

> We do not think of ourselves as having a human resource strategy per se. We just see it as one aspect of the overall business strategy. From what I have observed going on in the business I find it quite difficult to separate a strand of activity which I would call HR strategy because it is so integral to everything which is going on... HR strategy is effectively a part of the overall vision.

He gave the example of the Technical Director who is developing technical route maps, and the personnel function which is working with technical management to produce forecasts as a basis for finding and developing the right people with the right skills. His own role is to explain the nature of the competences required in the business groups, including business management, programme management and sales and marketing: 'Only by understanding these can we equip ourselves for the future'.

At Midlands Manufacturing, the mission for the company as being 'internationally renowned for extraordinary customer satisfaction' is the integrating theme that unifies all aspects of strategy, including the people strategies. The Chief Executive stated that:

> The whole question of the contribution of people to our business has been so open in terms of our strategies and enabling processes over the last few years that probably a large part of our population would suggest that people strategies have actually led processes at the very front end of our thinking, whether it is explicit or implicit... We have a company culture which requires everyone when formulating their strategies to recognize the implications for individuals and their job security in whatever they are planning to do.

The Director of Finance for Welland Water pointed out that:

> The HR side is a fundamental part of the business planning process, and it's not something you just bolt on somewhere along the way. There's a lot of interaction, prior to and during the top board discussion which tends to be concerned with culturally based issues and the way we manage people.

On the basis of these comments and other observations made by the directors interviewed by Armstrong and Long, integration is most likely to be achieved when:

- there are well-articulated corporate or business strategies operating in the context of a clear mission;
- there is a powerful driving force in the shape of commitment to certain values and overall strategies for change;
- the chief executive or managing director recognizes the contribution that people make to increasing added value and achieving competitive advantage, and ensures that people issues are fully taken into account *at the time corporate or business strategies are being prepared*;
- the other members of the top team generally share the views of their chief executive on the added value that can be created by considering HR and corporate/business issues simultaneously;
- the HR director is capable of making a full contribution to the formulation of corporate/business strategies as well as those relating to people;
- the views of the HR director are listened to, respected and acted upon.

SUMMARY

To summarize, the most characteristic features of strategic HRM in action in the case study companies mentioned above were:

- A clear and purposeful corporate or business strategy exists.
- The HR strategies in most cases are fully integrated and owned by the whole of the top management team.
- The HR strategies are very much concerned with developing the organization and the people in it.
- Most if not all of the organizations could be described as 'unitarist' in their approach (ie they believed in the commonality of the interests of management and employees), and they are all striving to develop a 'commitment-oriented' culture. But in many cases they have still taken pains to involve the trade unions in their change strategies on a partnership basis.
- HR strategies relate to the critical success factors of the organization and the impact high-quality and committed people can make on the delivery of the results the organization is expected to achieve.

7

The strategic contribution of HRM to organizational success

Many writers (eg Arthur, 1990, 1992, 1994; Becker *et al*, 1997; Chadwick and Cappelli, 1998; Delaney and Huselid, 1996; Delery and Doty, 1996; Guest and Hoque, 1994; Huselid, 1995; Huselid and Becker, 1996; Huselid *et al*, 1997; Ichniowski *et al*, 1997; Koch and McGrath, 1996; MacDuffie, 1995; Patterson *et al*, 1997; Youndt *et al*, 1996) have conducted research that demonstrated that HRM practices can improve company performance. Typically, the ways in which this contribution has been made have included:

- developing a positive psychological contract;
- increasing motivation and commitment;
- increasing employee skills and extending the skills base;
- providing employees with extended responsibilities so that they can make full use of their skills and abilities;
- spelling out career opportunities and defining competence requirements;

■ instituting processes of performance management and continuous development;

■ using reward management systems to convey messages about what the organization believes to be important and what it is prepared to provide financial and non-financial rewards for;

■ developing employee relations strategies that provide employees with a voice.

HR can contribute to the achievement of competitive advantage and added value and to total quality initiatives in the ways described below. The key outcomes of research into the impact of HRM are summarized at the end of this chapter.

CONTRIBUTION TO ADDED VALUE

In accounting language, added value is the difference between the income of the business arising from sales (output) and the amount spent on materials and other purchased goods and services (input). In more general terms, it is the development and use of any resource in a way that ensures that it yields a substantial and sustainable higher return on whatever has been invested in it. Added value often means the creation of more out of less, and an increasingly popular index of overall organizational performance is added value per £ of employment costs.

Added value is created by people. It is people at various levels in the organizations who create visions, define values and missions, set goals, develop strategic plans, and implement those plans in accordance with the underpinning values. Added value will be enhanced by anything that is done to obtain and develop the right sort of people, to motivate and manage them effectively, to gain their commitment to organizational values, to build and maintain stable relationships with them, to develop the right sort of organization structure, and to deploy them effectively and productively in that structure.

The HR function contributes to the creation of added value by ensuring that people with the required competences and levels of motivation are available, and by helping to create a culture and environment that stimulates quality performance. An added value approach to HR will be directed positively to improve employee motivation, commitment, skill, performance and contribution. It can aim to get better value for money from HR expenditure in such areas as training, reward and employee benefits.

Obtaining added value

There are four ways in which the HR function can take the lead and make the most of its opportunity to add value:

1. By facilitating change and by proposing strategies and programmes for developing a more positive quality, customer-focused and performance-oriented culture, and by playing a major part in their implementation.
2. By making specific contributions in the areas of human resource planning, resourcing, training and development, performance management, reward and employee relations.
3. By ensuring that any HR initiatives in such fields as training and development are treated as investments on which a proper return will be obtained, which will increase added value.
4. By delivering cost-effective HR services, ie providing value for money.

CONTRIBUTION TO COMPETITIVE ADVANTAGE

The concept of sustainable competitive advantage as formulated by Porter (1985) arises when a firm creates value for its customers, selects markets in which it can excel and presents a moving target to its competitors by continually improving its position. According to Porter, three of the most important factors are innovation, quality, and cost leadership, but he recognizes that all these depend on the quality of an organization's human resources. The ability to gain and retain competitive advantage is crucial to a business's growth and prosperity.

Unique talents among employees, including superior performance, productivity, flexibility, innovation and the ability to deliver high levels of personal customer service are ways in which people provide a critical ingredient in developing an organization's competitive position. People also provide the key to managing the pivotal interdependencies across functional activities and the important external relationships. It can be argued that one of the clear benefits arising from competitive advantage based on the effective management of people is that such an advantage is hard to imitate. An organization's HR strategies, policies and practices are a unique blend of processes, procedures, personalities, styles, capabilities and organizational culture. One of the keys to competitive advantage is the ability to differentiate what the business supplies to its customers from those supplied by its competitors. Such differentiation can be achieved by having higher-quality people than those competitors, by developing and nurturing the intellectual capital possessed by the business and by functioning as a 'learning organization'.

Achieving competitive advantage

Competitive advantage is achieved by developing core competences in the workforce through traditional services (recruitment, reward, career pathing, employee development), and by dealing effectively with macro concerns such as corporate culture, management development and organizational structure.

THE IMPACT OF HRM ON BUSINESS PERFORMANCE

The outcomes of key research projects on HRM and organization performance are summarized below.

Arthur (1990, 1992, 1994)

The research conducted by Arthur collected data from 30 US steel mini-mills. He investigated the impact on labour efficiency and scrap rate of either a control strategy or a commitment strategy. According to Arthur, in a control strategy there is enforced employee compliance through rules and procedures, little employee participation, little general training, low wages, and a high proportion of employees on bonus schemes. In a commitment strategy the focus is on shaping employee behaviours by creating psychological links between organizational and employee goals, moderate employee participation, moderate general training, high wages, and fewer employees on bonus schemes or incentives.

Comparing steel mills with a high-commitment strategy with those having a low-commitment strategy, Arthur found that the former had significantly higher levels of both productivity and quality. The average turnover rate in high-commitment mills was less than half that in firms with a low-commitment strategy.

Arthur also examined the performance effects associated with a fit between business and HR strategy. He defined fit as occurring when a cost-based business strategy was combined with a control-oriented HR strategy and when a differentiating-based business strategy was combined with a commitment-type HR strategy. The results were not statistically significant but he did find that those mills practising a differentiation-based strategy with fit had 25 per cent higher productivity than those without fit. Thus some modest support was provided for the contingency hypothesis.

Huselid (1995)

Huselid conducted research into the impact of human resource management practices on company performance by analysing the responses of 968 US firms to a questionnaire. In general, he found that if firms increased their high-performance work practices, the result was significant reductions in employee turnover and significant increases in productivity and profits. The three hypotheses he tested were that diminished employee turnover, increased productivity and corporate financial performance would result from:

■ the use of systems of high-performance work practices;
■ the development of complementarities or synergies among high-performance work practices;
■ the alignment of a firm's system of high-performance work practices with its competitive strategy.

The 13 questions he asked firms were:

1. What proportion of the workforce are included in a formal information program?
2. What is the proportion of the total workforce whose jobs have been subjected to a formal job analysis?
3. What proportion of non-entry jobs have been filled from within in recent years?
4. What proportion of the workforce are administered attitude surveys on a regular basis?
5. What proportion of the workforce participate in Quality of Work Life programmes, quality circles and/or labour-management participation teams?
6. What proportion of the workforce have access to company incentive plans, profit-sharing plans and/or gain-sharing plans?
7. What is the average number of hours training received by a typical employee over the last 12 months?

8. What proportion of the workforce have access to a formal grievance procedure and/or complaint resolution system?
9. What proportion of the workforce is administered an employment test prior to hiring?
10. What is the proportion of the workforce whose performance appraisals are used to determine their compensation?
11. What proportion of the workforce receive formal appraisals?
12. Which of the following promotion-decision rules do you use most often? a) merit or performance rating alone; b) seniority among employees who meet a minimum merit requirement; c) seniority.
13. For the five positions that your firm hires most frequently, how many qualified applicants do you have per position (on average)?

The dependent variables were the average annual rate of employee turnover, sales per employee, and corporate financial performance as measured by economic profits (the net cash flow that accrues to shareholders) and accounting profits (the profit figures as published in company accounts).

The main findings were that:

- turnover is determined by employee skills and organizational structures, motivation has an insignificant effect;
- productivity is determined by employee motivation;
- financial performance is determined by employee skills, motivation and organization structure;
- one standard deviation decrease in the use of each practice reduces turnover by 1.3 per cent;
- one standard deviation increase in the use of the practices raises sales by an average of $27,044 per employee;
- one standard deviation increase in the use of the practices produces an increase in profit of $18,641 per employee.

As Huselid comments, the impact of high-performance work practices on corporate financial performance 'is in part due to their influence on employee turnover and productivity'.

However, his research produced little or no evidence that internal or external fit will increase firm performance and he concludes that the simple adoption of high-performance work practices is more important than efforts to ensure that these are internally consistent or aligned with firm competitive strategy. But he does believe that 'the theoretical arguments for internal and external fit remain compelling'.

Becker, Huselid, Pickus and Spratt (1997)

These writers summarized the outcomes of a number of research projects into the relationship between HR and company performance that they have conducted or been associated with. The focus was on the strategic impact on shareholder value of high-performance work systems (HPWS) as defined in Chapter 4. Their model of the relationship is shown in Figure 7.1.

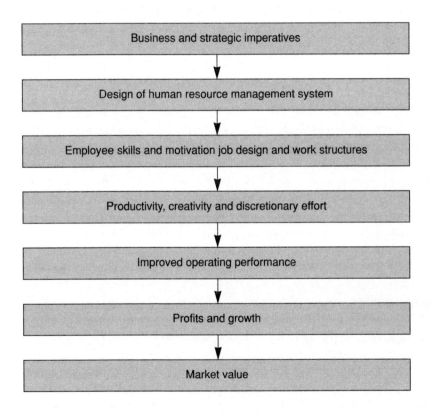

Figure 7.1 A model of the HR-shareholder value relationship
(source: Becker *et al*, 1997)

Huselid and Becker (1996) created an index of the HRM systems in 740 firms, reflecting the degree to which the firm adopted an HPWS. They found that firms with higher values on this index, other things being equal, have economically and statistically significant higher levels of firm performance. They further estimated that significant changes in the quality of a firm's HPWS system are associated with changes in market value of $15,000 to $60,000 per employee. They suggest that a properly designed and deployed HRM system represents a significant economic asset for an organization, although the research has not identified precisely *how* such a system creates that value. But Becker *et al* (1997) did point out that:

> HRM systems only have a systematic impact on the bottom line when they are embedded in the management infrastructure and help the firm achieve important business priorities such as shortening product development cycle times, increasing customer service, lowering turnover among high quality employees, etc.

Patterson, West, Lawthom and Nickell (1997)

Research conducted by the Institute of Work Psychology at Sheffield University on behalf of the IPD (Patterson *et al*, 1997) addressed the question of what factors most influence business performance. The study looked at the impact of employee attitudes, organizational culture, human resource management practices, and various other managerial activities. An assessment was made of the extent to which each of these factors predicted company performance as measured by productivity and profits per employee.

The human resource management variables used in the study are shown in Table 7.1. They broadly reflect the approaches typical of high-performance practices. The measures used to assess company performance were labour productivity in the firm relative to the industry in which the firm belongs, and profits per employee.

The results were expressed in terms of the percentage variation in performance attributable to a particular factor, as follows:

- Job satisfaction explained 5 per cent of the variation between companies in change of profitability and 16 per cent of the variation in productivity.
- Organizational culture explained 10 per cent of the variation in profitability and 29 per cent of the variation in productivity.
- Human resource management practices explained 19 per cent of the variation in profitability and 18 per cent of the variation in productivity.

These analyses revealed very strong relationships between employee attitudes, organizational culture, HRM practices and company performance. This was particularly convincing in the case of the link between HRM practices and performance.

The analysis of the links between managerial practices and performance

Table 7.1 Human resource management variables

HRM area	Measurement dimensions
Selection and recruitment	Sophistication of processes (eg use of psychometric tests, clear criteria for selection)
Induction	Sophistication in running and evaluating induction programmes for new employees
Training	Sophistication and coverage of training
Appraisal	Coherence and coverage of appraisal system
Skill flexibility	Flexibility of workforce skills
Job variety	Variety in shop floor (eg job rotation)
Job responsibility	Responsibility in shop floor jobs for various tasks and problem-solving
Teamworking	Use of formal teams
Communication	Frequency and comprehensiveness of communication to workforce (eg, newsletter, briefing groups, meetings between top management and work force)
Quality improvement teams	Use of quality improvement teams
Harmonization	Extent of harmonized terms and conditions
Comparative pay	Extent to which basic pay is higher or lower than the competition
Incentive compensation systems	Use of individual or group compensation (eg merit pay)

revealed that the impact on performance was much lower – between 1 and 3 per cent for strategy, technology and quality, 6 per cent for the link between R & D and productivity, and 8 per cent for the link between R & D and profitability. These figures are not statistically significant.

As the report on the research states:

> Overall these results very clearly indicate the importance of people management practices in predicting company performance. The results suggest that, if managers wish to influence the performance of their companies, the most important area they should emphasize is the management of people.

The conclusion reached by the IPD on this research was that employee commitment and a positive psychological contract are fundamental to improving performance. Two HR practices were identified as being particularly significant: first, acquisition and development of employee skills (including selection, induction and the use of appraisals) and second, job design (including skill flexibility, job responsibility, variety and the use of formal teams).

8

The strategic role of the HR function

PHILOSOPHY

The philosophy of CIBA, the pharmaceuticals company, of business-driven human resource management, as described by Morton (1999), is as follows:

- quality improvement depends on high-quality personnel at all levels;
- staff retention is important to support growth;
- the balance of motivation and cost reduction requires a clearly thought out reward strategy that has maximum impact without sending costs out of control;
- new HR technology can be used to capture process efficiencies and control costs;
- HR specialists will become subject experts in a team of internal consultants rather than members of the old-style hierarchy.

THE NEW MANDATE FOR HR   (NB)

According to Ulrich (1998): 'HR should not be defined by what it does but by what it delivers – results that enrich the organization's value to customers, investors and employees'. Ulrich believes that for HR to deliver excellence it should:

- become a partner with senior and line managers in strategy execution, helping to improve planning from the conference room to the market-place;
- become an expert in the way work is organized and executed, delivering administrative efficiency to ensure that costs are reduced while quality is maintained;
- become a champion for employees, vigorously representing their concerns to senior management and at the same time working to increase employee contribution, that is, employees' commitment to the organization and their ability to deliver results;
- become an agent of continuous transformation, shaping processes and a culture that together improve an organization's capacity for change;
- communicate the importance of the soft, people-centred issues;
- define HR deliverables and be accountable for them;
- invest in innovative HR practices.

HR SPECIALISTS AS STRATEGIC PARTNERS

To be fully-fledged strategic partners with senior management, Ulrich's (1998) view is that HR executives should:

impel and guide serious discussion of how the company should be organized to carry out its strategy. HR must take stock of its own work and set clear priorities. At any given moment, the HR staff might have a dozen initiatives in its sights such as pay-for-performance, global teamwork, and action-learning development experiences. But to be truly tied to business outcomes, HR needs to join forces with operating managers to systematically assess the impact and importance of each one of these initiatives. Which ones are really aligned with strategy implementation? Which ones should receive immediate attention and which ones can wait? Which ones, in short, are really linked to business results?

The answers must be obtained to six questions:

1. *Shared mind-set.* To what extent does our company have the right culture to achieve our goals?
2. *Competence.* To what extent does our company have the required knowledge, skills, and abilities?
3. *Consequence.* To what extent does our company have the appropriate measures, rewards and incentives?
4. *Governance.* To what extent does our company have the right organization structure, communication systems and policies?
5. *Capacity for change.* To what extent does our company have the ability to improve work processes, to change and to learn?
6. *Leadership.* To what extent does our company have the leadership to achieve its goals?

HR AS A BUSINESS PARTNER

The four roles of HR as a business partner as defined by Morton (1999) are:

1. *Strategic partner* – the management of strategic human resources, aligning HR and business strategy.
2. *Change agent* – the management of transformation and change, creating a renewed organization.
3. *Administrative expert* – management of firm infrastructure, re-engineering organizational processes.
4. *Employee champion* – management of employee contribution, increasing employee commitment and capability.

The key roles of strategist, business partner, innovator and change manager are discussed in more detail below.

KEY ROLES

The strategist role

As strategists, HR practitioners address major long-term issues concerning the management and development of people and the employment relationship. They are guided by the business plans of the organization but they also contribute to the formulation of the business plans. This is achieved by ensuring that top managers focus on the human resource implications of their strategies. HR strategists persuade top managers that they must develop plans that make the best use of the organization's human resources in terms of the required core competences. They emphasize, in the words of Hendry and Pettigrew (1986), that people are a strategic resource for the achievement of competitive advantage.

A strategic approach to managing people as described above means that HR strategists strive to achieve strategic integration and fit. Vertical integration or fit takes place when HR strategies are linked to and support business strategies. Horizontal integration or fit is achieved when a range or 'bundle' of coherent, interconnected and mutually reinforcing HR strategies are established.

The business partner role

As business partners, HR practitioners share responsibility with their line management colleagues for the success of the enterprise. As defined by Tyson (1985), HR specialists as business partners integrate their activities closely with top management and ensure that they serve a long-term strategic purpose, and have the capacity to identify business opportunities, to see the broad picture and to see how their HR role can help to achieve the company's business objectives.

HR practitioners in their role as business partners are aware of business strategies and the opportunities and threats facing the organization. They are capable of analysing organizational strengths and weaknesses and diagnosing the issues facing the enterprise (PESTLE analysis) and their human resource implications. They know about the critical success factors that will create competitive advantage and they can draw up a convincing business case for innovations that will add value.

In becoming a business partner, however, HR must still deliver effective administrative services.

The innovator role

A strategic approach to HRM will mean that HR specialists will want to innovate – to introduce new processes and procedures that they believe will increase organizational effectiveness.

The need for innovation should be established by processes of analysis and diagnosis which identify the business need and the issues to be addressed. 'Benchmarking' can take place to identify 'best practice' as adopted by other organizations. But in the interests of achieving 'best fit', the innovation should meet the particular needs of the business, which are likely to differ from those of other 'best practice' organizations. It has to be demonstrable that the innovation is appropriate, beneficial and practical in the circumstances, and can be implemented without too much difficulty in the shape of opposition from those affected by it or the unjustifiable use of resources – financial and the time of those involved.

The danger, according to Marchington (1995), is that HR people may go in for 'impression management' – aiming to make an impact on senior managers and colleagues through publicizing high-profile innovations. HR specialists who aim to draw attention to themselves simply by promoting the latest flavour of the month, irrespective of its relevance or practicality, are falling into the trap that Drucker (1955), anticipating Marchington by 40 years, described as follows:

> The constant worry of all HR administrators is their inability to prove that they are making a contribution to the enterprise. Their pre-occupation is with the search for a 'gimmick' that will impress their management colleagues.

As Marchington points out, the risk is that people believe 'all can be improved by a wave of the magic wand and the slaying of a few evil characters along the way'. This facile assumption means that people can too readily devise elegant solutions that do not solve the problem because of the hazards encountered during implementation – for example, indifference or open hostility. These have to be anticipated and catered for.

The change manager role

As Purcell (1999) has pointed out: 'We need to be much more sensitive to the processes of organizational change and avoid being caught in the trap of logical choice'. Johnson and Scholes (1993) in their classic book on strategy, suggest that 'organizations that successfully manage change are those that have integrated their human resource management policies with their strategies and the strategic change process'.

Strategies involve change, and failure to implement strategies often arises because the changes involved have not been managed effectively. HR practitioners can play a major part in developing and implementing organizational change strategies, as described in Chapter 11.They must pay particular attention to managing change when implementing HR initiatives. This means considering:

- who will be affected by the change;
- how they will react to it;
- barriers to implementation (eg resistance or indifference to change) and how they will be overcome;
- resource requirements for implementing change (these resources include the commitment and skill of those involved in the change as well as people, time and money);
- who is available to champion the change;
- how people will be involved in the change process, including the formulation as well as the implementation of changed policies;
- how the purpose and impact of change will be communicated to all concerned;
- what different skills and behaviours will be required and how they are to be developed;
- how the change process will be monitored;
- how the effectiveness of the change will be measured;
- what steps will be taken to evaluate the impact of change.

A change model used by HR staff at GE in the US to guide a transformation process in the company is shown in Table 8.1. The model is based on the statement that 'change begins by asking who, why, what and how'.

HR COMPETENCIES

The three competencies HR staff should possess if they want to function as strategic business partners as defined by Morton (1999) are:

1. *Knowledge of the business:*
   - strategic capability;
   - financial capability;
   - technological capability.
2. *Knowledge of HR practices:*
   - staffing;
   - development;
   - appraisal;

Table 8.1 Change model (source: Ulrich, 1998)

Key success factors in change	Questions to assess and accomplish the key success factors for change
Leading change (who is responsible?)	Do we have a leader: ■ who owns and champions change? ■ who publicly commits to making it happen? ■ who will garner the resources necessary to sustain it? ■ who will put in the personal time and attention needed to follow through?
Creating a shared need (why do it?)	Do employees: ■ see the reason for the change? ■ understand why it is important? ■ see how it will help them and the business in the short and long term?
Shaping a vision (what will it look like when it is done?)	Do employees: ■ see the outcomes of the change in behavioural terms (ie in terms of what people will do differently as a result of the change)? ■ get excited about the results of accomplishing the change? ■ understand how it will benefit customers and other stakeholders?
Mobilizing commitment (who else needs to be involved?)	Do the sponsors of the change: ■ recognize who else has to be committed to the change to make it happen? ■ know how to build a coalition of support for the change? ■ have the ability to enlist the support of key individuals in the organization? ■ have the ability to build a responsibility matrix to make it happen?
Modifying systems and structures (how will it be institutionalized?)	Do the sponsors of the change: ■ understand how to link it to other HR systems such as staffing, training, appraisal, rewards, structure and communications? ■ recognize the systems implications of the change?
Monitoring progress (how will it be measured?)	Do the sponsors of the change: ■ have a means of measuring its success? ■ plan to benchmark progress against both the results of the change and the process of implementing it?
Making it last (how will it get started and last?)	Do the sponsors of the change: ■ recognize the first steps in getting it started? ■ have a short-term and long-term plan to keep attention focused on the change? ■ have a plan to adapt the change over time?

- rewards;
- organization design;
- communication.
3. *Management of change:*
   - knowledge of change processes;
   - skills as change agents;
   - ability to deliver change.

A more detailed competence map is shown in Table 8.2.

Table 8.2   HR competence map

Strategic capability	Seeks involvement in strategy formulation and contributes to the development of business strategy	Has a clear strategic vision of how HR can support the achievement of the business strategy	Understands the critical success of the business and the implications for HR strategy	Develops and implements integrated and coherent HR strategies
Business cultural awareness	Understands the business's environment and the competitive pressures it faces	Understands activities and processes of the business and how these affect HR strategies	Understands culture (values and norms) of the business as the basis for developing culture change strategies	Adapts HR strategies to fit business and cultural imperatives
Organizational effectiveness	Understands key factors which contribute to organizational effectiveness and acts accordingly	Contributes to planning transformational change programmes and managing change	Helps to develop a high-quality, skilled, committed and flexible workforce	Facilitates team building
Internal consultancy	Analyses and diagnoses people issues and suggets practical solutions	Adapts intervention style to fit internal client needs; acts as catalyst facilitator or expert as required	Uses processes consultancy approaches to help resolve people problems and issues	Coaches clients to deal with own problems; transfers skills

Table 8.2 (*contd*)

Service delivery	Anticipates requirements and sets up services to meet	Responds promptly and efficiently to requests for help and advice	Empowers line managers to make HR decisions but provides guidance as required	Provides cost-effective services in each HR area
Quality	Contributes to the development of a total quality approach throughout the organization	Identifies internal customer requirements for HR services and responds to their needs	Demonstrates a concern for total quality and continuous improvement in own work	Promotes total quality and continuous improvement in HR function
Continuous professional development	Continually develops professional knowledge and skills	Benchmarks best HR practice and keeps in touch with new HR developments	Demonstrates understanding of relevant HR practices	Promotes awareness in own function

THE STRATEGIC ROLE OF THE HR DIRECTOR

HR directors have a key role in strategic HRM, especially if they are – as they should be – on the board. They are there to envision how HR strategies can be integrated with the business strategy, to prepare strategic plans, and to oversee their implementation. They should play a major part in organization development and change management and in the achievement of coherence in the different aspects of HR policy. HR directors who will most probably play a full strategic role as business partners are likely to be:

■ very much part of the top management team;
■ involved in business planning and the integration of human resource plans with business plans;
■ well placed to exert influence on the way in which the enterprise is organized, managed and staffed – all with a view to helping it achieve its strategic objectives;

- professionally competent in HR techniques; however, their contribution and credibility will depend mainly on their business awareness and skills and their ability to play a full part as members of the top team;
- involved in resourcing at top and senior levels and in so doing be in a strong position to improve organizational effectiveness and, therefore, bottom-line performance;
- able to convince others of the need for change and to act as champions of change and as effective change agents;
- involved in shaping corporate culture and values;
- fully aware of the need to develop a vision of what the HR function exists to do, to define its mission, to provide leadership and guidance to the members of the function (without getting over-involved in day-to-day HR matters) and to maintain the quality of the support that the HR function provides to line managers;
- enablers and facilitators, but ones who are well placed to make a significant contribution to end-results by adopting an innovatory approach to the improvement of organizational effectiveness and by intervening as necessary on any matters where there are HR implications that will affect performance;
- essentially pragmatists who know about the theory of HRM but also know what is right for their organization and what will work there;
- good at defining and achieving deliverables.

Part 3

Organizational strategies

9

Strategies for organizational development

Strategies for organizational development (OD) are concerned with the planning and implementation of programmes designed to enhance the effectiveness with which an organization functions. They may involve strategies for developing organizational processes, and OD programmes for organizational transformation and for managing the transition between the present and the desired state.

Overall, the aim of organizational development strategies is to adopt a planned and coherent approach to improving organizational effectiveness. An effective organization can be defined broadly as one that achieves its purpose by meeting the wants and needs of its stakeholders, matching its resources to opportunities, adapting flexibly to environmental changes and creating a culture that promotes commitment, creativity, shared values and mutual trust.

Organizational development strategies are concerned with process, as well as structure or systems. They address *how* things are done as well as *what* is done. Process refers to the ways in which people act and interact. It is about the roles they play on a continuing basis to deal with events and with situations involving other people, and to adapt to changing circumstances.

STRATEGIES FOR IMPROVING ORGANIZATIONAL EFFECTIVENESS

Strategies for improving organizational effectiveness will focus on developing processes that support the achievement of business goals and a positive culture. There are no universal prescriptions for the development of strategies. Some of the areas that might be considered are listed in Table 9.1, but these are generalities and would have to be turned into specifics in accordance with an assessment of the particular business environment and needs.

Table 9.1   Areas for developing organizational effectiveness

---

- Clearly defined goals and strategies to accomplish them.
- A value system that emphasizes performance, productivity, quality, customer service, teamwork and flexibility.
- Strong visionary leadership from the top.
- A powerful management team.
- A well-motivated, committed, skilled and flexible workforce.
- Effective teamwork throughout the organization, with win/lose conflict well under control.
- Continuous pressure to innovate and grow.
- The ability to respond fast to opportunities and threats.
- The capacity to manage, indeed thrive, on change.
- A sound financial base and good systems for management accounting and cost control.

Kanter (1984) recalled how Apple Computer devised a three-pronged approach to improving organizational effectiveness as follows:

1. Develop an organizational structure that produces synergies, not conflict.
2. Create more cooperative alliances with suppliers and customers.
3. Find ways to maintain a flow of new ideas toward new products and new ventures.

She notes that corporations are being pushed in ever less bureaucratic and ever more entrepreneurial directions, cutting out unnecessary layers of the hierarchy and forging closer ties with employees. She emphasizes, however, that the pursuit of excellence has multiplied the number of demands on executives and managers. Kanter (1989) has described this as the 'post-entrepreneurial corporation'. This represents 'a triumph of process over structure'. She suggests that relationships and communication, and the flexibility to combine resources, are more important than the formal channels and reporting relationships represented in an organization chart: 'What is important is not how responsibilities are divided but how people can pull together to pursue new opportunities'.

In *Managing on the Edge*, Pascale (1990) suggested a new 'paradigm' for organizations in which they are:

- placing increased emphasis on the 'soft' dimensions of style and shared values;
- operating as networks rather than hierarchies;
- moving from the status-driven view that managers think and workers do as they are told, to a belief in managers as 'facilitators' with workers empowered to initiate improvements and change;
- placing less emphasis on vertical tasks within functional units and more on horizontal tasks and collaboration across units;
- focusing less on content and the prescribed use of specific tools and techniques and more on 'process' and an holistic synthesis of techniques;
- changing the military command model to a commitment model.

STRATEGIES FOR DEVELOPING ORGANIZATIONAL PROCESSES

Strategies for developing organizational processes can involve preparing and implementing organization development programmes. OD has been defined by French and Bell (1990) as:

> A planned systematic process in which applied behavioural science principles and practices are introduced into an ongoing organization towards the goals of effecting organizational improvement, greater organizational competence, and greater organizational effectiveness. The focus is on organizations and their improvement or, to put it another way, *total systems change*. The orientation is on action – achieving desired results as a result of planned activities.

OD was originally based on behavioural science concepts, but during the 1980s and 1990s the focus shifted to a number of other approaches. Some of these, such as organizational transformation, are not entirely dissimilar to OD. Others such as team building, change management and culture change or management are built on some of the basic ideas developed by OD writers and practitioners. Yet other approaches such as total quality management, business process re-engineering and performance management would be described as holistic processes which attempt to improve overall organizational effectiveness from a particular perspective.

Characteristics of OD strategies

OD concentrates on *how* things are done as well as what is done. It is concerned with system-wide change. The organization is considered as a total system and the emphasis is on the interrelationships, interactions and interdependencies of different aspects of how systems operate as they transform inputs and outputs and use feedback mechanisms for self-regulation. OD practitioners talk about 'the client system' – meaning that they are dealing with the total organizational system.

Assumptions and values of OD

OD is based upon the following assumptions and values:

- Most individuals are driven by the need for personal growth and development as long as their environment is both supportive and challenging.
- The work team, especially at the informal level, has great significance for feelings of satisfaction and the dynamics of such teams have a powerful effect on the behaviour of their members.
- OD programmes aim to improve the quality of working life of all members of the organization.
- Organizations can be more effective if they learn to diagnose their own strengths and weaknesses.
- Managers often do not know what is wrong and need special help in diagnosing problems, although the outside 'process consultant' ensures that decision making remains in the hands of the client.

Features of OD strategies

OD strategies are developed as programmes with the following features:

- They are managed, or at least strongly supported, from the top but often make use of third parties or 'change agents' to diagnose problems and to manage change by various kinds of planned activity or 'intervention'.

- The plans for organization development are based upon a systematic analysis and diagnosis of the circumstances of the organization and the changes and problems affecting it.
- They use behavioural science knowledge and aim to improve the way the organization copes in times of change through such processes as interaction, communications, participation, planning and conflict management.

OD activities

The activities that may be incorporated in an OD programme are summarized below.

Action research

This is an approach developed by Lewin (1947) which takes the form of systematically collecting data from people about process issues and feeding it back in order to identify problems and their likely causes. This provides the basis for an action plan to deal with the problem, which can be implemented cooperatively by the people involved. The essential elements of action research are data collection, diagnosis, feedback, action planning, action and evaluation.

Survey feedback

This is a variety of action research in which data is systematically collected about the system and then fed back to groups to analyse and interpret as the basis for preparing action plans. The techniques of survey feedback include the use of attitude surveys, and workshops to discuss implications.

Interventions

The term 'intervention' in OD refers to core structured activities involving clients and consultants. The activities can take the form of action research, survey feedback or any of those mentioned below. Argyris (1970) summed up the three primary tasks of the OD practitioner or interventionist as being to:

1. Generate and help clients to generate valid information that they can understand about their problems.

2. Create opportunities for clients to search effectively for solutions to their problems, to make free choices.
3. Create conditions for internal commitment to their choices and opportunities for the continual monitoring of the action taken.

Process consultation

As described by Schein (1969), this involves helping clients to generate and analyse information that they can understand and, following a thorough diagnosis, act upon. The information will relate to organizational processes such as inter-group relations, interpersonal relations and communications. The job of the process consultant was defined by Schein as being to 'help the organization to solve its own problems by making it aware of organizational processes, of the consequences of these processes, and of the mechanisms by which they can be changed'.

Team-building interventions

These deal with permanent work teams or those set up to deal with projects or to solve particular problems. Interventions are directed towards the analysis of the effectiveness of team processes such as problem solving, decision making and interpersonal relationships, a diagnosis and discussion of the issues and joint consideration of the actions required to improve effectiveness.

Inter-group conflict interventions

As developed by Blake *et al* (1964) these aim to improve inter-group relations by getting groups to share their perceptions of one another and to analyse what they have learnt about themselves and the other group. The groups involved meet each other to share what they have learnt, to agree on the issues to be resolved and the actions required.

Personal interventions

These include sensitivity training laboratories (T-groups), transactional analysis and, more recently, neuro-linguistic programming (NLP). Another approach is behaviour modelling, which is based on Bandura's (1977) social learning theory. This states that for people to engage successfully in a behaviour, they must: 1) perceive a link between the behaviour and certain outcomes;

2) desire those outcomes (this is termed 'positive valence'); and 3) believe they can do it (termed 'self-efficacy'). Behaviour-modelling training involves getting a group to identify the problem and develop and practise the skills required by looking at videos showing what skills can be applied, role playing, practising the use of skills on the job and discussing how well they have been applied.

Use of OD

The decline of traditional OD, as mentioned earlier, has been partly caused by disenchantment with the jargon used by consultants and the unfulfilled expectations of significant improvements in organizational effectiveness. There was also a reaction in the hard-nosed 1980s against the perceived softness of the messages preached by the behavioural scientists. Managements in the later 1980s and 1990s wanted more specific strategies that would impact on processes they believed to be important as means of improving performance, such as total quality management, business process re-engineering and performance management. The need to manage change to processes, systems or culture was still recognized as long as it was results-driven, rather than activity-centred. Teambuilding activities in the new process-based organizations were also regarded favourably as long as they were directed towards measurable improvements in the shorter term. It was also recognized that organizations were often compelled to transform themselves in the face of massive challenges and external pressures, and traditional OD approaches would not make a sufficient or speedy impact. Many of the techniques as described below were, however, developed during the heyday of OD – the philosophy may have been rejected but the practices that worked, based on action learning and survey feedback techniques, were often retained.

STRATEGIES FOR ORGANIZATIONAL TRANSFORMATION

Transformation, according to *Webster's Dictionary*, is: 'A change in the shape, structure, nature of something'. Organizational transformation strategies are concerned with the development of programmes that will ensure that it responds strategically to new demands and continues to function effectively in the dynamic environment in which it operates.

Organizational transformation strategic plans may involve radical changes to the structure, culture and processes of the organization. This may be in response to competitive pressures, mergers, acquisitions, investments, disinvestments, changes in technology, product lines, markets, cost-reduction exercises and decisions to downsize or outsource work. Transformational change may be forced on an organization by investors or government decisions. It may be initiated by a new chief executive and top management team with a remit to 'turn round' the business.

Transformational change strategies involve planning and implementing significant and far-reaching developments in corporate structures and organization-wide processes. The change is neither incremental (bit by bit) nor transactional (concerned solely with systems and procedures). Transactional change, according to Pascale (1990), is merely concerned with the alteration of ways in which the organization does business and people interact with one another on a day-to-day basis, and 'is effective when what you want is more of what you've already got'. He advocates a 'discontinuous improvement in capability' and this he describes as transformation.

A distinction can also be made between first order and second order transformational development. First order development is concerned with changes to the ways in which particular parts of the organization function. Second order change aims to make an impact on the whole organization.

Types of transformational strategies

Four strategies for transformational change have been identified by Beckhard (1989):

1. *A change in what drives the organization* – for example, a change from being production-driven to being market-driven would be transformational.
2. *A fundamental change in the relationships between or among organizational parts* – for example, decentralization.
3. *A major change in the ways of doing work* – for example, the introduction of new technology such as computer-integrated manufacturing.
4. *A basic, cultural change in norms, values or research systems* – for example, developing a customer-focused culture.

Transformation through leadership

Transformation programmes are led from the top within the organization. They do not rely on an external 'change agent' as did traditional OD interventions, although specialist external advice might be obtained on aspects of the transformation such as strategic planning, re-organization or developing new reward processes.

The prerequisite for a successful programme is the presence of a transformational leader who, as defined by Burns (1978), motivates others to strive for higher-order goals rather than merely short-term interest. Transformational leaders go beyond dealing with day-to-day management problems: they commit people to action and focus on the development of new levels of awareness of where the future lies, and commitment to achieving that future. Burns contrasts transformational leaders with transactional leaders who operate by building up a network of interpersonal transactions in a stable situation and who enlist compliance rather than commitment through the reward system and the exercise of authority and power. Transactional leaders may be good at dealing with here-and-now problems but they will not provide the vision required to transform the future.

Managing the transition

Strategies need to be developed for managing the transition from where the organization is to where the organization wants to be. This is the critical part of a transformation programme. It is during the transition period of getting from here to there that change takes place. Transition management starts from a definition of the future state and a diagnosis of the present state. It is then necessary to define what has to be done to achieve the transformation. This means deciding on the new processes, systems, procedures, structures, products and markets to be developed. Having defined these, the work can be programmed and the resources required (people, money, equipment and time) can be defined. The strategic plan for managing the transition should include provisions for involving people in the process and for communicating to them what is happening, why it is happening and how it will affect them. Clearly the aims are to get as many people as possible committed to the change.

The transformation programme

The eight steps required to transform an organization have been summed up by Kotter (1995) as follows:

1. *Establishing a sense of urgency*
   - examining market and competitive realities;
   - identifying and discussing crises, potential crises, or major opportunities.

2. *Forming a powerful guiding coalition*
   - assembling a group with enough power to lead the change effort;
   - encouraging the group to work together as a team.
3. *Creating a vision*
   - creating a vision to help direct the change effort;
   - developing strategies for achieving that vision.
4. *Communicating the vision*
   - using every vehicle possible to communicate the new vision and strategies;
   - teaching new behaviours by the example of the guiding coalition.
5. *Empowering others to act on the vision*
   - getting rid of obstacles to change;
   - changing systems or structures that seriously undermine the vision;
   - encouraging risk-taking and non-traditional ideas, activities and actions.
6. *Planning for and creating short-term wins*
   - planning for visible performance improvement;
   - creating those improvements;
   - recognizing and rewarding employees involved in the improvements.
7. *Consolidating improvements and producing still more change*
   - using increased credibility to change systems, structures and policies that don't fit the vision;
   - hiring, promoting and developing employees who can implement the vision;
   - reinvigorating the process with new projects, themes and change agents.
8. *Institutionalizing new approaches*
   - articulating the connections between the new behaviours and corporate success;
   - developing the means to ensure leadership development and succession.

Transformation capability

The development and implementation of transformation strategies require special capabilities. As Gratton (1999) points out:

Transformation capability depends in part on the ability to create and embed processes that link business strategy to the behaviours and performance of individuals and teams. These clusters of processes link vertically (to create alignment with short-term business needs), horizontally (to create cohesion), and temporally (to transform to meet future business needs).

The strategic role of HR in organizational transformation

HR can and should play a key strategic role in developing and implementing organizational transition and transformation strategies. It can provide help and guidance in analysis and diagnosis, highlighting the people issues that will fundamentally affect the success of the strategy. HR can advise on resourcing programmes and planning and implementing the vital training, reward, communications and involvement aspects of the process. It can anticipate people problems and deal with them before they become serious. If the programme does involve restructuring and downsizing, HR can advise on how this should be done humanely and with the minimum disruption to people's lives.

10

Strategies for culture management

WHAT ARE CULTURE MANAGEMENT STRATEGIES?

Strategies for culture management are about the achievement of longer-term objectives for either changing the culture in specified ways or for reinforcing the existing culture of an organization – its values and 'the way things are done around here'.

Culture change strategies will be concerned with how the culture of the organization can be moved from a present state to a future desired state. The strategy will be based on an analysis of the present culture and the extent to which it supports the achievement of business goals. This should identify areas where changes are deemed to be desirable. Those changes can then be specified and plans developed for them to be implemented.

Culture reinforcement strategies are also based on an analysis of the existing culture and how it supports the attainment of goals. In so far as it is seen to be supportive, steps can be taken to ensure that the desirable features of the culture are maintained.

Culture change or reinforcement strategies should be based on an understanding of the meaning of organizational culture and climate and how they can be analysed. It is then a matter of being aware of the various approaches that can be adopted to manage the culture.

Culture management often focuses on the development of shared values and gaining commitment to them. These values will be concerned with the sort of behaviour the management believes is appropriate in the interests of the organization. The core values of a business express the beliefs about what management regards as important with regard to how the organization functions and how people should behave. The aim is to ensure that these beliefs are also held and acted upon by employees. As Hailey (1999) suggests:

> The business case for inculcating shared values through managing culture is based on the idea that ultimately employees could then be given licence to innovate in the confidence that their adherence to corporate values would prevent them from acting against the interests of the company.

The case for culture management therefore rests on the belief that the prescription of shared values results in appropriate behaviour. It is argued by Hailey, however, that instead of focusing on values initially (and hoping that behaviour would change), organizations should focus on behaviours first so that values would then emerge. Values are abstract and can be espoused but not acted upon. Behaviour is real and if it is the right sort of behaviour, it will produce the desired results. It follows therefore that culture management strategies should be concerned with analysing what behaviours are appropriate and then bringing in processes such as performance management, which will encourage the development of those behaviours. If, for example, it is important for people to behave effectively as members of teams, then team performance management processes can be introduced (self-managed teams setting their own standards and monitoring their own performance against those standards) and behaviour conducive to good teamwork rewarded by financial or non-financial means.

But Hailey refers with approval to the approach to culture management adopted by Hewlett Packard which is based on a values statement, 'The HP Way'. This focuses on a 'belief in our people' which incorporates:

> Confidence and respect for our people as opposed to depending on extensive rules, procedures and so on; which depends upon people doing their job right (individual freedom) without constant directives.

As Hailey comments: '[The] two critical issues of managing performance through business planning and the "HP Way" are inextricably connected and account for the success and performance of Hewlett Packard'. Middle managers believe that the culture is 'supportive' and 'very, very open', with a 'team ethic'.

Strategies for managing culture may therefore concentrate on operational-izing values as at Hewlett Packard. But organizations without the deeply embedded culture of that firm may concentrate first on shaping or reinforcing appropriate behaviours. These should, however, be developed against the background of an understanding of what organizational culture and climate are and how they can be analysed. and assessed. This analysis and assessment process provides the basis for the culture management programme.

This chapter explores the approach to strategic culture management against the background of definitions of organizational culture and the associated concept of organizational climate. It continues with comments on the signifi-cance of the concept to organizations. The components of culture and methods of analysing and describing culture and the climate are then considered. The chapter concludes with a review of approaches to supporting or changing cultures.

Definitions

Organizational culture

Organizational culture has been defined by Furnham and Gunter (1993) as 'the commonly held beliefs, attitudes and values that exist in an organization; put more simply, culture is "the way we do things around here" '.

This pattern of values, norms, beliefs, attitudes and assumptions may not have been articulated but will shape the ways in which people behave and things get done. Values refer to what is believed to be important about how people and organizations behave. Norms are the unwritten rules of behaviour.

The definition emphasizes that organizational culture is concerned with the subjective aspect of what goes on in organizations. It refers to abstractions such as values and norms which pervade the whole or part of a business. These may not be defined, discussed or even noticed. Nevertheless, culture can have a significant influence on people's behaviour.

Summing up the various definitions of culture, Furnham and Gunter (1993) list, among others, the following areas of agreement on the concept:

■ it is difficult to define (often a pointless exercise);
■ it is multi-dimensional, with many different components at different levels;
■ it is not particularly dynamic and ever-changing (being relatively stable over short periods of time);
■ it takes time to establish and therefore time to change a corporate culture.

Organizational climate

The term 'organizational climate' is sometimes confused with 'organizational culture' and there has been much debate on what distinguishes the concept of climate from that of culture. In his analysis of this issue, Denison (1996) suggested that *culture* refers to the deep structure of organizations, which is rooted in the values, beliefs and assumptions held by organizational members. In contrast, *climate* refers to those aspects of the environment that are consciously perceived by organizational members. Rousseau (1988) stated that climate is a perception and is descriptive. Perceptions are sensations or realizations experienced by an individual. Descriptions are what a person reports of these sensations.

The debate about the meanings of these terms can become academic. It is easiest to regard organizational climate as how people perceive (see and feel about) the culture existing in their organization. As defined by French *et al* (1985) it is 'the relatively persistent set of perceptions held by organization members concerning the characteristics and quality of organizational culture'. They distinguish between the actual situations (ie culture) and the perception of it (climate).

The significance of culture

As Furnham and Gunter (1993) comment:

> Culture represents the 'social glue' and generates a 'we-feeling', thus counter-acting processes of differentiation which are an unavoidable part of organizational life. Organizational culture offers a shared system of meanings which is the basis for communications and mutual understanding. If these functions are not fulfilled in a satisfactory way, culture may significantly reduce the efficiency of an organization.

ANALYSING ORGANIZATIONAL CULTURE

There have been many attempts to classify or categorize organizational culture as a basis for the analysis of cultures in organizations and for taking action to support or change them. Most of these classifications are expressed in four dimensions and two of the best-known ones are summarized below.

Harrison

Harrison (1972) categorized what he called 'organization ideologies'. These are:

1. *Power-oriented* – competitive, responsive to personality rather than expertise.
2. *People-oriented* – consensual, management control rejected.
3. *Task-oriented* – focus on competency, dynamic.
4. *Role-oriented* – focus on legality, legitimacy and bureaucracy.

Handy

Handy (1981) based his typology on Harrison's classification, although Handy preferred the word 'culture' to 'ideology' because in his view, culture conveyed more of the feeling of a pervasive way of life or set of norms. His four types of culture are:

1. *The power culture*, in which there is a central power source that exercises control. There are few rules or procedures and the atmosphere is competitive, power-oriented and political.
2. *The role culture*, in which work is controlled by procedures and rules and the role, or job description, is more important than the person who fills it. Power is associated with positions not people.
3. *The task culture*, in which the aim is to bring together the right people and let them get on with it. Influence is based more on expert power than in position or personal power. The culture is adaptable and teamwork is important.
4. *The person culture*, in which the individual is the central point. The organization exists only to serve and assist the individuals in it.

ASSESSING ORGANIZATIONAL CULTURE

A number of instruments exist for assessing organizational culture. This is not easy because culture is concerned with both subjective beliefs and unconscious assumptions (which might be difficult to measure), and with observed phenomena such as behavioural norms and artefacts. One of the best-known instruments is the Organizational Ideology Questionnaire (Harrison, 1972), which deals with the four orientations referred to earlier (power, role, task, self). The questionnaire is completed by ranking statements according to views on what is closest to the organization's actual position. Statements include:

- A good boss is strong, decisive and firm but fair.
- A good subordinate is compliant, hard working and loyal.
- People who do well in the organization are shrewd and competitive, with a strong need for power.
- The basis of task assignment is the personal needs and judgements of those in authority.
- Decisions are made by people with the most knowledge and expertise about the problem.

Another well-known instrument is the Organizational Culture Inventory (Cooke and Lafferty, 1989), which was described in Chapter 5.

MEASURING ORGANIZATIONAL CLIMATE

Organizational climate measures attempt to assess organizations in terms of dimensions that are thought to capture or describe perceptions about the climate. Perceptions about climate can be measured by questionnaires such as that developed by Litwin and Stringer (1968), covering eight categories:

1. *Structure* – feelings about constraints and freedom to act and the degree of formality or informality in the working atmosphere.
2. *Responsibility* – the feeling of being trusted to carry out important work.
3. *Risk* – the sense of riskiness and challenge in the job and in the organization; the relative emphasis on taking calculated risks or playing it safe.
4. *Warmth* – the existence of friendly and informal social groups.
5. *Support* – the perceived helpfulness of managers and co-workers; the emphasis (or lack of emphasis) on mutual support.

6. *Standards* – the perceived importance of implicit and explicit goals and performance standards; the emphasis on doing a good job; the challenge represented in personal and team goals.
7. *Conflict* – the feeling that managers and other workers want to hear different opinions; the emphasis on getting problems out into the open rather than smoothing them over or ignoring them.
8. *Identity* – the feeling that you belong to a company; that you are a valuable member of a working team.

APPROPRIATE CULTURES

It could be argued that a 'good' culture exerts a positive influence on organizational behaviour. It could help to create a 'high-performance' culture, one that will produce a high level of business performance. As described by Furnham and Gunter (1993), 'a good culture is consistent in its components and shared amongst organizational members, and it makes the organization unique, thus differentiating it from other organizations'.

However, a high-performance culture means little more than any culture that will produce a high level of business performance. The attributes of cultures vary tremendously by context. The qualities of a high-performance culture for an established retail chain, a growing service business and a consumer products company that is losing market share may be very different. Further, in addition to context differences, all cultures evolve over time. Cultures that are 'good' in one set of circumstances or period of time may be dysfunctional in different circumstances or different times.

Because culture is developed and manifests itself in different ways in different organizations, it is not possible to say that one culture is better than another, only that it is dissimilar in certain ways. There is no such thing as an ideal culture, only an appropriate culture. This means that there can be no universal prescription for a culture management strategy, although there are certain approaches that can be helpful, as described in the next section.

STRATEGIES FOR SUPPORTING AND CHANGING CULTURES

While it may not be possible to define an ideal structure or to prescribe how it can be developed, it can at least be stated with confidence that embedded cultures exert considerable influence on organizational behaviour and there-fore performance. If there is an appropriate and effective culture, it would be desirable to develop a strategy for supporting or reinforcing it. If the culture is inappropriate, attempts should be made to determine what needs to be changed and to develop and implement plans for change.

Culture analysis

In either case, the first step is to analyse the existing culture. This can be done through questionnaires, surveys and discussions in focus groups or work-shops. It is often helpful to involve people in analysing the outcome of surveys, getting them to produce a diagnosis of the cultural issues facing the organiza-tion and to participate in the development and implementation of plans and programmes to deal with any issues. This could form part of an organizational development programme, as described in Chapter 9. Groups can analyse the culture through the use of measurement instruments. Extra dimensions can be established by the use of group exercises such as 'rules of the club' (partici-pants brainstorm the 'rules' or norms that govern behaviour) or 'shield' (participants design a shield, often quartered, which illustrates major cultural features of the organization). Joint exercises like this can lead to discussions on appropriate values, which are much more likely to be 'owned' by people if they have helped to create them rather than having them imposed from above.

While involvement is highly desirable, there will be situations when management has to carry out the analysis and determine the actions required without the initial participation of employees. But the latter should be kept informed and brought into discussion on developments as soon as possible.

Culture support and reinforcement

Culture support and reinforcement programmes aim to preserve and underpin what is good and functional about the present culture. Schein (1985) has suggested that the most powerful primary mechanisms for culture embedding and reinforcement are:

- what leaders pay attention to, measure and control;
- leaders' reactions to critical incidents and crises;
- deliberate role modelling, teaching and coaching by leaders;
- criteria for allocation of rewards and status;
- criteria for recruitment, selection, promotion and commitment.

Other means of underpinning the culture are:

- re-affirming the behaviours believed to be important;
- encouraging appropriate behaviours by providing financial and non-financial rewards for behaviour which is in accordance with expectations and through actions designed, for example, to implement total quality and customer care programmes, to improve productivity, to promote and reward good teamwork, to develop a learning organization;
- developing a statement of core values which describe the basis for the desired behaviours, using the value set as headings for reviewing individual and team performance and emphasizing that people are expected to behave in ways that will uphold the values;
- ensuring that induction procedures cover expected behaviours and core values and how people are expected to act upon them;
- reinforcing induction training through further training courses set up as part of a continuous development programme.

Culture change

Focus

In theory, culture change programmes start with an analysis of the existing culture. The desired culture is then defined, which leads to the identification of a 'culture gap' that needs to be filled. This analysis can identify behavioural expectations so that development and reward processes can be used to define and reinforce them. In real life, it is not quite as simple as that.

A comprehensive change programme may be a fundamental part of an organizational transformation exercise, as described in Chapter 9. But culture change programmes can focus on particular aspects of the culture, for example, performance, commitment, quality, customer service, teamwork, organizational learning. In each case the underpinning values would need to be defined. It would probably be necessary to prioritize by deciding which areas need the most urgent attention. There is a limit to how much can be done at once except in crisis conditions.

Levers for change

Having identified what needs to be done and the priorities, the next step is to consider what levers for change exist and how they can be used. The levers could include, as appropriate:

- *Performance* – performance-related or competence-related pay schemes; performance management processes; gainsharing; leadership training, skills development.
- *Commitment* – communication, participation and involvement programmes; developing a climate of cooperation and trust; clarifying the psychological contract.
- *Quality* – total quality programmes.
- *Customer service* – customer care programmes.
- *Teamwork* – team building; team performance management; team rewards.
- *Organizational learning* – taking steps to enhance intellectual capital and the organization's resource-based capability by developing a learning organization.
- *Values* – gaining understanding, acceptance and commitment through involvement in defining values, performance management processes and employee development interventions, although it is often the case that values are embedded by changing behaviours, not the other way round.

11

Change management strategies

Strategic change

Strategic change is concerned with organizational transformation, as described in Chapter 9. It deals with broad, long-term and organization-wide issues. It is about moving to a future state that has been defined generally in terms of strategic vision and scope. It will cover the purpose and mission of the organization, its corporate philosophy on such matters as growth, quality, innovation and values concerning people, the customer needs served and the technologies employed. This overall definition leads to specifications of competitive positioning and strategic goals for achieving and maintaining competitive advantage and for product-market development. These goals are supported by policies concerning marketing, sales, manufacturing, product and process development, finance and human resource management.

Strategic change takes place within the context of the external competitive, economic and social environment, and the organization's internal resources, capabilities, culture, structure and systems. Its successful implementation requires thorough analysis and understanding of these factors in the formulation and planning stages. The ultimate achievement of sustainable competitive advantage relies on the qualities defined by Pettigrew and Whipp (1991), namely:

> The capacity of the firm to identify and understand the competitive forces in play and how they change over time, linked to the competence of a business to mobilize and manage the resources necessary for the chosen competitive response through time.

Strategic change, however, should not be treated simplistically as a linear process of getting from A to B which can be planned and executed as a logical sequence of events. Pettigrew and Whipp (1991) issued the following warning based on their research into competitiveness and managing change in the motor, financial services, insurance and publishing industries:

> The process by which strategic changes are made seldom move directly through neat, successive stages of analysis, choice and implementation. Changes in the firm's environment persistently threaten the course and logic of strategic changes: dilemma abounds. We conclude that one of the defining features of the process, in so far as management action is concerned, is ambiguity; seldom is there an easily isolated logic to strategic change. Instead, that process may derive its motive force from an amalgam of economic, personal and political imperatives. Their introduction through time requires that those responsible for managing that process make continual assessments, repeated choices and multiple adjustments.

Change management strategies may be mainly directed towards strategic change, but it may also be necessary to adopt a strategic approach to operational change.

Operational change

Operational change relates to new systems, procedures, structures or technology which will have an immediate effect on working arrangements within a part of the organization. But their impact on people can be more significant than broader strategic change and they have to be handled just as carefully.

Fundamentals of change management strategy

To develop and implement change management strategies, it is necessary to understand what constitutes the process of change, why people resist change and how resistance can be overcome. It is important to bear in mind that while those wanting change need to be constant about ends, they have to be flexible about means. This requires them to come to an understanding of the various models of change that have been developed. In the light of an understanding of these models they will be better equipped to make use of the guidelines for change, which are set out at the end of this chapter.

THE CHANGE PROCESS

Conceptually, the change process starts with an awareness of the need for change. An analysis of this situation and the factors that have created it leads to a diagnosis of their distinctive characteristics and an indication of the direction in which action needs to be taken and therefore the change strategy. Possible courses of action can then be identified and evaluated and a choice made of the preferred action.

It is then necessary to decide how to get from here to there. Managing change during this transition state is a critical phase in the change process. It is here that the problems of introducing change emerge and have to be managed. These problems can include resistance to change, low stability, high levels of stress, misdirected energy, conflict and loss of momentum. Hence the need to do everything possible when formulating the strategy to anticipate reactions and likely impediments to the introduction of change.

The installation stage may not be straightforward and can also be painful. As described by Pettigrew and Whipp (1991), the implementation of change is an 'iterative, cumulative and reformulation-in-use process'. All the evidence collated by Gratton *et al* (1999) revealed a gap between the rhetoric of strategic aspirations and the reality of what happened subsequently. It seems likely that this gap arose because of a failure to adopt a strategic approach to managing change that recognized the problems of making things happen. One of the most significant of these problems is resistance to change.

RESISTANCE TO CHANGE

Why people resist change

People resist change because it is seen as a threat to familiar patterns of behaviour as well as to status and financial rewards. Woodward (1968) made this point clearly:

> When we talk about resistance to change we tend to imply that management is always rational in changing its direction, and that employees are stupid, emotional

or irrational in not responding in the way they should. But if an individual is going to be worse off, explicitly or implicitly, when the proposed changes have been made, any resistance is entirely rational in terms of his own best interest. The interests of the organization and the individual do not always coincide.

Specifically, the main reasons for resisting charge are as follows:

- *The shock of the new* – people are suspicious of anything that they perceive will upset their established routines, methods of working or conditions of employment. They do not want to lose the security of what is familiar to them. They may not trust management, which means that they will not believe statements that the change is for their benefit as well as that of the organization and they may have good reason from past experience to adopt this viewpoint. They may feel that management has ulterior motives and sometimes, the more powerful the rhetoric, the louder the protestations of managements, the greater the suspension of belief.
- *Economic fears* – loss of money, threats to job security.
- *Inconvenience* – the change will make life more difficult.
- *Uncertainty* – change can be worrying because of uncertainty about its likely impact.
- *Symbolic fears* – a small change that may affect some treasured symbol, such as a separate office or a reserved parking space, may symbolize big ones, especially when employees are uncertain about how extensive the programme of change will be.
- *Threat to interpersonal relationships* – anything that disrupts the customary social relationships and standards of groups of employees will be resisted.
- *Threat to status or skill* – the change is perceived as reducing the status of individuals or as de-skilling them.
- *Competence fears* – concern about the ability to cope with new demands or to acquire new skills.

Overcoming resistance to change

Resistance to change can be difficult to overcome even when it is not detrimental to those concerned. But the attempt must be made and this is the key element in the development of a change strategy. The first step is to analyse the potential impact of change by considering how it will affect people in their jobs. The analysis should indicate what aspects of the proposed change may be supported generally or by specified individuals, and which aspects may be resisted. So far as possible, the potentially hostile or negative reactions of people should be identified, taking into account all the possible reasons for resisting change listed above. It is necessary to try and understand the likely feelings and fears of those affected so that unnecessary worries can be relieved and, as far as possible, ambiguities can be resolved. In making this analysis, the individual introducing the change, who is sometimes called the 'change agent', should recognize that new ideas are likely to be suspect and should make ample provision for the discussion of reactions to proposals to ensure complete understanding of them.

Involvement in the change process gives people the chance to raise and resolve their concerns and make suggestions about the form of the change and how it should be introduced. The aim is to get 'ownership' – a feeling among people that the change is something that they are happy to live with because they have been involved in its planning and introduction – it has become *their* change. People accept what they have helped to create.

Communications about the proposed change should be carefully prepared and worded so that unnecessary fears are allayed. All the available channels as described – written documents, newsletters and the intranet should be used. But face-to-face communications direct from managers to individuals or through a team briefing system are best.

CHANGE MODELS

The change management strategy should be based on an understanding of the various change models. These provide a framework within which strategic choices can be made.

The best-known change models are those developed by Lewin (1951) and Beckhard (1969). But other important contributions to an understanding of the mechanisms for change have been made by Thurley (1979) and Beer *et al* (1990).

Lewin

The basic mechanisms for managing change, according to Lewin (1951), are as follows:

- █ *Unfreezing* – altering the present stable equilibrium that supports existing behaviours and attitudes. This process must take account of the inherent threats change presents to people and the need to motivate those affected to attain the natural state of equilibrium by accepting change.

■ *Changing* – developing new responses based on new information.
■ *Refreezing* – stabilizing the change by introducing the new responses into the personalities of those concerned.

Beckhard

According to Beckhard (1969), a change programme should incorporate the following processes:

■ setting goals and defining the future state or organizational conditions desired after the change;
■ diagnosing the present condition in relation to these goals;
■ defining the transition state activities and commitments required to meet the future state;
■ developing strategies and action plans for managing this transition in the light of an analysis of the factors likely to affect the introduction of change.

Thurley

Thurley (1979) described the following five approaches to managing change:

1. *Directive* – the imposition of change in crisis situations or when other methods have failed. This is done by the exercise of managerial power without consultation.
2. *Bargained* – this approach recognizes that power is shared between the employer and the employed and change requires negotiation, compromise and agreement before being implemented.
3. *'Hearts and minds'* – an all-embracing thrust to change the attitudes, values and beliefs of the whole workforce. This 'normative' approach (ie one that starts from a definition of what management thinks is right or 'normal') seeks 'commitment' and 'shared vision' but does not necessarily include involvement or participation.
4. *Analytical* – a theoretical approach to the change process using models of change such as those described above. It proceeds sequentially from the analysis and diagnosis of the situation, through the setting of objectives,

the design of the change process, the evaluation of the results and, finally, the determination of the objectives for the next stage in the change process. This is the rational and logical approach much favoured by consultants – external and internal. But change seldom proceeds as smoothly as this model would suggest. Emotions, power politics and external pressures mean that the rational approach, although it might be the right way to start, is difficult to sustain.

5. *Action-based* – this recognizes that the way managers behave in practice bears little resemblance to the analytical, theoretical model. The distinction between managerial thought and managerial action blurs in practice to the point of invisibility. What managers think is what they do. Real life therefore often results in a 'ready, aim, fire' approach to change management. This typical approach to change starts with a broad belief that some sort of problem exists, although it may not be well defined. The identification of possible solutions, often on a trial-or-error basis, leads to a clarification of the nature of the problem and a shared understanding of a possible optimal solution, or at least a framework within which solutions can be discovered.

Beer et al

Beer *et al* (1990) suggested in a seminal *Harvard Business Review* article, 'Why change programs don't produce change', that most such programmes are guided by a theory of change that is fundamentally flawed. This theory states that changes in attitudes lead to changes in behaviour. 'According to this model, change is like a conversion experience. Once people "get religion", changes in their behaviour will surely follow.' They believe that this theory gets the change process exactly backwards:

> In fact, individual behaviour is powerfully shaped by the organizational roles people play. The most effective way to change behaviour, therefore, is to put people into a new organizational context, which imposes new roles, responsibilities and relationships on them. This creates a situation that in a sense 'forces' new attitudes and behaviour on people.

They prescribe six steps to effective change which concentrate on what they call 'task alignment' – reorganizing employee's roles, responsibilities and relationships to solve specific business problems in small units where goals and tasks can be clearly defined. The aim of following the overlapping steps is to build a self-reinforcing cycle of commitment, coordination and competence.

The steps are:

1. Mobilize commitment to change through the joint analysis of problems.
2. Develop a shared vision of how to organize and manage to achieve goals such as competitiveness.
3. Foster consensus for the new vision, competence to enact it, and cohesion to move it along.
4. Spread revitalization to all departments without pushing it from the top – don't force the issue, let each department find its own way to the new organization.
5. Institutionalize revitalization through formal policies, systems and structures.
6. Monitor and adjust strategies in response to problems in the revitalization process.

GUIDELINES FOR CHANGE MANAGEMENT STRATEGIES

The above models can be distilled into the following guidelines for planning and implementing change strategies:

■ The achievement of sustainable change requires strong commitment and visionary leadership from the top.
■ There is a need to understand the culture of the organization and the levers for change that are most likely to be effective in that culture.
■ Those concerned with managing change at all levels should have the temperament and leadership skills appropriate to the circumstances of the organization and its change strategies.
■ It is important to build a working environment that is conducive to change. This means developing the firm as a 'learning organization'.
■ Commitment to change is improved if those affected by change are allowed to participate as fully as possible in planning and implementing it. The aim should be to get them to 'own' the change as something they want and will be glad to live with.
■ The reward system should encourage innovation and recognize success in achieving change.
■ Strategies for change must be adaptable – the ability to respond swiftly to new situations and demands, which will inevitably arise, is essential.

- Change will always involve failure as well as success. The failures must be expected and learnt from.
- Hard evidence and data on the need for change are the most powerful tools for its achievement, but establishing the need for change is easier than deciding how to satisfy it.
- The emphasis must be on changing behaviour, not trying to enforce corporate values.
- It is easier to change behaviour by changing processes, structure and systems than to change attitudes.
- It is necessary to anticipate problems of implementation; these will include:
  - resource dependency (shortages in the resources required, people and time as well as money, will inhibit change);
  - the capacity and willingness of middle managers to support the change (without their cooperation, change strategies are likely to fail);
  - the capacity and willingness of HR to ensure that the change is embedded in spite of indifference or negative reactions (this includes the ability of HR to provide guidance, advice and training as well as developing procedures that are user-friendly and not over-engineered).
- There are usually people in organizations who can act as champions of change. They will welcome the challenges and opportunities that change can provide. They are the ones to be chosen as change agents.
- Resistance to change is inevitable if the individuals concerned feel that they are going to be worse off – implicitly or explicitly. The inept management of change will produce that reaction.
- In an age of global competition, technological innovation, turbulence, discontinuity, even chaos, change is inevitable and necessary. The organization must do all it can to explain why change is essential and how it will affect everyone. Moreover, every effort must be made to protect the interests of those affected by change.

12

Strategies for developing the employment relationship

The employment relationship between managements and employees is a factor that can make a significant impact on the degree to which organizational effectiveness is achieved. Although relationships between employers and employees are subject to continuous day-to-day development, negotiation and change, it is necessary to take a strategic view on how a lasting and positive relationship can be established. In this chapter:

- the employment relationship and its nature are defined and described;
- the features of the psychological contract that play an important part in defining the employment relationship are described;
- strategic approaches to creating and maintaining a positive psychological contract, increasing commitment and developing trust are discussed.

THE EMPLOYMENT RELATIONSHIP

The term 'employment relationship' describes the relationships that exist between employers and employees in the workplace. These may be formal, eg contracts of employment, procedural agreements. Or they may be informal, in the shape of the psychological contract that expresses certain assumptions and expectations about what managers and employees have to offer and are willing to deliver (Kessler and Undy, 1996). They can have an individual dimension, which refers to individual contracts and expectations, or a collective dimension, which refers to relationships between management and trade unions, staff associations or members of joint consultative bodies such as works councils.

Nature of the employment relationship

The dimension of the employment relationship as described by Kessler and Undy (1996) are shown in Figure 12.1.

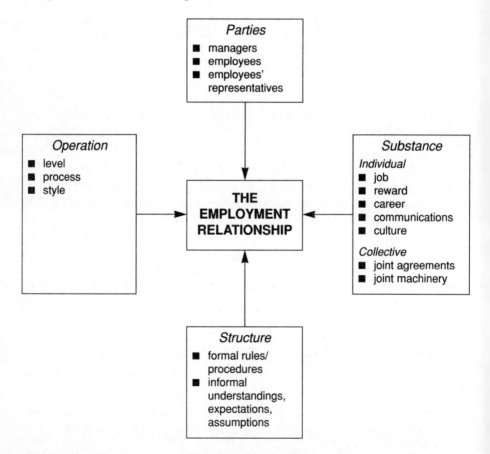

Figure 12.1   Dimensions of the employment relationship

The parties are managers, employees and employee representatives. The 'substance' incorporates the job, reward and career of individuals and the communications and culture of the organization as it affects them. It can also include collective agreements and joint employee relations machinery (works councils and the like). The formal dimensions include rules and procedures, and the informal aspect covers understanding, expectations and assumptions. Finally, the employment relationship exists at different levels in the organization (management to employees generally, and managers to individual employees and their representatives or groups of people). The operation of the relationship will also be affected by processes such as communications and consultation, and by the management style prevailing throughout the organization or adopted by individual managers.

Basis of the employment relationship

The starting point of the employment relationship is an undertaking by an employee to provide skill and effort to the employer in return for which the employer provides the employee with a salary or a wage. Initially the relationship is founded on a legal contract. This may be a written contract but the absence of such a contract does not mean that no contractual relationship exists. Employers and employees still have certain implied legal rights and obligations. The employer's obligations include the duty to pay salary or wages, provide a safe workplace, to act in good faith towards the employee and not to act in such a way as to undermine the trust and confidence of the employment relationship. The employee has corresponding obligations, which include obedience, competence, honesty and loyalty.

An important factor to remember about the employment relationship is that generally it is the employer who has the power to dictate the contractual terms unless they have been fixed by collective bargaining. Individuals, except when they are much in demand, have little scope to vary the terms of the contract imposed upon them by employers.

Defining the employment relationship

Two types of contracts defining the employment relationship have been distinguished by MacNeil (1985) and Rousseau and Wade-Benzoni (1994). There are *transactional contracts*, which have well-described terms of exchange and which are usually expressed financially. They are of limited duration with specified performance requirements. There are also *relational contracts*, which are less well defined with more abstract terms and refer to an open-ended membership of the organization. Performance requirements attached to this continuing membership are incomplete or ambiguous.

However, the employment relationships can also be expressed in terms of a *psychological contract* which, according to Guzzo and Noonan (1994), has both transactional and relational qualities. The concept of a psychological contract expresses the view that at its most basic level the employment relationship consists of a unique combination of beliefs held by an individual and his or her employer about what they expect of one another.

Changes in the employment relationship

As noted by Gallie *et al* (1998) in their analysis of the outcome of their Employment in Britain research programme, while there have been shifts in the ways in people are employed, 'the evidence for a major change in the nature of the employment relationship was much less convincing'. But they did note the following characteristics of employment as revealed by the survey:

- New forms of management, often based explicitly or implicitly on HRM principles and emphasizing individual contracts rather than collective bargaining.
- There was some increase in task discretion but there was no evidence of a significant decline in managerial control, indeed, in some important respects control was intensified.
- Supervisory activity was still important.
- Integrative forms of management policy were centred on non-manual employees.
- The great majority of employees continued to attach a high level of importance to the intrinsically motivating aspects of work.
- The higher the level of skill, the more people were involved with their work.
- The raising of skill levels and the granting of increased discretion to employees are key factors in improving the quality of work experience.
- High levels of commitment to the organization can reduce absenteeism and labour turnover, but there was no evidence that organizational commitment 'added anything over and above other organizational and task characteristics with regard to the quality of work performance'.

THE PSYCHOLOGICAL CONTRACT

The employment relationship is governed to a considerable extent by the psychological contract.

This expresses the combination of beliefs held by an individual and his or her employer about what they expect of one another. It can be described as the set of reciprocal but unwritten expectations that exist between individual employees and their employers. As described by Guest *et al* (1996): 'It is concerned with assumptions, expectations, promises and mutual obligations'. It creates attitudes and emotions that form and govern behaviour. A psychological contract is implicit. It is also dynamic – it develops over time as experience accumulates, employment conditions change and employees re-evaluate their expectations. The notion of a psychological contract implies that there is an unwritten set of expectations operating at all times between every member of an organization and the various managers and others in that organization.

The psychological contract may provide some indication of the answers to the two fundamental employment relationship questions that individuals pose: 'What can I reasonably expect from the organization?' and 'What should I reasonably be expected to contribute in return?'. But it is unlikely that the psychological contract and therefore the employment relationship will ever be fully understood by either party.

The aspects of the employment relationship covered by the psychological contact will include, from the employee's point of view:

- trust in the management of the organization to keep their promises – to 'deliver the deal' (Guest *et al*, 1996);
- how they are treated in terms of fairness, equity and consistency;
- security of employment;
- scope to demonstrate competence;
- career expectations and the opportunity to develop skills;
- involvement and influence.

From the employer's point of view, the psychological contact covers such aspects of the employment relationship as:

- commitment;
- competence;
- effort;
- compliance;
- loyalty.

As Guest *et al* (1996) point out:

> While employees may want what they have always wanted – security, a career,
> fair rewards, interesting work and so on – employers no longer feel able or obliged
> to provide these. Instead, they have been demanding more of their employees in
> terms of greater input and tolerance of uncertainty and change, while providing
> less in return, in particular less security and more limited career prospects.

The significance of the psychological contract

As suggested by Spindler (1994): 'A psychological contract creates emotions
and attitudes which form and control behaviour'. The significance of the
psychological contract was further explained by Sims (1994) as follows:

> A balanced psychological contract is necessary for a continuing, harmonious rela-
> tionship between the employee and the organization. However, the violation of
> the psychological contract can signal to the participants that the parties no longer
> shared (or never shared) a common set of values or goals.

The concept highlights the fact that employee/employer expectations take the
form of unarticulated assumptions. Disappointments on the part of management as well as employees may therefore be inevitable. These disappointments
can, however, be alleviated if managements appreciate that one of their key
roles is to manage expectations, which means clarifying what they believe
employees should achieve, the competences they should possess and the
values they should uphold. And this is a matter not just of articulating and
stipulating these requirements but of discussing and agreeing them with individuals and teams.

The psychological contract governs the continuing development of the
employment relationship, which is constantly evolving over time. But how the
contract is developing and the impact it makes may not be fully understood by
any of the parties involved. As Spindler (1994) comments:

> In a psychological contract the rights and obligations of the parties have not been
> articulated much less agreed to. The parties do not express their expectations and,
> in fact, may be quite incapable of doing so.

People who have no clear idea about what they expect may, if such unex-
pressed expectations have not been fulfilled, have no clear idea why they have
been disappointed. But they will be aware that something does not feel right.
And a company staffed by 'cheated' individuals who expect more than they
get is heading for trouble.

EMPLOYMENT RELATIONSHIP STRATEGIES

Strategies for developing the employment relationship aim to:

- develop a positive psychological contract;
- increase commitment;
- create a climate of trust.

None of these aims can be achieved overnight if the situation is one of a negative psychological contract, poor commitment and an absence of trust. That is why a strategic approach is necessary, which sets out longer-term aims and the programmes to accomplish them but recognizes that the programmes will have to be flexible in the sense of being able to respond rapidly to new circumstances.

Strategies for developing a positive psychological contract

As Guest *et al* (1996) point out:

> A positive psychological contract is worth taking seriously because it is strongly linked to higher commitment to the organization, higher employee satisfaction and better employment relations. Again this reinforces the benefits of pursuing a set of progressive HRM practices.

They also emphasize the importance of a high-involvement climate and suggest HRM strategies for developing the contract, such as the provision of opportunities for learning, training and development; focus on job security, promotion and careers; minimizing status differentials; fair reward systems; and comprehensive communication and involvement processes.

The particular practices that can be incorporated in the strategy include:

- during *recruitment interviews* – presenting the unfavourable as well as the favourable aspects of a job in a 'realistic job preview';
- in *induction programmes* – communicating to new starters the organization's personnel policies and procedures and its core values, indicating to them the standards of performance expected in such areas as quality and customer service, and spelling out requirements for flexibility;

- by issuing and updating *employee handbooks* that reinforce the messages delivered in induction programmes;
- by encouraging the development of *performance management* processes that ensure that performance expectations are agreed and reviewed regularly;
- by encouraging the use of *personal development plans* that spell out how continuous improvement of performance can be achieved, mainly by self-managed learning;
- by using *training and management development programmes* to underpin core values and define performance expectations;
- by ensuring through *manager and team leader training* that managers and team leaders understand their role in managing the employment relationship through such processes as performance management and team leadership;
- by encouraging the maximum amount of *contact* between managers and team leaders and their team members to achieve mutual understanding of expectations and to provide a means of two-way communications;
- by adopting a general policy of *transparency* – ensuring that on all matters which affect them, employees know what is happening, why it is happening and the impact it will make on their employment, development and prospects;
- by developing *HR procedures* covering grievance handling, discipline, equal opportunities, promotion and redundancy and ensuring that they are implemented fairly and consistently;
- by developing and communicating *HR policies* covering the major areas of employment, development, reward and employee relations;
- by ensuring that the *reward system* is developed and managed to achieve equity, fairness and consistency in all aspects of pay and benefits;
- generally, by advising on *employee relations* procedures, processes and issues that further good collective relationships.

These strategies for managing the employment relationship by developing a positive psychological contract cover all aspects of people management. It is important to remember, however, that this is a continuous process. The effective management of the relationship means ensuring that values are upheld and that a transparent, consistent and fair approach is adopted in dealing with all aspects of employment.

Commitment strategy

The concept of commitment refers to feelings of attachment and loyalty and as such plays an important part in HRM philosophy. As defined by Porter *et al* (1974), commitment is the relative strength of the individual's identification with, and involvement in, a particular organization. It consists of three factors:

1. A strong desire to remain a member of the organization.
2. A strong belief in, and acceptance of, the values and goals of the organization.
3. A readiness to exert considerable effort on behalf of the organization.

An alternative, although closely related, definition of commitment emphasizes the importance of behaviour in creating commitment. As Salancik (1977) put it: 'Commitment is a state of being in which an individual becomes bound by his actions to beliefs that sustain his activities and his own involvement'. Three features of behaviour are important in binding individuals to their acts: the visibility of the acts, the extent to which the outcomes are irrevocable, and the degree to which the person undertakes the action voluntarily. Commitment, according to Salancik, can be increased and harnessed 'to obtain support for organizational ends and interests' through such ploys as participation in decisions about actions.

The significance of commitment

The importance of commitment was highlighted by Walton (1985). His theme was that improved performance would result if the organization moved away from the traditional control-oriented approach to workforce management, which relies upon establishing order, exercising control and 'achieving efficiency in the application of the workforce'. He argued that this approach should be replaced by a commitment strategy. He suggested that workers respond best – and most creatively – not when they are tightly controlled by management, placed in narrowly defined jobs, and treated like an unwelcome necessity, but, instead, when they are given broader responsibilities, encouraged to contribute and helped to achieve satisfaction in their work.

Problems with the concept of commitment

A comment frequently made about the concept of commitment is that it is too simplistic in adopting a unitary frame of reference; in other words, it assumes unrealistically that an organization consists of people with shared interests. It has been suggested by people like Cyert and March (1963) that an organization is really a coalition of interest groups where political processes are an inevitable part of everyday life. The pluralistic perspective recognizes the legitimacy of different interests and values and therefore asks the question, 'Commitment to what?'. Thus, as Coopey and Hartley (1991) put it, 'commitment is not an all-or-nothing affair (though many managers might like it to be) but a question of multiple or competing commitments for the individual'.

It was also pointed out by Coopey and Hartley that:

> The problem for a unitarist notion of organizational commitment is that it fosters a conformist approach, which not only fails to reflect organizational reality, but can be narrowing and limiting for the organization.

They argue that if employees are expected and encouraged to commit themselves tightly to a single set of values and goals, they will not be able to cope with the ambiguities and uncertainties that are endemic in organizational life in times of change. Conformity to 'imposed' values will inhibit creative problem solving, and high commitment to present courses of action will increase both resistance to change and the stress that invariably occurs when change takes place.

A further key issue is that of mutual commitment. Management may ask employees to be committed to the organization but will that have any meaning if there is no evidence that management is committed to employees in such fundamental aspects of the employment relationship as security and fair dealing? A sudden decision to downsize does not deliver a good message about mutual commitment.

Creating a commitment strategy

In spite of these reservations, it is difficult to deny that it is desirable for management to have defined strategic goals and values. And it is equally desirable from management's point of view for employees to behave in ways that support these strategies and values.

But in enlisting this support by means of a commitment strategy, account should be taken of the points discussed above. Firstly, it has to be accepted that the interests of the organization and of its members do not necessarily coincide. It can be asserted by management that everyone will benefit from organizational success in terms of security, pay, opportunities for advancement, etc. But employees and their trade unions may be difficult to convince that this is the case if they believe that the success is to be achieved by such actions as disinvestments, downsizing, cost reductions affecting pay and employment, tougher performance standards or tighter management controls. And when defining values, it is important not to impose them on employees. They should be involved in their formulation and in discussing with management how they are to be upheld. This avoids what Legge (1989) refers to as a process of 'co-optation' in which management forces its own set of values down the throats of its employees. Involving employees makes sense in that they are thus much more likely to own and practise the values.

Secondly, management must not define and communicate values in such a way as to inhibit flexibility, creativity and the ability to adapt to change. Strategies have to be defined in broad terms with caveats that they will be amended if circumstances change. Values have to emphasize the need for flexibility, innovation and teamworking as well as the need for performance and quality.

Thirdly, too much should not be expected from campaigns to increase commitment. They may reduce employee turnover, increase identification with the organization and develop feelings of loyalty among its employees. They may increase job satisfaction, but there is no evidence that higher levels of job satisfaction necessarily improve performance. They may provide a context within which motivation and therefore performance will increase. But there is no guarantee that this will take place, although the chances of gaining improvements will be increased if the campaign is focused upon a specific value such as quality.

It may be naive to believe that 'hearts and minds' campaigns to win commitment will transform organizational behaviour overnight. But it is surely useful for organizations to do what they can along the lines described below to influence behaviour, to support the achievement of objectives and to uphold values that are inherently worthwhile. It is good management practice to define expectations in terms of objectives and standards of performance. It is even better management practice to discuss and agree these objectives and standards with employees.

A commitment strategy will be concerned with the development of communication, education and training programmes, initiatives to increase involvement and 'ownership', and the introduction of performance and reward management processes.

Communication programmes

It seems to be strikingly obvious that commitment will only be gained if people understand what they are expected to commit to. But managements too often fail to pay sufficient attention to delivering the message in terms that recognize that the frame of reference for those who receive it is likely to be quite different from their own. Management's expectations will not necessarily coincide with those of employees. Pluralism prevails. And in delivering the message, the use of different and complementary channels of communication such as newsletters, briefing groups, videos, the intranet, notice boards, etc is often neglected.

Education

Education is another form of communication. An educational programme is designed to increase both knowledge and understanding of, for example, total quality management. The aim will be to influence behaviour and thereby progressively change attitudes.

Training

Training is designed to develop specific competences. For example, if one of the values to be supported is flexibility, it will be necessary to extend the range of skills possessed by members of work teams through multi-skilling programmes. Commitment is enhanced if managers can gain the confidence and respect of their teams, and training to improve the quality of management should form an important part of any programme for increasing commitment. Management training can also be focused on increasing the competence of managers in specific areas of their responsibility for gaining commitment, for example, performance management.

Developing ownership

A sense of belonging is enhanced if there is a feeling of 'ownership' among employees, not just in the literal sense of owning shares (although this can help) but in the sense of believing they are genuinely accepted by management as a key part of the organization. This concept of 'ownership' extends to participating in decisions on new developments and changes in working practices that affect the individuals concerned. They should be involved in making those decisions and feel that their ideas have been listened to and that they have contributed to the outcome. They will then be more likely to accept the decision or change because it is owned by them rather than being imposed by management.

Developing a sense of excitement in the job

A sense of excitement in the job can be created by concentrating on the intrinsic motivating factors such as responsibility, achievement and recognition, and using these principles to govern the way in which jobs are designed. Excitement in the job is also created by the quality of leadership and the will-ingness of managers and team leaders to recognize that they will obtain increased motivation and commitment if they pay continuous attention to the ways in which they delegate responsibility and give their staff the scope to use their skills and abilities.

Performance management

Performance management strategies, as described in Chapter 14, can help to cascade corporate objectives and values throughout the organization so that consistency is achieved at all levels. Expectations of individuals are defined in terms of their own job, which they can more readily grasp and act upon than if they were asked to support some remote and, to them, irrelevant overall objec-tives. But individual objectives can be described in ways that support the achievement of those defined for higher levels in the organization.

Reward management

Reward management processes can make it clear that individuals will be rewarded in accordance with the extent to which they achieve objectives and uphold corporate values. This can reinforce the messages delivered through other channels of communication.

Strategies for developing a climate of trust

The Institute of Personnel and Development suggested in its statement, *People Make the Difference* (1994) that a strategy for building trust is the only basis upon which commitment can be generated. The IPD commented that: 'In too many organizations inconsistency between what is said and what is done undermines trust, generates employee cynicism and provides evidence of contradictions in management thinking'.

It has also been suggested by Herriot *et al* (1998) that trust should be regarded as social capital – the fund of goodwill in any social group that enables people within it to collaborate with one another. Thompson (1998) sees trust as a 'unique human resource capability that helps the organization fulfil its competitive advantage' – a core competency that leads to high business performance. Thus there is a business need to develop a climate of trust, as there is a business need to introduce effective pay-for-contribution processes that are built on trust.

The meaning of trust

Trust, as defined by the *Oxford English Dictionary*, is a firm belief that a person may be relied on. An alternative definition has been provided by Shaw (1997) to the effect that trust is the 'belief that those on whom we depend will meet our expectations of them'. These expectations are dependent on 'our assessment of another's responsibility to meet our needs'.

A climate of trust

A high-trust organization has been described by Fox (1973) as follows:

> Organizational participants share certain ends or values; bear towards each other a diffuse sense of long-term obligations; offer each other spontaneous support without narrowly calculating the cost or anticipating any short-term reciprocation; communicate honestly and freely; are ready to repose their fortunes in each other's hands; and give each other the benefit of any doubt that may arise with respect to goodwill or motivation.

This ideal state may seldom, if ever, be attained, but it does represent a picture of an effective organization in which, as Thompson (1998) notes, trust 'is an outcome of good management'.

When do employees trust management?

A strategy for creating a climate of trust should be based on the understanding that management is more likely to be trusted by employees when the latter:

- believe that the management means what it says;
- observe that management does what it says it is going to do – suiting the action to the word;
- know from experience that management delivers the deal – it keeps its word and fulfils its side of the bargain;
- feel they are treated fairly, equitably and consistently.

Developing a high-trust organization

As Thompson (1998) comments, a number of writers have generally concluded that trust is 'not something that can, or should, be directly managed'. He cites Sako (1994) who wrote that: 'Trust is a cultural norm which can rarely be created intentionally because attempts to create trust in a calculative manner would destroy the effective basis of trust'.

It may not be possible to 'manage' trust but, as Thompson points out, trust is an outcome of good management. It is created and maintained by managerial behaviour and by the development of better mutual understanding of expectations – employers of employees, and employees of employers. Issues of trust are not in the end to do with managing people or processes, but are more about relationships and mutual support through change, as Herriot et al (1998) point out.

Clearly, the sort of behaviour that is most likely to engender trust is when management is honest with people, keeps its word (delivers the deal) and practices what it preaches. Organizations that espouse core values ('people are our greatest asset') and then proceed to ignore them will be low-trust organizations.

More specifically, trust will be developed if management acts fairly, equitably and consistently, if a policy of transparency is implemented, if intentions and the reasons for proposals or decisions are communicated both to employees generally and to individuals, if there is full involvement in developing reward processes, and if mutual expectations are agreed through performance management.

Failure to meet these criteria, wholly or in part, is perhaps the main reason why so many performance-related pay schemes have not lived up to expectations.

Renewing trust

As suggested by Herriot et al (1998), if trust is lost, a four-step renewal strategy is required:

1. Admission by top management that it has paid insufficient attention in the past to employees' diverse needs.
2. A limited process of contracting whereby a particular transition to a different way of working for a group of employees is done in a form that takes individual needs into account.

3. Establishing 'knowledge-based' trust, which is based not on a specific transactional deal but on a developing perception of trustworthiness.
4. Achieving trust based on identification in which all parties empathize with each other's needs and therefore takes them on board themselves (although this final state is seldom reached in practice).

Part 4

Functional strategies

13

Employee resourcing strategy

Employee resourcing strategy is concerned with ensuring that the organization obtains and retains the people it needs and employs them efficiently. It is a key part of the HRM process.

HRM is fundamentally about matching human resources to the strategic and operational needs of the organization and ensuring the full utilization of those resources. It is concerned not only with obtaining and keeping the number and quality of staff required, but also with selecting and promoting people who 'fit' the culture and the strategic requirements of the organization.

THE OBJECTIVE OF RESOURCING STRATEGY

The objective of HRM resourcing strategies as expressed by Keep (1989) is:

> To obtain the right basic material in the form of a workforce endowed with the appropriate qualities, skills, knowledge and potential for future training. The selection and recruitment of workers best suited to meeting the needs of the organization ought to form a core activity upon which most other HRM policies geared towards development and motivation could be built.

The concept that the strategic capability of a firm depends on its resource capability in the shape of people (resource-based strategy, as explained in Chapter 2) provides the rationale for resourcing strategy. The aim of this strategy is therefore to ensure that a firm achieves competitive advantage by employing more capable people than its rivals. These people will have a wider and deeper range of skills and will behave in ways that will maximize their contribution. The organization attracts such people by being 'the employer of choice'. It retains them by providing better opportunities and rewards than others and by developing a positive psychological contract that increases commitment and creates mutual trust. Furthermore, the organization deploys its people in ways that maximize the added value they supply.

THE STRATEGIC HRM APPROACH TO RESOURCING

HRM places more emphasis than traditional personnel management on finding people whose attitudes and behaviour are likely to be congruent with what management believes to be appropriate and conducive to success. In the words of Townley (1989), organizations are concentrating more on 'the attitudinal and behavioural characteristics of employees'. This tendency has its dangers. Innovative and adaptive organizations need non-conformists, even mavericks, who can 'buck the system'. If managers recruit people 'in their own image' there is the risk of staffing the organization with conformist clones and of perpetuating a dysfunctional culture – one that may have been successful in the past but is no longer appropriate in the face of new challenges. As Pascale (1990) puts it, 'nothing fails like success'.

The HRM approach to resourcing therefore emphasizes that matching resources to organizational requirements does not simply mean maintaining the status quo and perpetuating a moribund culture. It can and often does mean radical changes in thinking about the skills and behaviours required in the future to achieve sustainable growth and cultural change.

INTEGRATING BUSINESS AND RESOURCING STRATEGIES

The philosophy behind the strategic HRM approach to resourcing is that it is people who implement the strategic plan. As Quinn Mills (1983) has put it, the process is one of 'planning with people in mind'.

The integration of business and resourcing strategies is based on an understanding of the direction in which the organization is going and the determination of:

- the numbers of people required to meet business needs;
- the skills and behaviour required to support the achievement of business strategies;
- the impact of organizational restructuring as a result of rationalization, decentralization, delayering, mergers, product or market development, or the introduction of new technology – for example, cellular manufacturing;
- plans for changing the culture of the organization in such areas as ability to deliver, performance standards, quality, customer service, team-working and flexibility, which indicate the need for people with different attitudes, beliefs and personal characteristics.

These factors will be strongly influenced by the type of business strategies adopted by the organization and the sort of business it is in. These may be expressed in such terms as the Boston Consulting Group's classification of businesses as wild cat, star, cash cow or dog; or Miles and Snow's (1978) typology of defender, prospector and analyser organizations.

Resourcing strategies exist to provide the people and skills required to support the business strategy, but they should also contribute to the formulation of that strategy. HR directors have an obligation to point out to their colleagues the human resource opportunities and constraints that will affect the achievement of strategic plans. In mergers or acquisitions, for example, the ability of management within the company to handle the new situation and the quality of management in the new business will be important considerations.

BUNDLING RESOURCING STRATEGIES AND ACTIVITIES

Employee resourcing is not just about recruitment and selection. It is concerned with any means available to meet the needs of the firm for certain skills and behaviours. A strategy to enlarge the skill base may start with recruitment and selection but would also extend into training and development to enhance skill and modify behaviours and methods of rewarding people for the acquisition of extra skills. Performance management processes can be used to identify development needs (skill and behavioural) and motivate people to make the most effective use of their skills. Competence frameworks and profiles can be prepared to define the skills and behaviours required and used in selection, employee development and employee reward processes. The aim should be to develop a reinforcing bundle of strategies along these lines.

THE COMPONENTS OF EMPLOYEE RESOURCING STRATEGY

The components of employee resourcing strategy as considered in this chapter are:

- *Human resource planning* – assessing future business needs and deciding on the numbers and types of people required.
- *Resourcing plans* – preparing plans for finding people from within the organization and/or for training programmes to help people learn new skills. If needs cannot be satisfied from within the organization, preparing longer-term plans for ensuring that recruitment and selection processes will satisfy them.
- *Retention strategy* – preparing plans for retaining the people the organization needs.
- *Flexibility strategy* – planning for increased flexibility in the use of human resources to enable the organization to make the best use of people and adapt swiftly to changing circumstances.

Human resource planning

Human resource planning determines the human resources required by the organization to achieve its strategic goals. As defined by Bulla and Scott (1994), it is 'the process for ensuring that the human resource requirements of an organization are identified and plans are made for satisfying those requirements'. Human resource planning is based on the belief that people are an organization's most important strategic resource. It is generally concerned with matching resources to business needs in the longer term, although it will sometimes address shorter-term requirements. It addresses human resource needs both in quantitative and qualitative terms. This means answering two basic questions: 1) How many people? and 2) What sort of people? Human resource planning also looks at broader issues relating to the ways in which people are employed and developed in order to improve organizational effectiveness. It can therefore play an important part in strategic human resource management.

Link to business planning

Human resource planning should be an integral part of business planning. The strategic planning process defines projected changes in the types of activities carried out by the organization and the scale of those activities. It identifies the core competences the organization needs to achieve its goals and therefore its skill and behavioural requirements.

Human resource planning interprets these plans in terms of people require-
ments. But it may influence the business strategy by drawing attention to ways in which people could be developed and deployed more effectively to further the achievement of business goals, as well as focusing on any problems that might have to be resolved in order to ensure that the people required will be available and will be capable of making the necessary contribution. As Quinn Mills (1983) indicates, human resource planning is:

> a decision-making process that combines three important activities: 1) identifying and acquiring the right number of people with the proper skills; 2) motivating them to achieve high performance; and 3) creating interactive links between business objectives and people-planning activities.

Hard and soft human resource planning

A distinction can be made between 'hard' and 'soft' human resource planning. The former is based on quantitative analysis in order to ensure that the right number of the right sort of people is available when needed. The latter, as described by Marchington and Wilkinson (1996), 'is more explicitly focused on creating and shaping the culture of the organization so that there is a clear integration between corporate goals and employee values, beliefs and behaviours'. But as they point out, the soft version becomes virtually synonymous with the whole subject of human resource management.

Human resource planning is indeed concerned with broader issues about the employment of people than the traditional quantitative approach of 'manpower planning'. But it also addresses those aspects of human resource management that are primarily about the organization's requirements for people from the viewpoint of numbers, skills and how they are deployed. This is the sense in which human resource planning is discussed in this chapter.

Limitations

However, it must be recognized that although the notion of human resource planning is well established in the HRM vocabulary it does not seem to be embedded as a key HR activity. As Rothwell (1995) suggests: 'Apart from isolated examples, there has been little research evidence of increased use or of its success'. She explains the gap between theory and practice as arising from:

- the impact of change and the difficulty of predicting the future – 'the need for planning may be in inverse proportion to its feasibility';
- the 'shifting kaleidoscope' of policy priorities and strategies within organizations;
- the distrust of theory or planning that is displayed by many managers – they often prefer pragmatic adaptation to conceptualization;
- the lack of evidence that human resource planning works.

Research conducted by Cowling and Walters (1990) indicated that the only formal and regular activities carried out by respondents were the identification of future training needs, analysis of training costs and analysis of productivity. Fewer than half produced formal labour supply-and-demand forecasts, and less than 20 per cent formally monitored HR planning practices.

Summarizing the problem, Taylor (1998) comments that:

> It would seem that employers, quite simply, prefer to wait until their view of the future environment clears sufficiently for them to see the whole picture before committing resources in preparation for its arrival. The perception is that the more complex and turbulent the environment, the more important it is to wait and see before acting.

Be that as it may, it is difficult to reject out of hand the belief that some attempt should be made broadly to determine future human resource requirements as a basis for strategic planning and action.

Approaches to human resource planning

Resourcing strategies show the way forward through the analysis of business strategies and demographic trends. They are converted into action plans based on the outcome of the following interrelated planning activities:

- *Demand forecasting* – estimating future needs for people and competences by reference to corporate and functional plans and forecasts of future activity levels.

- *Supply forecasting* – estimating the supply of people by reference to analyses of current resources and future availability, after allowing for wastage. The forecast will also take account of labour market trends relating to the availability of skills and to demographics.
- *Forecasting requirements* – analysing the demand and supply forecasts to identify future deficits or surpluses with the help of models, where appropriate.
- *Action planning* – preparing plans to deal with forecast deficits through internal promotion, training or external recruitment. If necessary, preparing plans for unavoidable downsizing so as to avoid any compulsory redundancies, if that is possible. Developing retention and flexibility strategies.

Although these are described as separate areas they are closely interrelated and often overlap. For example, demand forecasts are estimates of future requirements and these may be prepared on the basis of assumptions about the productivity of employees. But the supply forecast will also have to consider productivity trends and how they might affect the supply of people.

A flow chart of the process of human resource planning is shown in Figure 13.1.

Resourcing plans

The analysis of future requirements should indicate what steps need to be taken to appoint people from within the organization and what training programmes should be planned. The analysis will also establish how many people will need to be recruited in the absence of qualified employees within the organization or the impossibility of training people in the new skills in time.

Internal resourcing

Ideally, internal resourcing should be based on data already available about skills and potential. This should have been provided by regular skills audits and the analysis of the outcomes of performance management reviews. A 'trawl' can then be made to locate available talent which can be accompanied by an internal advertising campaign.

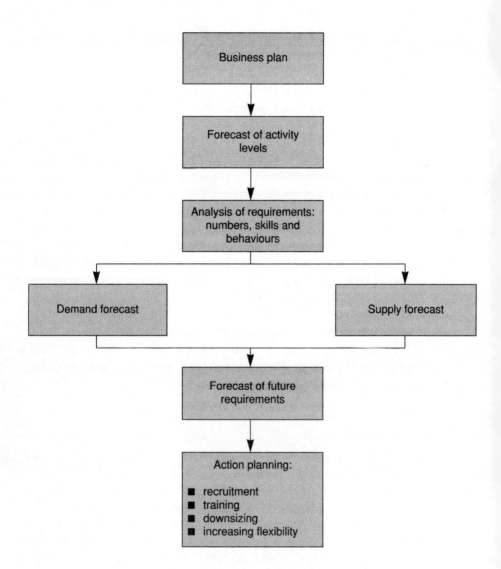

Figure 13.1   Human resource planning flow chart

External resourcing

External resourcing requirements can be met by developing a recruitment strategy. The aims of this strategy would be, first, to make the organization 'the employer of choice' in its particular field or for the people it wants to recruit (eg, graduates). Secondly, the strategy should plan the best methods of defining precisely what is needed in terms of skills and competencies. Finally, the strategy should be concerned with planning the use of the most effective methods of obtaining the number and type of people required.

As indicated by Spellman (1992), the strategy should be concerned with the following activities:

1. *Define skill and competency (behavioural) requirements* – ideally this should be carried out by the use of systematic skill and competence analysis techniques. These can form the material upon which focused and structured interviews can take place and be used as criteria for selection. They may also indicate where and how psychometric tests could be helpful.
2. *Analyse the factors affecting decisions to join the organization* – these include:
   - the pay and total benefits package: this may have a considerable effect on decisions to join the organization but it is by no means the only factor; those set out below can be just as important, even more significant for some people;
   - career opportunities;
   - the opportunity to use existing skills or to acquire new skills;
   - the opportunity to use the latest technology and equipment with which the organization is well supplied (of particular interest to research scientists and engineers);
   - access to high-level training;
   - a responsible and intrinsically rewarding job;
   - a belief that what the organization is doing is worthwhile;
   - the reputation of the organization as an employer;
   - the opportunity the job will provide to further the individual's career, for example, the scope to achieve and have achievements recognized; increase in employability, a respected company name to put on a CV.
3. *Competitive resourcing* – this will start from an analysis of the basis upon which the organization competes with other firms for employees. The factors mentioned above should be covered and the aim would be to seek competitive advantage by exploiting those that are superior to rivals. One of the factors will be pay. This may not be the only one, but it can be important. It is necessary to track market rates and make a policy decision on where the organization wants to be in relation to the market.
4. *Alternative strategies for satisfying human resource requirements* – these consist of:
   - outsourcing;
   - re-engineering;
   - increasing flexibility, as discussed later in this chapter;

- skills training;
- multi-skilling;
- downsizing.

Recruitment and selection techniques

The strategy should explore methods not only of recruiting the number of people required, but also of finding staff who have the necessary skills and experience, who are likely to deliver the sort of behaviour required and will fit into the organization's culture readily. These processes and techniques will include the use of:

- skills analysis;
- competence mapping;
- the Internet for recruitment;
- biodata;
- structured interviews;
- psychometric testing;
- assessment centres.

The aim of the strategy is to develop the best mix of recruitment and selection tools. It has been demonstrated that a 'bundle' of selection techniques is likely to be more effective as a method of predicting the likely success of candidates than relying on a single method such as an interview.

Retention strategy

Retention strategies aim to ensure that key people stay with the organization and that wasteful and expensive levels of employee turnover are reduced. They will be based on an analysis of why people stay and why they leave.

Analysis of reasons for staying or leaving

The reasons why people remain with the organization can be established through attitude surveys. These could segment respondents according to their length of service and analyse the answers of longer-serving employees to establish if there are any common patterns. The survey results could be supplemented by focus groups, which would discuss why people stay and identify any problems. An analysis of why people leave through exit interviews may provide some information but they are unreliable – people rarely give the full reasons why they are going.

The retention plan should address each of the areas in which lack of commitment and dissatisfaction can arise. The actions to be considered under each heading are listed below:

- ■ *Pay* – problems arise because of uncompetitive, inequitable or unfair pay systems. Possible actions include:
  - reviewing pay levels on the basis of market surveys;
  - introducing job evaluation or improving an existing scheme to provide for equitable grading decisions;
  - ensuring that employees understand the link between performance and reward;
  - reviewing performance-related pay schemes to ensure that they operate fairly;
  - adapting payment-by-results systems to ensure that employees are not penalized when they are engaged only on short runs;
  - tailoring benefits to individual requirements and preferences;
  - involving employees in developing and operating job evaluation and performance-related pay systems.
- ■ *Job design* – dissatisfaction may be caused by jobs that are unrewarding in themselves. Jobs should be designed to maximize skill variety, task significance, autonomy and feedback, and they should provide opportunities for learning and growth.
- ■ *Performance* – employees can be demotivated if they are unclear about their responsibilities or performance standards, are uninformed about how well they are doing, or feel that their performance assessments are unfair. The following actions can be taken:
  - express performance requirements in terms of hard but attainable goals;
  - get employees and managers to agree on those goals and the steps required to achieve them;
  - encourage managers to praise employees for good performance but also get them to provide regular, informative and easily interpreted feedback: performance problems should be discussed as they happen in order that immediate corrective action can be taken;
  - train managers in performance review techniques such as counselling; brief employees on how the performance management system works and obtain feedback from them on how it has been applied.

■ *Training* – resignations and turnover can increase if people are not trained properly, or feel that demands are being made upon them that they cannot reasonably be expected to fulfil without proper training. New employees can go through an 'induction crisis' if they are not given adequate training when they join the organization. Learning programmes and training schemes should be developed and introduced which:

  – give employees the competence and confidence to achieve expected performance standards;
  – enhance existing skills and competences;
  – help people to acquire new skills and competences so that they can make better use of their abilities, take on greater responsibilities, undertake a greater variety of tasks and earn more under skill- and competence-based pay schemes;
  – ensure that new employees quickly acquire and learn the basic skills and knowledge needed to make a good start in their jobs;
  – increase employability, inside and outside the organization.

■ *Career development* – dissatisfaction with career prospects is a major cause of turnover. To a certain extent, this has to be accepted. More and more people recognize that to develop their careers they need to move on, and there is little their employers can do about it, especially in today's flatter organizations where promotion prospects are more limited. These are the individuals who acquire a 'portfolio' of skills and may consciously change direction several times during their careers. To a certain degree, employers should welcome this tendency. The idea of providing 'cradle to grave' careers is no longer as relevant in the more changeable job markets of today, and this self-planned, multi-skilling process provides for the availability of a greater number of qualified people. But there is still everything to be said in most organizations for maintaining a stable core workforce, and in this situation employers should still plan to provide career opportunities by:

  – providing employees with wider experience;
  – introducing more systematic procedures for identifying potential such as assessment or development centres;
  – encouraging promotion from within;
  – developing more equitable promotion procedures;
  – providing advice and guidance on career paths.

■ *Commitment* – this can be increased by:

  – explaining the organization's mission, values and strategies and encouraging employees to discuss and comment on them;

- communicating with employees in a timely and candid way, with the emphasis on face-to-face communications through such means as briefing groups;
- constantly seeking and taking into account the views of people at work;
- providing opportunities for employees to contribute their ideas on improving work systems;
- introducing organization and job changes only after consultation and discussion.

■ *Lack of group cohesion* – employees can feel isolated and unhappy if they are not part of a cohesive team or if they are bedevilled by disruptive power politics. Steps can be taken to tackle this problem through:
- teamwork: setting up self-managing or autonomous work groups or project teams;
- team building: emphasizing the importance of teamwork as a key value, rewarding people for working effectively as members of teams and developing teamwork skills.

■ *Dissatisfaction and conflict with managers and supervision* – a common reason for resignations is the feeling that management in general, or individual managers and team leaders in particular, are not providing the leadership they should, or are treating people unfairly, or are bullying their staff (not an uncommon situation). This problem should be remedied by:
- selecting managers and team leaders with well-developed leadership qualities;
- training them in leadership skills and in methods of resolving conflict and dealing with grievances;
- introducing better procedures for handling grievances and discipli- nary problems, and training everyone in how to use them.

■ *Recruitment, selection and promotion* – rapid turnover can result simply from poor selection or promotion decisions. It is essential to ensure that selection and promotion procedures match the capacities of individuals to the demands of the work they have to do.

■ *Over-marketing* – creating expectations about career development oppor- tunities, tailored training programmes, increasing employability and varied and interesting work can, if not matched with reality, lead directly to dissatisfaction and early resignation. Care should be taken not to over- sell the firm's employee development policies.

Flexibility strategy

The aims of the flexibility strategy should be to develop a 'flexible firm' (Atkinson, 1984) by providing for greater operational and role flexibility.

The steps to be considered when formulating a flexibility strategy are as follows:

- take a radical look at traditional employment patterns to find alternatives to full-time, permanent staff – this may take the form of segregating the workforce into a 'core group' and one or more peripheral groups;
- outsourcing – getting work done by external firms or individuals;
- multi-skilling to increase the ability of people to switch jobs or carry out any of the tasks that have to be undertaken by their team.

14

Strategies for managing performance

Strategies for managing performance aim to achieve increased organizational effectiveness, better results for individuals and teams, and higher levels of skill, competence, commitment and motivation. Managing performance is a continuing responsibility for managers and team leaders. It is not achieved by a once-a-year performance appraisal meeting. Individual employees are responsible for managing their own performance but may need guidance and support in doing so.

Managing performance strategies needs to recognize, in the words of Purcell (1999), that in circumstances of lean production, employees increasingly come to possess knowledge and skills that management lacks. 'Employees need to be motivated to apply these skills through discretionary effort. And it is often the case that the firm's business or production strategy can only be achieved when this discretionary effort is contributed.'

Strategies for managing performance are concerned with how the business should be managed to achieve its goals. They will refer to performance measures such as the balanced scorecard (Kaplan and Norton, 1992) which direct attention to four related questions:

1. How do customers see us?
2. What must we excel at?
3. Can we continue to improve?
4. How do we look to shareholders?

But performance comes from people, and performance management processes as described in this chapter focus on how the performance of individuals and teams can be improved through performance and personal development planning.

PERFORMANCE MANAGEMENT

Performance management processes have come to the fore in recent years as means of providing a more integrated and continuous approach than was provided by previous isolated and often inadequate merit rating or performance appraisal schemes. Performance management is based on the principle of management by agreement or contract rather than management by command. It emphasizes development and the initiation of self-managed learning plans as well as the integration of individual and corporate objectives. It can, in fact, play a major role in providing for an integrated and coherent range of human resource management processes that are mutually supportive and contribute as a whole to improving organizational effectiveness.

Performance management can be defined as a strategic and integrated approach to delivering sustained success to organizations by improving the performance of the people who work in them and by developing the capabilities of teams and individual contributors.

Performance management is strategic in the sense that it is concerned with the broader issues facing the business if it is to function effectively in its environment, and with the general direction in which it intends to go to achieve longer-term goals. It is integrated in four senses:

1. *vertical integration* – linking or aligning business, team and individual objectives;
2. *functional integration* – linking functional strategies in different parts of the business;
3. *HR integration* – linking different aspects of human resource management, especially organizational development, human resource

development and reward, to achieve a coherent approach to the management and development of people;

4. *the integration of individual needs* with those of the organization, as far as this is possible.

PURPOSE OF PERFORMANCE MANAGEMENT

Performance management strategy aims to provide the means through which better results can be obtained from the organization, teams and individuals, by understanding and managing performance within an agreed framework of planned goals, standards and competence requirements. It involves the development of processes for establishing shared understanding about what is to be achieved, and an approach to managing and developing people in a way that increases the probability that it *will* be achieved in the short and longer term. It is owned and driven by line management.

Performance management strategy is concerned, firstly, with *performance improvement* in order to achieve organizational, team and individual effectiveness. Organizations, as stated by Lawson (1995) have 'to get the right things done successfully'.

Secondly, performance management strategy is concerned with *employee development*. Performance improvement is not achievable unless there are effective processes of continuous development. This addresses the core competences of the organization and the capabilities of individuals and teams. Performance management should really be called 'performance and development management'.

Thirdly, performance management strategy is concerned with satisfying the needs and expectations of all the organization's *stakeholders* – owners, management, employees, customers, suppliers and the general public. In particular, employees are treated as partners in the enterprise whose interests are respected and who have a voice on matters that concern them, whose opinions are sought and listened to. Performance management should respect the needs of individuals and teams as well as those of the organization, although it must be recognized that they will not always coincide.

Finally, performance management strategy is concerned with *communication* and *involvement*. It aims to creates a climate in which a continuing dialogue between managers and the members of their teams take place to define expectations and share information on the organization's mission, values and objectives. Performance management can contribute to the development of a high-involvement organization by getting teams and individuals to participate in defining their objectives and the means to achieve them. Performance management strategy aims to provide the means through which better results can be obtained from the organization, teams and individuals by understanding and managing performance within an agreed framework of planned goals, standards and competence requirements.

THE SCOPE OF PERFORMANCE MANAGEMENT STRATEGY

Performance management strategy focuses on what is involved in managing the organization. It is a natural process of management, not a system or a technique (Fowler, 1990). It is also about managing within the context of the business (its internal and external environment). This will affect how performance management processes are developed, what they set out to do and how they operate. The context is important, and Jones (1995) goes as far as to say, 'manage context not performance'.

Performance management strategy concerns everyone in the business – not just managers. It rejects the cultural assumption that only managers are accountable for the performance of their teams and replaces it with the belief that responsibility is *shared* between managers and team members. In a sense, managers should regard the people who report to them as customers for the managerial contribution and services they can provide. Managers and their teams are jointly accountable for results and are jointly involved in agreeing what they need to do and how they need to do it, in monitoring performance and in taking action.

Performance management processes are part of an holistic approach to managing for performance which is the concern of everyone in the organization.

The holistic approach to performance management

'Holistic' means being all-embracing, covering every aspect of a subject. In the case of performance management strategy, this means being concerned with the whole organization. A comprehensive view is taken of the constituents of performance, how these contribute to desired outcomes at the organizational, departmental, team and individual levels, and what needs to be done to improve these outcomes. Performance management in its fullest sense is based on the belief that everything that people do at work at any level contributes to achieving the overall purpose of the organization. It is therefore concerned with what people do (their work), how they do it (their behaviour) and what they achieve (their results). It embraces all formal and informal measures adopted by an organization to increase corporate, team and individual effectiveness and continuously to develop knowledge, skill and competence. It is certainly not an isolated system run by the HR department that functions once a year (the annual appraisal) and is then forgotten. The combined impact of a number of related aspects of performance management may be expected to achieve more to improve organizational effectiveness than the various parts if they functioned separately. When designing and operating performance management, it is necessary to consider the interrelationships of each process.

The concept of performance management as an integrating force

As stated by Hartle (1995), performance management:

> should be integrated into the way the performance of the business is managed and it should link with other key processes such as business strategy, employee development, and total quality management.

Integration is achieved vertically with the business strategy and business plans and goals. Team and individual objectives are agreed that support the achievement of corporate goals. These take the form of interlocking objectives from the corporate level to the functional or business unit level, and down to teams and the individual level. Steps need to be taken to ensure that these goals are in alignment. This can be a cascading process so that objectives flow down from the top, and at each level team or individual objectives are defined in the light of higher-level goals. But it should also be a bottom-up process, individuals and teams being given the opportunity to formulate their own goals within the framework provided by the overall purpose and values of the organization. Objectives should be *agreed* not set, and this agreement should be reached through the open dialogues that take place between managers and individuals throughout the year. In other words, this needs to be seen as a partnership in which responsibility is shared and mutual expectations are defined.

Chris Bones (1996), Human Resource Director of United Distillers, explains their approach to integration:

> Setting up appraisal systems in a vacuum adds no value. They are merely a record of a convention that must take place in the context of the business strategy and annual plans. Creating the right context for the conversation is an essential part of successful performance management. In HR we have to develop and implement a range of strategies across the organization which enable excellent performance from all our employees.

In United Distillers, performance management initiatives are driven by the business vision and strategic imperatives. The initiatives and the ways in which they inter-connect are illustrated in Figure 14.1.

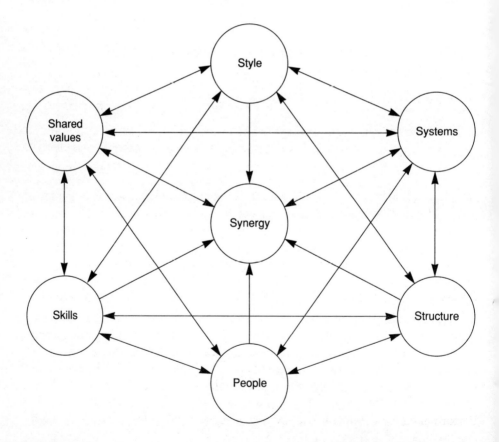

Figure 14.1   Integration at United Distillers (adapted from Bones, 1996)

Horizontal integration

Horizontal integration means aligning performance management strategies with other HR strategies concerned with valuing, paying, involving and developing people, as modelled in Figure 14.2. It can act as a powerful force in integrating these activities.

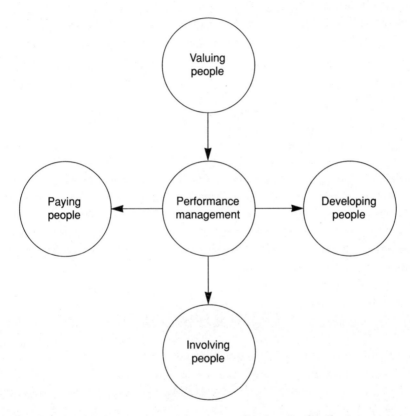

Figure 14.2 Performance management as a focal point for the integration of HR activities

THE PROCESS OF PERFORMANCE MANAGEMENT

Performance management strategy has to focus on developing a continuous and flexible process that involves managers and those whom they manage acting as partners within a framework. This should set out how they can best work together to achieve the required results. It focuses on future performance planning and improvement rather than on retrospective performance appraisal. It provides the basis for regular and frequent dialogues between managers and individuals or teams about performance and development needs. Performance management is mainly concerned with individual performance and development, but it can also be applied to teams.

Performance management reviews (individual and 360-degree feedback) provide the inputs required to create personal or team development plans, and to many people performance management is essentially a developmental process. Performance reviews can, however, produce data in the form of individual ratings that may be used as the basis for performance-related pay decisions. There are, however, strong arguments against linking performance management with performance-related pay.

Performance management is a process for measuring outputs in the shape of delivered performance compared with expectations expressed as objectives. In this respect, it focuses on targets, standards and performance measures or indicators. But it is also concerned with inputs – the knowledge, skills and competencies required to produce the expected results. It is by defining these input requirements and assessing the extent to which the expected levels of performance have been achieved by using skills and competencies effectively, that developmental needs are identified.

CONCLUSION

In conclusion, it must be emphasized that performance management strategy is not about establishing a top-down, backward-looking form of appraising people. Neither is it just a method of generating information for pay decisions. Performance management is a strategic process because it is forward-looking and developmental. It provides a framework in which managers can *support* their team members rather than dictate to them, and its impact on results will be much more significant if it is regarded as a transformational rather than as an appraisal process.

15

Strategic human resource development

Strategic human resource development (SHRD) is concerned with the development of a learning organization and the provision of learning, development and training opportunities in order to improve individual, team and organizational performance. SHRD is defined by Walton (1999) as follows:

> Strategic human resource development involves introducing, eliminating, modifying, directing and guiding processes and responsibilities in such a way that all individuals and teams are equipped with the skills, knowledge and competences they require to undertake current and future tasks required by the organization.

As described by Harrison (1997): 'Strategic HRD is a development that arises from a powerful vision about the people's abilities and potential and arises within the overall strategic framework of the business'.

SHRD takes a broad and long-term view about how HRD strategies can support the achievement of business strategies. HRD strategies flow from business strategies, but they have a positive role in helping to ensure that the business attains its goals. To do this, it is essential to develop the skills base and intellectual capital the organization requires as well as ensuring that the right quality of people are available to meet present and future needs.

SHRD AIMS

SHRD aims to produce a coherent and comprehensive framework for developing people. Much of the HRD process will be geared to providing an environment in which employees are encouraged to learn and develop. HRD activities may include traditional training programmes, but the emphasis is much more on developing intellectual capital and promoting organizational, team and individual learning. The focus is on creating a learning organization within which knowledge is managed systematically. SHRD is also about planning approaches to the encouragement of self-development (self-managed learning) with appropriate support and guidance from within the organization.

Although SHRD is business led, its policies have to take into account individual aspirations and needs. The importance of increasing employability outside as well as within the organization should be a major HRD policy consideration.

HRD and HRM

HRD policies are closely associated with that aspect of HRM that is concerned with investing in people and developing the organization's human capital. As Keep (1989) says:

> One of the primary objectives of HRM is the creation of conditions whereby the latent potential of employees will be realized and their commitment to the causes of the organization secured. This latent potential is taken to include, not merely the capacity to acquire and utilize new skills and knowledge, but also a hitherto untapped wealth of ideas about how the organization's operations might be better ordered.

THE PRINCIPAL CONCERNS OF SHRD

SHRD as described in this chapter is concerned with:

- the development of individual learning strategies;
- the development of organizational learning and the learning organization;
- knowledge management;

- the development of intellectual capital;
- developing managers;
- the development of emotional intelligence;
- the development of strategic capability.

Individual learning strategies

The individual learning strategies of an organization are driven by its human resource requirements, the latter being expressed in terms of the sort of skills and behaviours that will be required to achieve business goals. The starting point should be the approaches adopted to the provision of learning and development opportunities, bearing in mind the distinction between learning and development made by Pedler *et al* (1989), who see learning as being concerned with an increase in knowledge or a higher degree of an existing skill, whereas development is more of a different state of being or functioning.

The strategy should cover:

- how learning needs will be identified;
- the role of personal development planning and self-managed learning;
- the support that should be provided for individual learning in the form of guidance, coaching, learning resource centres, mentoring, external courses designed to meet the particular needs of individuals, internal or external training programmes and courses designed to meet the needs of groups of employees.

Organizational learning strategies

Organizations can be described as continuous learning systems (Harrison, 1997) and organizational learning has been defined by Marsick (1994) as a process of:

> Co-ordinated systems change, with mechanisms built in for individuals and groups to access, build and use organizational memory, structure and culture to develop long-term organizational capacity.

Organizational learning strategy aims to develop a firm's resource-based capability. This is in accordance with one of the basic principles of human resource management, namely that it is necessary to invest in people in order to develop the human capital required by the organization and to increase its stock of knowledge and skills. As stated by Ehrenberg and Smith (1994), human capital theory indicates that: 'The knowledge and skills a worker has – which come from education and training, including the training that experience brings – generate a certain stock of productive capital'.

Harrison (1997) has defined five principles of organizational learning:

1. The need for a powerful and cohering vision of the organization to be communicated and maintained across the workforce in order to promote awareness of the need for strategic thinking at all levels.
2. The need to develop strategy in the context of a vision that is not only powerful but also open-ended and unambiguous. This will encourage a search for a wide rather than a narrow range of strategic options, will promote lateral thinking and will orient the knowledge-creating activities of employees.
3. Within the framework of vision and goals, frequent dialogue, communication and conversations are major facilitators of organizational learning.
4. It is essential continuously to challenge people to re-examine what they take for granted.
5. It is essential to develop a conducive learning and innovation climate.

Single- and double-loop learning

Argyris (1992) suggests that organizational learning occurs under two conditions: first, when an organization achieves what is intended and second, when a mismatch between intentions and outcomes is identified and corrected. But organizations do not perform the actions that produce the learning: it is individual members of the organization who behave in ways that lead to it, although organizations can create conditions that facilitate such learning.

Argyris distinguishes between single-loop and double-loop learning. Single-loop learning organizations define the 'governing variables', ie what they expect to achieve in terms of targets and standards. They then monitor and review achievements and take corrective action as necessary, thus completing the loop. Double-loop learning occurs when the monitoring process initiates action to redefine the 'governing variables' to meet the new situation, which may be imposed by the external environment. The organization has learnt something new about what has to be achieved in the light of changed circumstances and can then decide how this should be achieved.

Developing a learning organization

The process of organizational learning is the basis for the concept of a learning organization. Wick and Leon (1995) have defined a learning organization as one that 'continually improves by rapidly creating and refining the capabilities required for future success'. Senge (1990) calls the learning organization: 'An organization that is continually expanding to create its future'. It has been described by Pedler *et al* (1989) as 'an organization which facilitates the learning of all its members and continually transforms itself'. As Burgoyne (1994) has pointed out, learning organizations have to be able to adapt to their context and develop their people to match the context.

Garvin (1993) defines a learning organization as one that is 'skilled at creating, acquiring, and transferring knowledge, and at modifying its behaviour to reflect new knowledge and insights'. He has suggested that learning organizations are good at doing five things:

1. *Systematic problem-solving* which rests heavily on the philosophy and methods of the quality movement. Its underlying ideas include:
   - relying on scientific method, rather than guesswork, for diagnosing problems – what Deming (1986) calls the 'plan-do-check-act' cycle and others refer to as 'hypothesis-generating, hypothesis-testing' techniques;
   - insisting on data rather than assumptions as the background to decision-making – what quality practitioners call 'fact-based management';
   - using simple statistical tools such as histograms, Pareto charts and cause-and-effect diagrams to organize data and draw inferences.
2. *Experimentation* – this activity involves the systematic search for and testing of new knowledge. Continuous improvement programmes ('kaizen') are an important feature in a learning organization.
3. *Learning from past experience* – learning organizations review their successes and failures, assess them systematically and record the lessons learnt in a way that employees find open and accessible. This process has been called the 'Santayana principle', quoting the philosopher George Santayana who coined the phrase: 'Those who cannot remember the past are condemned to repeat it'.
4. *Learning from others* – sometimes the most powerful insights come from looking outside one's immediate environment to gain a new perspective. This process has been called SIS – 'steal ideas shamelessly'. Another more acceptable word for it is benchmarking – a disciplined process of

identifying best practice organizations and analysing the extent to which what they are doing can be transferred, with suitable modifications, to one's own environment.

5. *Transferring knowledge quickly and efficiently throughout the organization* by seconding people with new expertise, or by education and training programmes, as long as the latter are linked explicitly with implementation.

One approach, as advocated by Senge (1990), is to focus on collective problem-solving within an organization. This is achieved using team learning and a 'soft systems' methodology whereby all the possible causes of a problem are considered in order to define more clearly those that can be dealt with and those that are insoluble.

A learning organization strategy will be based on the belief that learning is a continuous process rather than a set of discrete training activities (Sloman, 1999). It will incorporate strategies for individual and organizational learning and also for knowledge management.

Knowledge management strategies

Knowledge is the outcome of learning, but organizational learning will be enhanced if a systematic strategy of knowledge management is developed and implemented.

Knowledge management is concerned with treating knowledge as a key resource. It involves transforming knowledge resources by identifying relevant information and then sharing it so that learning can take place. The aim is to unlock the flow of knowledge and then make it flow faster in the direction of individual learners and away from the organization.

Knowledge management strategies promote the sharing of knowledge by linking people with people and by linking them to information so that they learn from other documented experiences.

Knowledge can be found in presentations, reports, databanks, libraries, policy documents and manuals. It can be moved around the organization by traditional methods such as meetings, workshops, courses, 'master classes', written publications, videos and tapes. The intranet provides an additional and very effective medium for communicating knowledge. An important aim is to unlock tacit or hidden knowledge. This can be done through knowledge interviews, which enable tacit knowledge to be articulated and then shared around the organization.

The development of intellectual capital

Intellectual capital consists of the intangible assets an organization possesses. These can be related to customers (brands, loyalty), to the organization (corporate expertise, accumulated knowledge, trade secrets, systems and methodologies) and to individuals (know-how, capability, special skills). The latter constitutes the human capital of the business and this is where HR strategies for developing intellectual capital concentrate.

The balance sheet of human capital as set out by Mayo (1998) is shown in Table 15.1.

Table 15.1 The balance sheet of human capital

Examples of assets	Examples of liabilities
■ continuous learning	■ spasmodic training
■ up-to-date expertise	■ out-of-date experience
■ continuity of teams	■ constant instability
■ shared accessible knowledge	■ knowledge localized
■ mistakes shared/learnt from	■ blame culture
■ extensive collaboration	■ insularity
■ low loss rate of talent	■ high staff turnover
■ cross-boundary careers	■ 'silo' progression
■ open and customer-focused	■ consumed with internal issues
■ flexible organization	■ rigid hierarchy

Clearly, a strategy for developing intellectual capital will concentrate on maximizing the assets and minimizing the liabilities. The basis of the strategy should be information on existing capabilities and assessments of future requirements. The scope for developing the capabilities to meet future needs can then be identified and a learning strategy can be developed.

Strategies for management development

Strategic aims

Management development strategies take a long-term view about approaches to increase the effectiveness of the organization by:

- ensuring that managers understand what is expected of them; agreeing with them objectives against which their performance will be measured and areas where competence levels need to be improved;
- identifying managers with potential, encouraging them to prepare and implement personal development plans and ensuring that they receive the required development, training and experience to equip them for more demanding responsibilities within their own locations and elsewhere in the organization;
- providing for management succession and creating a system whereby this is kept under regular review.

Management development as a business-led process

The most important thing to remember about the process of management development is that it must be business-led even though it will be concerned with the development of individual performance and potential. The business has to decide what sort of managers it needs to achieve its strategic goals and how it can best obtain and develop these managers. Even when the emphasis is on self-development, as it should be, the business must still indicate the directions in which self-development in terms of the acquisition of skills and knowledge and behavioural modification should go, possibly in the broadest of terms, but explicitly none the less.

The impact of management development

The capacity of the organization to achieve its business strategies in the light of the critical success factors for the business (innovation, quality, cost leadership, etc) depends largely on the capability of its managers as developed within the organization to meet its particular demands and circumstances. Fonda (1989) emphasizes the far-reaching nature of the management capabilities required:

- setting challenging ambitions;
- developing product-market strategies which sustain the competitiveness of the business;
- creating functional strategies that support strategic ambitions and product-market strategies;
- developing and effectively using systems for managing the business;
- shaping organizational culture for the future;
- structuring and restructuring the parts and the whole of the business in line with emerging priorities;

- optimizing profits by continually improving sales and service with today's customers and today's products.

The processes of management development

As suggested by Harrison (1997) the three essential management development activities that have to be considered when formulating the strategy are the:

- analysis of present and future management needs;
- assessment of existing and potential skills and effectiveness of managers against those needs;
- production of policy, strategy and plans to meet those needs.

Strategies for developing emotional intelligence

Leadership development strategies, according to Goleman (1999), should take account of the concept of emotional intelligence. He defines this as: 'The capacity for recognizing our own feelings and those of others, for motivating ourselves, for managing emotions well in ourselves and in our relationships'. The possession of high levels of emotional intelligence is a necessary attribute for success as a leader.

Goleman has defined four components of emotional intelligence:

1. *Self-management* – the ability to control or redirect disruptive impulses and moods and regulate own behaviour, coupled with a propensity to pursue goals with energy and persistence. The six competencies associated with this component are self-control, trustworthiness/integrity, initiative, adaptability (comfort with ambiguity) openness to change and strong desire to achieve.
2. *Self-awareness* – the ability to recognize and understand your moods, emotions and drives as well as their effect on others. This is linked to three competencies: self-confidence, realistic self-assessment and emotional self-awareness.
3. *Social awareness* – the ability to understand the emotional make-up of other people and skill in treating people according to their emotional reactions. This is linked to six competencies: empathy, expertise in building and retaining talent, organizational awareness, cross-cultural sensitivity, valuing diversity and service to clients and customers.

4. *Social skills* – proficiency in managing relationships and building networks to get the desired result from others and reach personal goals, and the ability to find common ground and build rapport. The five competencies associated with this component are: leadership, effectiveness in leading change, conflict management, influence/communication and expertise in building and leading teams.

The steps required to develop emotional intelligence suggested by Goleman (1999) are:

- assess the requirements of jobs in terms of emotional skills;
- assess individuals to identify their level of emotional intelligence – 360-degree feedback can be a powerful source of data;
- gauge readiness – ensure that people are prepared to improve their level of emotional intelligence;
- motivate people to believe that the learning experience will benefit them;
- make change self-directed – encourage people to prepare a learning plan that fits their interests, resources and goals;
- focus on clear, manageable goals – the focus must be on immediate, manageable steps, bearing in mind that cultivating a new skill is gradual with stops and starts; the old ways will re-assert themselves from time to time;
- prevent relapse – show people how they can learn lessons from the inevitable relapses;
- give performance feedback;
- encourage practice, remembering that emotional competence cannot be improved overnight;
- provide models of desired behaviours;
- encourage and reinforce – create a climate that rewards self-improvement;
- evaluate – establish sound outcome measures and then assess performance against them.

Developing strategic capability

Strategic capability consists of the ability to select the most appropriate strategy and the courses of action required to implement it, including resource requirements. As suggested by Harrison (1997), a human resource development strategy for enhancing strategic capability involves planning the kind of learning activities that will improve:

- understanding of rapidly changing business environments;
- the ability to create a strategic vision;
- understanding of strategic decision-making tools and processes;
- understanding of strategy-making modes;
- the selection and assessment of strategic decision-makers;
- the link between strategy and operational implementation;
- the quality of strategic thinking and learning;
- the management and development of the firm's knowledge base.

16

Reward strategy

Reward strategy provides specific directions on how the organization will develop and design programmes that will ensure that it rewards the behaviours and performance outcomes supporting the achievement of its business goals.

As defined by Gomez-Mejia and Balkin (1992) a reward strategy is:

> The deliberate utilization of the pay system as an essential integrating mechanism through which the efforts of various sub-units and individuals are directed toward the achievement of an organization's strategic objectives.

Reward strategy should be founded on the proposition that the ultimate source of value is people. This means that reward processes must respond creatively to their needs as well as to those of the organization. The basis of the strategy will be the organization's requirements for performance in the short and longer term as expressed in its corporate strategy. Reward strategy can support change, reinforcing and validating the thrust of the business.

HOW REWARD STRATEGY CONTRIBUTES TO THE ACHIEVEMENT OF CORPORATE GOALS

A reward strategy can make an important contribution to the achievement of corporate goals if it:

- provides for the integration of reward policies and processes with key strategies for growth and improved performance;
- underpins the organization's values, especially those concerned with innovation, teamwork, flexibility, customer service and quality;
- fits the culture and management style of the organization as it is or as it is planned to be;
- drives and supports desired behaviour at all levels by indicating to employees what types of behaviour will be rewarded, how this will take place and how their expectations will be satisfied;
- provides the competitive edge required to attract and retain the level of skills the organization needs;
- enables the organization to obtain value for money from its reward practices.

CHARACTERISTICS OF REWARD STRATEGY

As Murlis (1996) points out: 'Reward strategy will be characterized by diversity and conditioned both by the legacy of the past and the realities of the present'. Reward strategy will mainly be concerned with the direction the organization should follow in developing the right mix and levels of financial and non-financial rewards in order to support the business strategy. It will deal with:

- the demands of the business strategy, including cost constraints;
- how business performance can be driven by influencing important individual and organizational behaviours;
- helping to achieve culture change;
- meeting objectives for ensuring the organization gets and keeps high-quality employees;
- aligning organizational core competences and individual competence;
- underpinning organizational changes, for example, introducing broad-banding following a delayering exercise;

- the development of competitive pay structures;
- ensuring that reward policies are used to convey messages about the expectations and values of the organization;
- achieving the right balance between rewards for individual, team and organizational performance;
- evolving total reward processes that incorporate the best mix of financial and non-financial rewards and employee benefits;
- achieving the flexibility required when administering reward processes within fast-changing organizations existing in highly competitive or turbulent environments;
- fitting reward processes to the individual needs and expectations of employees.

The reward strategy should be backed up by a realistic action plan and should incorporate an assessment of risks and contingency plans if things go wrong. Arrangements should also be made to ensure that the results of implementing a reward strategy are evaluated against its objectives and cost budgets.

DEVELOPING A REWARD STRATEGY

The aim is to develop a reward strategy that ensures that reward policies and processes are aligned to business and HR goals, point in the same direction and will work in practice. The basic questions to be asked are:

- Where is this organization going?
- How can reward programmes help it to get there and sustain success?
- What sort of behaviour do we want?
- How can reward processes promote and provide recognition for that behaviour?

The foundation for the strategy will be the business and human resource strategies, the culture, climate and management practices of the organization, the type of people employed, and the history and present arrangements for rewards. Market considerations and government regulations (including taxation) will influence the reward strategy. It leads on to the development of reward policies and practices.

Two of the major factors affecting the development of reward strategy will be contingency needs and the achievement of strategic integration.

Contingency needs

Contingency theory states that to be effective, policies and practices should be appropriate to the organization's unique characteristics, including its culture, management style and technology and its environmental conditions. It suggests that:

- diverse organizational strategies and cultures require different reward and HR strategies;
- the usefulness of different reward and HR strategies, policies and practices varies according to the context;
- business strategies may drive HR and reward strategies, but within an organizational context there will be, in Gomez-Mejia and Balkin's (1992) words: 'reciprocal effects because managers and employees will influence emergent (*ad hoc*) strategies at different levels in the organization'.

As Gomez-Mejia and Balkin also assert: 'The notion of general principles in personnel management is essentially bankrupt and, unless legally mandated, is bound to produce sub-optimal results'.

Integrating business and reward strategy

Lawler (1995) points out that:

> The business strategy in particular serves as a critical guide in designing organization systems because it specifies what the company wants to accomplish, how it wants to behave, and the kinds of performance and performance levels it must demonstrate to be effective. The strategy should strongly influence an organization's design and management style, both of which should drive the design of reward systems. These reward systems, in turn, help to drive performance by influencing important individual and organizational behaviours.

The need to link business and reward strategy to achieve strategic integration or fit may seem obvious. Reward strategy, so it is said, should be led by business needs. But recognizing this requirement is one thing; putting it into effect is another. As Corkerton and Bevan (1998) comment:

> Of all the 'holy grails' that HR professionals seek, the one that aligns reward strategy with business strategy offers the greatest prize. But in many ways it is also the most elusive. By aligning reward and business strategies, elements of the pay bill can be targeted at the employees who add most value. And it allows reward to

exert leverage over employees' behaviour and performance by sending a clear message about what outputs or skills attract most financial recognition and pay progression. As long as the leverage is on aspects of employee performance that lead directly and unambiguously to improved business performance, everyone (except poor performers) is bound to win.

The problem with the concept of integration is one of defining exactly what it means. Does it imply the existence of a well-articulated and detailed business strategy from which flows an equally well-articulated and detailed reward strategy? Or, more simply and possibly more realistically, does integrating mean no more than linking broad statements or understandings of the strategic intentions of the business with equally broad statements or understandings of the supporting reward strategy?

The latter alternative is probably more in line with the reality of the strategy formulation process. But broad business strategies can only generate broad reward strategies in these areas. The reward strategy may be no more than a declaration of intent expressed in fairly generalized terms.

However, strategic intentions may be actioned by means of strategic plans that specify programmes and actions, and these should provide more specific guidance on reward plans. The business plans and programmes may cover such initiatives as:

- restructuring;
- business process re-engineering;
- product/market development;
- technological development;
- rationalization or diversification;
- implementation of value-based approaches.

All of these will have implications for reward strategies and plans, especially if a 'resource-based' approach to strategic planning is adopted that views the firm as a collection of capabilities to be matched to the market it serves.

The following are examples of how different aspects of business strategy, programmes and plans can influence reward strategies and policies:

- *globalization* – the need to attract and retain the highest quality of 'global managers';
- *restructuring* – the need to develop pay structures that fit and support delayered and process-based organizations and to introduce methods of payment that support and reward effective teamwork;

- *culture change* – the use of reward processes to influence and reinforce desired changes in culture, values and management style;
- *flexibility* – the development of flexible reward policies and practices that fit the flexible firm (eg rewards for core and peripheral workers);
- *behaviour* – the development of reward processes that drive and support desired behaviour in order to promote 'value-added performance';
- *product/market and technological development* – the need for reward policies and practices that will provide people with the skills and competences required to match the organization's human resource requirements;
- *cost management* – developing affordable reward packages that will provide value for money.

When developing reward strategies and plans in each of these areas, there are three key questions to be answered:

1. How will they fit the business strategy and support the achievement of business goals?
2. How can the impact of reward strategies be maximized by integrating reward processes with other HR processes so that they are mutually supportive?
3. How can we be certain that the reward strategy will enhance the organization's strategic capability?

WHAT REWARD STRATEGY LOOKS LIKE

Reward strategies deal with issues concerning pay structures, the use of job evaluation, the approach to keeping pace with market rates, paying for individual performance, competence or skill, team pay, relating bonuses to organizational performance, and the provision of pensions and benefits, including the use of flexible benefits. In practice, reward strategies come in all shapes and sizes. The following are some examples.

Glaxo Wellcome

At Glaxo Wellcome the key features of the new reward strategy developed in 1995 were expressed as follows:

- competitive market rates to attract, develop, motivate and retain quality staff;
- levels of reward that vary, depending on the contribution of the individual, team, and operating company to overall business success;
- designed to maximize the potential contribution of all employees (a strong emphasis on continuous development);
- cost-effective employee choice in determining component parts of their own benefits package.

The strategic reward processes at Glaxo Wellcome are modelled in Figure 16.1.

Figure 16.1 Reward strategy at Glaxo Wellcome

Reward strategy at British Airways

The reward strategy at British Airways flows from an analysis of business requirements and people needs and the resulting people strategy. The aim is to achieve integration in order to engage people to satisfy business needs. BA emphasizes that reward strategy is about intrinsic motivation and non-financial rewards as well as pay. There is no 'holy grail' and no such thing as a tramline that takes you along in predetermined grooves. Strategy has to be a broad church. Its formulation is a living and evolving process. The strategic planning process is illustrated in Figure 16.2.

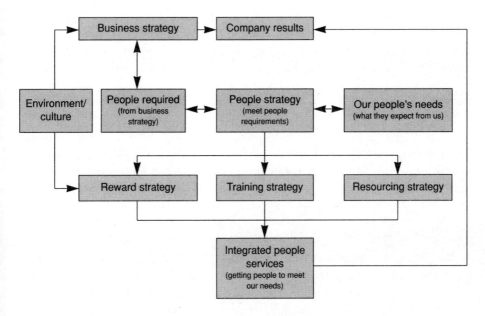

Figure 16.2   The paths to reward strategy: British Airways

BOC Gases (UK)

As described by Corkerton and Bevan (1998), the business strategy was to increase profitability. The reward strategy was to develop a new incentive pay plan based upon both the achievement of individual profit targets and wider business targets.

Customs and Excise

The aims of the pay strategy are to support departmental business needs, to secure the confidence of staff, to provide a clear link between performance and reward, to be consistent with other aspects of personnel policy (eg performance management and equal opportunities), to be affordable and to lie within the framework set by the government for public-sector pay.

First Direct

The overriding objective in developing the strategy was to ensure that it complemented the overall business objectives and that individuals all over the organization were involved in the development of its component parts. Above all, it was regarded as crucial that this strategy was seen not as a personnel initiative but rather as something that was owned by the company as a whole.

Guys' and St Thomas' Hospital Trust

To integrate reward with key strategies for growth and improved performance to underpin the organization's values, to indicate what behaviour will be rewarded and to provide the competitive edge to attract and retain the level of skills needed.

Halifax plc

- Change the emphasis from measuring the job and its accountabilities to recognizing the person and the contribution they make to the business.
- Reflect the way the organization is changing by encouraging staff to be more responsive and flexible to customers' needs.
- Improve reward for excellent performance by freeing up salary ranges.

IBM

The focus is on contribution pay – 'what you do counts'. Decisions on pay are primarily owned by line managers.

Rover Group

The pay strategy takes account of business needs, the views and aspirations of associates, and the collective bargaining environment. The strategy has to balance the following: individualism versus team approach, work groups versus overall performance, control of current processes versus innovation, achievement of goals versus calculated risk-taking, individual contribution versus market-related pay competitiveness.

Royal and Sun Alliance

To reward the acquisition and application of skills and competence and to give staff the opportunity to contribute to, and share in, the company's success.

17

Employee relations strategy

Employee relations consist of all those areas of HRM that involve general relationships with employees, through collective agreements where trade unions are recognized, and/or through commonly applied policies for employee involvement and communications.

Employee relations strategies define the intentions of the organization about what needs to be done and what needs to be changed in the ways in which the organization manages its relationships with employees and their trade unions. Like all other aspects of HR strategy, employee relations strategies will flow from the business strategy but will also aim to support it. For example, if the business strategy is to concentrate on achieving competitive edge through innovation and the delivery of quality to its customers, the employee relations strategy may emphasize processes of involvement and participation, including the implementation of programmes for continuous improvement and total quality management. If, however, the strategy for competitive advantage, or even survival, is cost-reduction, the employee relations strategy may concentrate on how this can be achieved by maximizing cooperation with the unions and employees and by minimizing detrimental effects on those employees and disruption to the organization.

Employee relations *strategies* should be distinguished from employee relations *policies*. Strategies are dynamic. They provide a sense of direction, and give an answer to the question, 'How are we going to get from here to there?'. Employee relations policies are more about the here and now. They express 'the way things are done around here' as far as dealing with unions and employees is concerned. Of course they will evolve, but this may not be a result of a strategic choice. It is when a deliberate decision is made to change policies that a strategy for achieving this change has to be formulated. Thus if the policy is to increase commitment, the strategy could consider how this might be achieved by involvement and participation processes.

CONCERNS OF EMPLOYEE RELATIONS STRATEGY

Employee relations strategy will be concerned with how to:

- build stable and cooperative relationships with employees that minimize conflict;
- achieve commitment through employee involvement and communications processes;
- develop mutuality – a common interest in achieving the organization's goals through the development of organizational cultures based on shared values between management and employees.

Strategic directions

The intentions expressed by employee relations strategies may direct the organization towards any of the following:

- changing forms of recognition, including single union recognition, or de-recognition;
- changes in the form and content of procedural agreements;
- new bargaining structures, including decentralization or single-table bargaining;
- the achievement of increased levels of commitment through involvement or participation – giving employees a voice;
- deliberately by-passing trade union representatives to communicate directly with employees;
- increasing the extent to which management controls operations in such areas as flexibility;

- generally improving the employee relations climate in order to produce more harmonious and cooperative relationships;
- developing a 'partnership' with trade unions as described at the end of this chapter, recognizing that employees are stakeholders and that it is to the advantage of both parties to work together (this could be described as a unitarist strategy aiming at increasing mutual commitment).

Four approaches to employee relations have been identified by Industrial Relations Services (1994):

1. *Adversarial:* the organization decides what it wants to do, and employees are expected to fit in. Employees only exercise power by refusing to cooperate.
2. *Traditional:* a good day-to-day working relationship, but management proposes and the workforce reacts through its elected representatives.
3. *Partnership:* the organization involves employees in the drawing up and execution of organization policies, but retains the right to manage.
4. *Power sharing:* employees are involved in both day-to-day and strategic decision-making.

Adversarial approaches are much less common than in the 1960s and 1970s. The traditional approach is still the most typical, but more interest is being expressed in partnership. Power sharing is rare.

Against the background of a preference for one of the four approaches listed above, employee relations strategy will be based on the philosophy of the organization regarding what sort of relationships between management and employees and their unions are wanted, and how they should be handled. A partnership strategy will aim to develop and maintain a positive, productive, cooperative and trusting climate of employee relations.

THE HRM APPROACH TO EMPLOYEE RELATIONS

The philosophy of HRM has been translated into the following prescriptions which constitute the HRM model for employee relations:

- a drive for commitment – winning the 'hearts and minds' of employees to get them to identify with the organization, to exert themselves more on its behalf and to remain with the organization, thus ensuring a return on their training and development;

- an emphasis on mutuality – getting the message across that 'we are all in this together' and that the interests of management and employees coincide (ie a unitarist approach);
- the organization of complementary forms of communication, such as team briefing, alongside traditional collective bargaining – ie approaching employees directly as individuals or in groups rather than through their representatives;
- a shift from collective bargaining to individual contracts;
- the use of employee involvement techniques such as quality circles or improvement groups;
- continuous pressure on quality – total quality management;
- increased flexibility in working arrangements, including multi-skilling, to provide for the more effective use of human resources, sometimes accompanied by an agreement to provide secure employment for the 'core' workers;
- emphasis on teamwork;
- harmonization of terms and conditions for all employees.

The key contrasting dimensions of traditional industrial relations and HRM have been presented by Guest (1995) and are shown in Table 17.1.

Table 17.1   The key contrasting dimensions of traditional industrial relations and HRM (based on Guest, 1995)

Dimension	Industrial Relations	HRM
Psychological contract	Compliance	Commitment
Behaviour references	Norms, custom and practice	Values/mission
Relations	Low trust, pluralist, collective	High trust, unitarist individual
Organization design	Formal roles, hierarchy, division of labour, managerial control	Flexible roles, flat structure, teamwork/autonomy, self-control

Guest notes that this model aims to support the achievement of the three main sources of competitive advantage identified by Porter (1985), namely, innovation, quality and cost leadership. Innovation and quality strategies require employee commitment, while cost leadership strategies are believed by many managements to be only achievable without a union. Guest contends that:

> The logic of a market-driven HRM strategy is that where high organizational commitment is sought, unions are irrelevant. Where cost advantage is the goal, unions and industrial relations systems appear to carry higher costs.

An HRM approach is still possible if trade unions are recognized by the organization. In this case, the strategy might be to marginalize or at least side-step them by dealing direct with employees through involvement and communications processes.

Policy options

There are a number of policy options that need to be considered when developing an employee relations strategy. The following four options have been described by Guest (1995):

1. *The new realism – a high emphasis on HRM and industrial relations.* The aim is to integrate HRM and industrial relations. This is the policy of such organizations as Rover, Nissan and Toshiba. New collaborative arrangements in the shape of single-table bargaining are usually the result of employer initiatives, but both employers and unions are often satisfied with them. They have facilitated greater flexibility, more multi-skilling, the removal of demarcations and improvements in quality. They can also extend consultation processes and accelerate moves towards single status.

2. *Traditional collectivism – priority to industrial relations without HRM.* This involves retaining the traditional pluralist industrial relations arrangements within an eventually unchanged industrial relations system. Management may take the view in these circumstances that it is easier to continue to operate with a union, since it provides a useful, well-established channel for communication and for the handling of grievance, discipline and safety issues.

3. *Individualized HRM – high priority to HRM with no industrial relations.* According to Guest, this approach is not very common, except in North American-owned firms. It is, he believes, 'essentially piecemeal and opportunistic'.

4. *The black hole – no industrial relations.* This option is becoming more prevalent in organizations in which HRM is not a policy priority for managements but where they do not see that there is a compelling reason to operate within a traditional industrial relations system. When such organizations are facing a decision on whether or not to recognize a union, they are increasingly deciding not to do so.

FORMULATING STRATEGIES

Like other business and HR strategies, those concerned with employee relations can, in Mintzberg's (1987) words, 'emerge in response to an evolving situation'. But it is still useful to spend time deliberately formulating strategies, and the aim should be to create a shared agenda that will communicate a common perspective on what needs to be done. This can be expressed in writing, but it can also be clarified through involvement and communication processes. A partnership agreement may well be the best way of getting employee relations strategies into action.

Partnership agreements

In industrial relations a partnership arrangement can be described as one in which both parties (management and the trade union) agree to work together to their mutual advantage and to achieve a climate of more cooperative and therefore less adversarial industrial relations. A partnership agreement may include undertakings from both sides; for example, management may offer job security linked to productivity and the union may agree to new forms of work organization that might require more flexibility on the part of employees.

Key values

Five key values for partnership have been set down by Rosow and Casner-Lotto (1998):

1. Mutual trust and respect.
2. A joint vision for the future and the means to achieve it.
3. Continuous exchange of information.
4. Recognition of the central role of collective bargaining.
5. Devolved decision-making.

Their research in the US indicated that if these matters were addressed success-fully by management and unions, then companies could expect productivity gains, quality improvements, a better motivated and committed workforce, and lower absenteeism and turnover rates.

The impact of partnership

The Department of Trade and Industry and Department for Education and Employment report on partnerships at work (1997) concludes that partnership is central to the strategy of successful organizations. A growing understanding that organizations must focus on customer needs has brought with it the desire to engage the attitudes and commitment of all employees in order to effectively meet those needs, says the report.

The report was based on interviews with managers and employees in 67 private and public sector organizations identified as 'innovative and successful'. It reveals how such organizations achieve significantly enhanced business performance through developing a partnership with their employees.

There are five main themes or 'paths' that the organizations identified as producing a balanced environment in which employees thrived and sought success for themselves and their organizations:

1. *Shared goals – 'understanding the business we are in'.* All employees should be involved in developing the organization's vision, resulting in a shared direction and enabling people to see how they fit into the organization and the contribution they are making. Senior managers in turn receive ideas from those who really understand the problems – and the opportu-nities.

2. *Shared culture – 'agreed values binding us together'.* In the research, 'organi-zation after organization acknowledged that a culture has to build up over time, it cannot be imposed by senior executives but must rather be developed in an atmosphere of fairness, trust and respect until it perme-ates every activity of the organization'. Once achieved, a shared culture means that employees feel respected and so give of their best.

3. *Shared learning – 'continuously improving ourselves'.* Key business benefits of shared learning include an increasing receptiveness to change, and the benefits of increased organization loyalty brought by career and personal development plans.

4. *Shared effort – 'one business driven by flexible teams'.* Change has become such an important part of our daily lives that organizations have learnt

that they cannot deal with it in an unstructured way, says the report. The response to change cannot be purely reactive, as business opportunities may be missed. While teamworking 'leads to essential cooperation across the whole organization', care must be taken to ensure that teams do not compete with each other in a counterproductive way. It is essential that the organization develops an effective communication system to ensure that the flow of information from and to teams enhances their effectiveness.

5. *Shared information* – *'effective communication throughout the enterprise'*. While most organizations work hard at downward communication, the most effective communication of all 'runs up, down and across the business in a mixture of formal systems and informal processes'. Many organizations with unions have built successful relationships with them, developing key partnership roles in the effective dissemination of information, communication and facilitation of change, while others have found representative works councils useful in consulting employees and providing information.

An important point which emerged from the research is that there are three levels, or stages, within each of these five paths. These are the levels 'at which certain elements of good practice must be established before the organization moves forward to break new ground'.

Forms of partnership agreements

There is no standard format for a partnership agreement. It will, as mentioned above, contain undertakings by both parties concerning such matters as job security, productivity, communications, involvement and working practices. But the scope of these undertakings will depend on the circumstances.

The agreement reached between the Legal and General management and the trade union MSF is an example of a partnership. It is seen by both sides as a way of improving employee relations and increasing the involvement and commitment of staff while addressing the rapidly changing business climate. It provides a workplace philosophy based on employer and union working together to achieve common goals, such as fairness and competitiveness. Both sides recognize that, although they have different constituencies and at times different interests, these can best be served by making common cause wherever possible.

18

Conclusions: getting into action

HR strategies are only as good as the effective action they produce. Formulating them is the easy part. The difficulties begin when they have to be implemented. To achieve effective action – to convert rhetoric into reality – it is necessary to:

- ensure that there is a good business case, bearing in mind the remark made by Wright (1998), a director of Mobil Services Company Limited, to the effect that 'the best HR strategy isn't an HR strategy at all. The most effective HR strategy is a *business* strategy that addresses all the important issues';
- be realistic about what can be achieved – do not attempt to do too much; incremental change is better than no change at all;
- understand what people want and what they will take by talking to them (networking) as well as conducting more formal surveys;
- be quite clear about the benefits of the strategy to the organization as a whole, to line managers and to individual employees, and be even clearer in convincing people that these benefits will accrue;

- anticipate the objections and the problems;
- identify supporters and opponents – bring the former alongside and do what you can to convince the latter;
- remember that line managers can easily ruin the implementation programme by indifference or open hostility, and you will depend on them, so get them on your side;
- bear in mind that line managers and others will need training and continued support and guidance if they are going to make the strategy happen;
- get people involved in preparing implementation plans – the more you can get line managers to do it for you the better;
- take particular care over communication;
- ensure that you have planned your resource requirements and that what you need will be available;
- prepare project plans, for any strategic innovation, which specify who does what, when and where;
- include precise objectives in your strategic plan and identify the measures that will indicate how well it is succeeding;
- monitor the implementation continuously and be prepared to step in if things are not going according to plan;
- set up formal review (milestone) meetings to assess progress and initiate corrective action when necessary;
- keep people informed of progress;
- evaluate the impact of the strategy at the first appropriate time and deal with any implementation problems that have arisen.

References

Andrews, K A (1987) *The Concept of Corporate Strategy*, Irwin, Georgetown, Ontario

Ansoff, H I (1987) *Corporate Strategy*, McGraw-Hill, New York

Argyris, C (1957) *Personality and Organization*, Harper & Row, New York

Argyris, C (1970) *Intervention Theory and Method*, Addison-Wesley, Reading, MA

Argyris, C (1992) *On Organizational Learning*, Blackwell, Cambridge, MA

Armstrong, M (1987) 'Human resource management: a case of the emperor's new clothes', *Personnel Management*, August, 30–35

Armstrong, M and Long, P (1994) *The Reality of Strategic HRM*, Institute of Personnel and Development, London

Arthur, J B (1990) 'Industrial Relations and Business Strategies in American Steel Minimills', unpublished PhD dissertation, Cornell University

Arthur, J B (1992) 'The link between business strategy and industrial relations systems in American steel mills', *Industrial and Labor Relations Review*, **45** (3), pp 488–506

Arthur, J B (1994) 'Effects of human resource systems on manufacturing performance and turnover', *Academy of Management Review*, **37** (4), pp 670–87

Atkinson, J (1984) 'Manpower strategies for flexible organizations', *Personnel Management*, August, pp 28–31

Bandura, A (1977) *Social Learning Theory*, Prentice-Hall, Englewood Cliffs, NJ

Bandura, A (1982) 'Self-efficacy mechanism in human agency', *American Psychologist*, **37**, pp 122–47

Bandura, A (1986) *Social Boundaries of Thought and Action*, Prentice-Hall, Englewood Cliffs, NJ

Barney, J (1991) 'Types of competition and the theory of strategy: towards an integrative approach', *Academy of Management Review*, **11** (4), pp 791–800

Barney, J (1995) 'Looking inside for competitive advantage', *Academy of Management Executive*, **9** (4), pp 49–61

Becker, B E, Huselid, M A, Pickus, P S and Spratt, M F (1997) 'HR as a source of shareholder value: research and recommendations', *Human Resource Management*, Spring, **36** (1), pp 39–47

Beckhard, R (1969) *Organization Development: Strategy and models*, Addison-Wesley, Reading, MA

Beckhard, R (1989) 'A model for the executive management of transformational change', in ed G Salaman, *Human Resource Strategies*, Sage, London

Beer, M, Eisenstat, R and Spector, B (1990) 'Why change programs don't produce change', *Harvard Business Review*, November–December, pp 158–66

Beer M, Spector B, Lawrence P, Quinn Mills D and Walton, R (1984) *Managing Human Assets*, The Free Press, New York

Blake, R, Shepart, H and Mouton, J (1964) 'Breakthrough in organizational development', *Harvard Business Review*, **42**, pp 237–58

Blyton, P and Turnbull, P (eds) (1992) *Reassessing Human Resource Management*, Sage, London

Bones C (1996) 'Performance management: the HR contribution', address at the Annual Conference of the Institute of Personnel and Development, Harrogate

Bower, J L (1982) 'Business policy in the 1980s', *Academy of Management Review*, **7** (4), pp 630–38

Boxall, P F (1992) 'Strategic HRM: a beginning, a new theoretical direction', *Human Resource Management Journal*, **2** (3), pp 61–79

Boxall, P F (1993) 'The significance of human resource management: a reconsideration of the evidence', *The International Journal of Human Resource Management*, **4** (3), pp 645–65

Boxall, P F (1994) 'Placing HR strategy at the heart of the business', *Personnel Management*, July, pp 32–5

Boxall, P F (1996) 'The strategic HRM debate and the resource-based view of the firm', *Human Resource Management Journal*, **6** (3), pp 59–75

Brewster, C (1993) 'Developing a "European" model of human resource management', *The International Journal of Human Resource Management*, **4** (4), pp 765–84

Bulla, D N and Scott, P M (1994) 'Manpower requirements forecasting: a case example', in eds D Ward, T P Bechet and R Tripp, *Human Resource Forecasting and Modeling*, The Human Resource Planning Society, New York

Burgoyne, J (1994) Reported in *Personnel Management Plus*, May, p 7

Burnes, B (1992) *Managing Change*, Pitman, London

Burns, J M (1978) *Leadership*, Harper & Row, New York

Cappelli, P and Crocker-Hefter, A (1996) *Organizational Dynamics*, Winter, pp 7–22

Chadwick, C and Cappelli, P (1998) 'Alternatives to generic strategy typologies in human resource management', in eds P Wright, L Dyer, J Boudreau and G Milkovich, Research in *Personnel and Human Resource Management*, JAI Press, Greenwich, CT

Chaffee, E E (1985) 'Three models of strategy', *Academy of Management Review*, **10**, 89–98

Chandler, A D (1962) *Strategy and Structure*, MIT Press, Boston, MA

Child, J (1972) 'Organizational structure, environment and performance: the role of strategic choice', *Sociology*, **6** (3), pp 1–22

Cooke, R and Armstrong, M (1990) 'Towards strategic HRM', *Personnel Management*, December, pp 30–33

Cooke, R and Lafferty, J (1989) *Organizational Culture Inventory*, Human Synergistic, Plymouth, MI

Coopey, J and Hartley, J (1991) 'Reconsidering the case for organizational commitment', *Human Resource Management Journal*, **3** (Spring), pp 18–31

Corkerton, R M and Bevan, S (1998) 'Paying hard to get', *People Management*, 13 August, pp 40–42

Cowling, A and Walters, M (1990) 'Manpower planning: where are we today?', *Personnel Review*, March

Cyert, R M and March, J G (1963) *A Behavioural Theory of the Firm*, Prentice-Hall, Englewood Cliffs, NJ

Delaney, J T and Huselid, M A (1996) 'The impact of human resource management practices on perceptions of organizational performance', *Academy of Management Journal*, **39** (4), pp 949–69

Delery, J E and Doty, H D (1996) 'Modes of theorizing in strategic human resource management: tests of universality, contingency and configurational performance predictions', *International Journal of Human Resource Management*, **6**, pp 656–70

Deming, W E (1986) *Out of the Crisis*, MIT Centre for Advanced Engineering Study, Cambridge, MA

Denison, D R (1996) 'What is the difference between organizational culture and organizational climate? A native's point of view on a decade of paradigm wars', *Academy of Management Review*, July, pp 619–54

Department of Trade and Industry and Department for Education and Employment (1997) *Partnerships at Work*, The Stationery Office, London

Digman, L A (1990) *Strategic Management – Concepts, decisions, cases*, Irwin, Georgetown, Ontario

Drucker, P E (1955) *The Practice of Management*, Heinemann, Oxford

Dyer, L (1984) 'Studying human resource strategy: an approach and an agenda', *Industrial Relations*, **23** (2), pp 156–69

Dyer, L and Holder, G W (1988) 'Strategic human resource management and planning', in ed L Dyer, *Human Resource Management: Evolving roles and responsibilities*, Bureau of National Affairs, Washington DC

Dyer, L and Reeves, T (1995) 'Human resource strategies and firm performance: what do we know and where do we need to go?', *The International Journal of Human Resource Management*, **6**, (3), pp 656–70

Eagleton, T (1983) *Literary Theory*, Blackwell, Oxford

Ehrenberg, R G and Smith, R S (1994) Modern Labor Economics. Harper Collins, New York

Evans, J (1998) 'HR Strategy in Practice', presentation at IPD National Conference, October

Faulkner, D and Johnson G (1992) *The Challenge of Strategic Management*, Kogan Page, London

Fombrun, C J, Tichy, N M and Devanna, M A (1984) *Strategic Human Resource Management*, Wiley, New York

Fonda, N (1989) 'Management development: the missing link in sustained business performance', *Personnel Management*, December, pp 50–53

Fowler, A (1987) 'When chief executives discover HRM', *Personnel Management*, January

Fowler, A (1990) 'Performance Management: the MBO of the 90s', *Personnel Management*, July, pp 47–51

Fox, A (1973) *Beyond Contract*, Faber and Faber, London

French, W L and Bell, C H (1990) *Organization Development*, Prentice-Hall, Englewood Cliffs, NJ

French, W L, Kast, F E and Rosenzweig, J E (1985) *Understanding Human Behaviour in Organizations*, Harper & Row, New York

Furnham, A and Gunter, B (1993) *Corporate Assessment*, Routledge, London

Gallie, D et al (1998) *Restructuring the Employment Relationship*, Clarendon Press, Oxford

Garratt, R (1990) *Creating a Learning Organization*, Institute of Directors, London

Garvin, D A (1993) 'Building a learning organization', *Harvard Business Review*, July–August, pp 78–91

Gennard, J and Judge, G (1997) *Employee Relations*, Institute of Personnel and Development, London

Goleman, D (1999) 'Emotional Intelligence', presentation at IPD Conference, October

Gomez-Mejia, L R and Balkin, D B (1992) *Compensation, Organizational Strategy, and Firm Performance*, Southwestern Publishing, Cincinnati, OH

Goold, M and Campbell, A (1986) *Strategies and Styles: The role of the centre in managing diversified corporations*, Blackwell, Oxford

Grant, R M (1991) 'The resource-based theory of competitive advantage: implications for strategy formulation', *California Management Review*, **33** (3), pp 114–35

Gratton, L (1999) 'People processes as a source of competitive advantage', in eds L Gratton, V H Hailey, P Stiles and C Truss, *Strategic Human Resource Management*, Oxford University Press, Oxford

Gratton, L and Hailey, V H (1999) 'The rhetoric and reality of new careers', in eds L Gratton, V H Hailey, P Stiles and C Truss, *Strategic Human Resource Management*, Oxford University Press, Oxford

Gratton, L, Hailey, V H, Stiles, P and Truss, C (1999) *Strategic Human Resource Management*, Oxford University Press, Oxford

Guest, D E (1987) 'Human resource management and industrial relations', *Journal of Management Studies*, **14** (5)

Guest, D E (1989a) 'Human resource management: its implications for industrial relations and trade unions', in ed J Storey, *New Perspectives in Human Resource Management*, Routledge, London

Guest, D E (1989b) 'Personnel and HRM: can you tell the difference?', *Personnel Management*, January, pp 48–51

Guest, D E (1990) 'Human resource management and the American dream', *Journal of Management Studies*, **27** (4), pp 378–97

Guest, D E (1991) 'Personnel management: the end of orthodoxy', British *Journal of Industrial Relations*, **29** (2), pp 149–76

Guest, D E (1992) 'Human resource management in the UK', in ed B Towers, *The Handbook of Human Resource Management*, Blackwell, Oxford

Guest, D E (1993) 'Current perspectives on human resource management in the United Kingdom', in ed C Brewster, *Current Trends in Human Resource Management in Europe*, Kogan Page, London

Guest, D E (1995) 'Human resource management: trade unions and industrial relations', in ed J Storey, *Human Resource Management; A critical text*, Routledge, London

Guest, D E (1997) 'Human resource management and performance; a review of the research agenda', *The International Journal of Human Resource Management*, **8** (3), pp 263–76

Guest, D E (1999) 'Human resource management: the workers' verdict', *Human Resource Management Journal*, **9** (2), pp 5–25

Guest, D E and Conway, N (1997) *Employee Motivation and the Psychological Contract*, Institute of Personnel and Development, London

Guest, D E and Hoque, K (1994) 'The good, the bad and the ugly: employment relationships in new non-union workplaces', *Human Resource Management Journal*, **5** (1), pp 1–14

Guest, D E and Peccei, R (1994) 'The nature and causes of effective human resource management', *British Journal of Industrial Relations*, June

Guest, D E *et al* (1996) *The State of the Psychological Contract in Employment*, Institute of Personnel and Development, London

Goold, M and Campbell, A (1986) *Strategies and Styles: The role of the centre in managing diversified corporations*, Blackwell, Oxford

Gunnigle, P and Moore, S (1994) 'Linking business strategy and human resource management: issues and implications', *Personnel Review*, **23** (1), pp 63–83

Guzzo, R A and Noonan, K A (1994) 'Human resource practices as communication and the psychological contract', *Human Resource Management*, Fall

Hailey, V H (1999) 'Managing culture', in eds L Gratton, V H Hailey, P Stiles and C Truss, *Strategic Human Resource Management*, Oxford University Press, Oxford

Hamel, G and Prahalad, C K (1989) 'Strategic intent', *The Harvard Business Review*, May–June, pp 63–76

Hamermesh, R G (1986) *Making Strategy Work – How senior managers produce results*, Wiley, New York

Handy, C (1981) *Understanding Organizations*, Penguin Books, Harmondsworth

Harrison, R (1972) 'Understanding your organization's character', *Harvard Business Review*, **5**, pp 119–28

Harrison, R (1997) *Employee Development*, 2nd edn, Institute of Personnel and Development, London

Hartle, F (1995) *Transforming the Performance Management Process*, Kogan Page, London

Heller, R (1972) *The Naked Manager*, Barrie & Jenkins, London

Hendry, C and Pettigrew, A (1986) 'The practice of strategic human resource management', *Personnel Review*, **15**, pp 2–8

Hendry, C and Pettigrew, A (1990) 'Human resource management: an agenda for the 1990s', *International Journal of Human Resource Management*, **1** (3), pp 17–43

Herriot, P, Hirsh, W and Riley, P (1998) *Trust and Transition: Managing the employment relationship*, Wiley, Chichester

Hickson, D G et al (1986) *Top Decisions: Strategic decision making in organizations*, Blackwell, Oxford

Hofer, C W and Schendel, D (1986) *Strategy Formulation: Analytical concepts*, West Publishing, New York

Huselid, M A (1995) 'The impact of human resource management practices on turnover, productivity and corporate financial performance', *Academy of Management Journal*, **38** (3), pp 635–72

Huselid, M A and Becker, B E (1996) 'Methodological issues in cross-sectional and panel estimates of the human resource-firm performance link', *Industrial Relations*, **35** (3), pp 400–422

Huselid, M A, Jackson, S E and Schuler, R S (1997) 'Technical and strategic human resource management effectiveness as determinants of firm performance', *Academy of Management Journal*, **40** (1)

Ichniowski, C (1990) 'Human resource management systems and the performance of US manufacturing businesses', *National Bureau of Economic Research*, September

Ichniowski, C, Shaw, K and Prennushi, G (1997) 'The effects of human resource management practices on productivity: a study of steel finishing lines', *The American Economic Review*, June

Institute of Personnel and Development (1994) *People Make the Difference*, IPD London

IRS (1994) 'Where are the unions going?', *Employment Trends*, (556) pp 14–16

Johnson, G (1987) *Strategic Change and the Management Process*, Blackwell, Oxford

Johnson, G and Scholes, K (1993) *Exploring Corporate Strategy*, Prentice-Hall, Hemel Hempstead

Jones, T W (1995) 'Performance management in a changing context', *Human Resource Management Fall*, pp 425–42

Kamoche, K (1996) 'Strategic human resource management within a resource capability view of the firm', *Journal of Management Studies*, **33** (2), pp 213–33

Kanter, R M (1984) *The Change Masters*, Allen & Unwin, London

Kanter, R M (1989) *When Giants Learn to Dance*, Simon & Schuster, London

Kaplan, R S and Norton, D P (1992) 'The balanced scorecard – measures that drive performance', *Harvard Business Review*, January–February, pp 71–9

Kay J (1999) 'Strategy and the illusions of grand designs', Mastering Strategy, *Financial Times*, 15 October, pp 2–4

Keenoy, T (1990a) 'HRM: a case of the wolf in sheep's clothing', *Personnel Review*, **19** (2), pp 3–9

Keenoy, T (1990b) 'HRM: rhetoric, reality and contradiction', *International Journal of Human Resource Management*, **1** (3), pp 363–84

Keenoy, T (1997) 'HRMism and the images of re-presentation', *Journal of Management Studies*, **4** (5), pp 825–41

Keenoy, T and Anthony, P (1992) 'HRM: metaphor, meaning and morality', in eds P Blyton and P Turnbull, *Reassessing Human Resource Management*, Sage Publications, London

Keep, E (1989) 'Corporate training strategies', in ed J Storey, *New Perspectives on Human Resource Management*, Blackwell, Oxford

Kessler, S and Undy, R (1996) *The New Employment Relationship: Examining the psychological contract*, Institute of Personnel and Development, London

Koch, M J and McGrath, G R (1996) 'Improving labour productivity: human resource management policies do matter', *Strategic Management Journal*, **17**, pp 335–54

Kotter, J J (1995) *A 20% Solution: Using rapid re-design to build tomorrow's organization today*, Wiley, New York

Lawler, E E (1990) *Strategic Pay*, Jossey-Bass, San Francisco, CA

Lawler, E E (1995) 'The new pay: a strategic approach', *Compensation & Benefits Review*, July–August, pp14–22

Lawson, P (1995) 'Performance management: an overview', in ed M Walters, *The Performance Management Handbook*, Institute of Personnel and Development, London

Legge, K (1978) *Power, Innovation and Problem Solving in Personnel Management*, McGraw-Hill, Maidenhead

Legge, K (1987) 'Women in personnel management: uphill climb or downhill slide?', in eds A Spencer and D Podmore, *Women in a Man's World*, Tavistock Publications, London

Legge, K (1989) 'Human resource management: a critical analysis', in ed J Storey, *New Perspectives in Human Resource Management*, Routledge, London

Legge, K (1995) *Human Resource Management; Rhetorics and realities*, Macmillan, London

Legge, K (1998) 'The morality of HRM', in eds C Mabey, D Skinner and T Clark, *Experiencing Human Resource Management*, Sage, London

Lengnick-Hall C A and Lengnick-Hall M L (1988) 'Strategic human resource management: a review of the literature and a proposed typology', *Academy of Management Review*, **13**, pp 454–70

Lengnick-Hall, C A and Lengnick-Hall, M L (1990) *Interactive Human Resource Management and Strategic Planning*, Quorum Books, Westport, CT

Lewin, K (1947) 'Frontiers in group dynamics', *Human Relations*, **1** (1), pp 5–42

Lewin, K (1951) *Field Theory in Social Science*, Harper & Row, New York

Likert, R (1961) *New Patterns of Management*, McGraw-Hill, New York

Litwin, G H and Stringer, R A (1968) *Motivation and Organizational Climate*, Harvard University Press, Boston, MA

Mabey, C, Skinner, D and Clark, T (1998) *Experiencing Human Resource Management*, Sage, London

MacDuffie, J P (1995) 'Human resource bundles and manufacturing performance', *Industrial Relations Review*, **48** (2), pp 199–221

MacMillan, I C (1983) 'Seizing strategic initiative', *Journal of Business Strategy*, pp 43–57

MacNeil, R (1985) 'Relational contract: what we do and do not know', *Wisconsin Law Review*, pp 483–525

Marchington, M (1995) 'Fairy tales and magic wands: new employment practices in perspective', *Employee Relations*, Spring, pp 51–66

Marchington, M and Parker, P (1990) *Changing Patterns of Employee Relations*, Harvester Wheatsheaf, Hemel Hempstead

Marchington, M and Wilkinson, A (1996) *Core Personnel and Development*, Institute of Personnel and Development, London

Marginson, P *et al* (1988) *Beyond the Workplace: Managing industrial relations in the multi-establishment enterprise*, Blackwell, Oxford

Marsick, V J (1994) 'Trends in managerial invention: creating a learning map' *Management Learning*, **21** (1), pp 11–33

Mayo, A (1998) 'The learning organization and knowledge management', presentation at the IPD annual conference, October

McGregor, D (1960) *The Human Side of Enterprise*, McGraw-Hill, New York

Miles, R E and Snow, C C (1978) *Organizational Strategy: Structure and process*, McGraw-Hill, New York

Miller, P (1987) 'Strategic industrial relations and human resource management: distinction, definition and recognition', *Journal of Management Studies*, **24**, pp 101–109

Miller, P (1989) 'Strategic human resource management: what it is and what it isn't', *Personnel Management*, February

Miller, P (1991) 'Strategic human resource management: an assessment of progress', *Human Resource Management Journal*, **1** (4)

Miller, A and Dess, G G (1996) *Strategic Management*, 2nd edn, McGraw-Hill, New York

Mintzberg, H (1978) 'Patterns in strategy formation', *Management Science*, May, pp 934–48

Mintzberg, H (1987) 'Crafting strategy', *Harvard Business Review*, July – August, pp 66–74

Mintzberg, H (1994) 'The rise and fall of strategic planning', *Harvard Business Review*, January – February, pp 107–14

Mintzberg, H, Quinn, J B and James, R M (1988) *The Strategy Process: Concepts, contexts and cases*, Prentice-Hall, New York

Monks, K (1992) 'Models of personnel management: a means of understanding the diversity of personnel practices?', *Human Resource Management Journal*, 3 (2), pp 29–41

Moore, J I (1992) *Writers on Strategic Management*, Penguin, Harmondsworth

Morton, R (1999) 'The Role of the HR Practitioner', presentation to IPD Professional Standards Conference, July

Murlis, H (ed.) (1996) *Pay at the Crossroads*, Institute of Personnel and Development, London

Nadler, D and Tushman, M (1980) 'A diagnostic model for organizational behaviour', in eds J R Hackman, E E Lawler and L W Porter, *Perspectives on Behaviour in Organizations*, McGraw-Hill, New York

Noon, M (1992) 'HRM: a map, model or theory?', in eds P Blyton and P Turnbull, *Reassessing Human Resource Management*, Sage, London

Pascale, R (1990) *Managing on the Edge*, Viking, London

Pascale, R and Athos, A (1981) *The Art of Japanese Management*, Simon & Schuster, New York

Patterson, M G et al (1997) *Impact of People Management Practices on Performance*, Institute of Personnel and Development, London

Pearce, J A and Robinson, R B (1988) *Strategic Management: Strategy formulation and implementation*, Irwin, Georgetown, Ontario

Pedler, M, Boydell, T and Burgoyne, J (1989) 'Towards the learning company', *Management Education and Development* 20 (1), pp 1–8

Peters, T (1988) *Thriving on Chaos*, Macmillan, London

Peters, T and Waterman, R (1982) *In Search of Excellence*, Harper & Row, New York

Pettigrew, A and Whipp, R (1991) *Managing Change for Strategic Success*, Blackwell, Oxford

Pfeffer, J (1994) *Competitive Advantage Through People*, Harvard Business School Press, Boston, MA

Pfeffer, J and Cohen, Y (1984) 'Determinants of internal labour markets in organizations', *Administrative Science Quarterly*, **29**, pp 550–72

Pfeffer, J and Salancik, G R (1978) *The External Control of Organizations: A resource dependence perspective*, Harper & Row, New York

Pickard, J (1993) 'From strife to plain sailing', *Personnel Management*, May, pp 28–31

Pil, F K and MacDuffie, J P (1996) 'The adoption of high-involvement work practices', *Industrial Relations*, **35** (3), pp 423–55

Poole, M (1990) 'Editorial: HRM in an international perspective', *International Journal of Human Resource Management*, **1** (1), pp 1–15

Porter, L W, Steers, R, Mowday, R and Boulian, P (1974) 'Organizational commitment, job satisfaction and turnover amongst psychiatric technicians', *Journal of Applied Psychology*, **59**, pp 603–9

Porter, M E (1985) *Competitive Advantage: Creating and sustaining superior performance*, The Free Press, New York

Prahalad, C K and Hamel, G (1990) 'The core competences of the organization', *Harvard Business Review*, May–June, pp 79–93

Purcell, J (1988) 'The structure and function of personnel management', in eds P Marginson *et al*, *Beyond the Workplace*, Blackwell, Oxford

Purcell, J (1989) 'The impact of corporate strategy on human resource management', in ed J Storey, *New Perspectives on Human Resource Management*, Routledge, London

Purcell, J, (1993) 'The challenge of human resource management for industrial relations research and practice', *The International Journal of Human Resource Management*, **4** (3), pp 511–27

Purcell, J (1994) 'Personnel earns a place on the board', *Personnel Management*, February, pp 26–9

Purcell, J (1999) 'Best practice or best fit: chimera or cul-de-sac', *Human Resource Management Journal*, **9** (3), pp 26–41

Purcell, J and Ahlstrand B (1994) *Human Resource Management in the Multidivisional Company*, Oxford University Press, Oxford

Quinn, J B (1980) *Strategies for Change: Logical Incrementalism*, Irwin, Georgetown, Ontario

Quinn Mills, D (1983) 'Planning with people in mind', *Harvard Business Review*, November–December, pp 97–105

Richardson, R and Thompson, M (1999) *The Impact of People Management Practices on Business Performance: A literature review*, Institute of Personnel and Development, London

Rosow, J and Casner-Lotto, J (1998) *People, Partnership and Profits: The new labor-management agenda*, Work in America Institute, New York

Rothwell, S (1995) 'Human resource planning', in ed J Storey, *Human Resource Management: A critical text*, Routledge, London

Rousseau, D M (1988) 'The construction of climate in organizational research', in eds L C Cooper and I Robertson, *International Review of Industrial and Organizational Psychology*, Wiley, Chichester

Rousseau, D M and Wade-Benzoni, K A (1994) 'Linking strategy and human resource practices: how employee and customer contracts are created', *Human Resource Management*, **33** (3), pp 463–89

Sako, M (1994) 'The informational requirement of trust in supplier relations: evidence from Japan, the UK and the USA', unpublished

Salancik, G R (1977) 'Commitment and the control of organizational behaviour and belief', in eds B M Staw and G R Salancik, *New Directions in Organizational Behaviour*, St Clair Press, Chicago, Ill

Sanchez, R (1995) 'Strategic flexibility in product competition', *Strategic Management Journal*, **16**, pp 135–59

Schein, E H (1969) *Process Consultation: Its role in organizational development*, Addison-Wesley, Reading, MA

Schein, E H (1985) *Organization Culture and Leadership*, Jossey-Bass, San Francisco, CA

Schuler, R S (1992) 'Strategic human resource management: linking people with the strategic needs of the business', *Organizational Dynamics*, **21** (1), pp 18–32

Schuler, R S and Jackson, S E (1987) 'Linking competitive strategies with human resource management practices', *Academy of Management Executive*, **9** (3), pp 207–19

Scott, A (1994) *Willing Slaves? British workers under human resource management*, Cambridge University Press, Cambridge

Senge, P (1990) *The Fifth Discipline: The art and practice of the learning organization*, Random Century, New York

Shaw, R B (1997) *Trust in the Balance*, Jossey-Bass, San Francisco, CA

Sims, R R (1994) 'Human resource management's role in clarifying the new psychological contract', *Human Resource Management*, **33** (3), pp 373–82

Sisson, K (1990) 'Introducing the Human Resource Management Journal', *Human Resource Management Journal*, **1** (1), pp 1–11

Sisson, K (1993) 'In search of HRM', *British Journal of Industrial Relations*, **31** (2), pp 201–10

Skinner, W (1981) 'Big hat no cattle: managing human resources', *Harvard Business Review*, **59**, pp 100–104

Sloman , M (1999) 'Seize the day', *People Management*, 20 May, p 31

Spellman, R (1992) 'Gaining a competitive advantage in the labour market', in ed M Armstrong, *Strategies for Human Resource Management*, Kogan Page, London

Spindler, G S (1994) 'Psychological contracts in the workplace: a lawyer's view', *Human Resource Management*, **33** (3), pp 325–33

Stacey, R D (1993) 'Strategy as order emerging from chaos', *Long Range Planning*, **26** (1), pp 10–17

Staehle, W H (1988) 'Human resource management', *Zeitshrift fur Betriebswirtschaft*, **5** (6), pp 26–37

Starkey K and McKinley, A (1993) *Strategy and the Human Resource*, Blackwell, Oxford

Stevens, J (1995) 'People management in transition', *Human Resources Management Yearbook*, AP Information Services, London

Stiles, P (1999) 'Transformation at the leading edge', in eds L Gratton, V H Hailey, P Stiles and C Truss, *Strategic Human Resource Management*, Oxford University Press, Oxford

Storey, J (1987) 'Developments in the management of human resources: an interim report', *Warwick Papers on Industrial Relations*, No 17, University of Warwick

Storey, J (1989) 'From personnel management to human resource management', in ed J Storey, *New Perspectives on Human Resource Management*, Routledge, London

Storey, J (1992a) *New Developments in the Management of Human Resources*, Blackwell, Oxford

Storey, J (1992b) 'HRM in action: the truth is out at last', *Personnel Management*, April

Storey, J (1993) 'The take-up of human resource management by mainstream companies: key lessons from research', *The International Journal of Human Resource Management*, **4** (3), pp 529–57

Storey, J and Sisson, K (1993) *Managing Human Resources and Industrial Relations*, Open University Press, Buckingham

Streek, W (1987) 'The uncertainties of management in the management of uncertainty: employer, labour relations and industrial adjustment in the 1980s', *Work, Employment and Society*, **1** (3), pp 281–308

Taylor, S (1998) *Employee Resourcing*, Institute of Personnel and Development, London

Teece, D, Pisano, G and Shuen A (1997) 'Dynamic capabilities and strategic management', *Strategic Management Journal*, **18**, pp 509–33

Thompson, A A and Strickland, A J (1990) *Strategic Management: Concepts and cases*, Irwin, Georgetown, Ontario

Thompson, M (1998) 'Trust and reward', in eds S Perkins and St John Sandringham, *Trust, Motivation and Commitment: A reader*, Strategic Remuneration Research Centre, Faringdon

Thurley, K (1979) *Supervision: A reappraisal*, Heinemann, Oxford

Torrington, D P (1989) 'Human resource management and the personnel function', in ed J Storey, *New Perspectives on Human Resource Management*, Routledge, London

Torrington, D and Hall, L (1995) *Personnel Management: A new approach*, Prentice-Hall, Englewood Cliffs, NJ

Townley, B (1989) 'Selection and appraisal: reconstructing social relations?', in ed J Storey, *New Perspectives in Human Resource Management*, Routledge, London

Truss, C (1999) 'Soft and hard models of HRM', in eds L Gratton, V H Hailey, P Stiles and C Truss, *Strategic Human Resource Management*, Oxford University Press, Oxford

Tyson, S (1985) 'Is this the very model of a modern personnel manager', *Personnel Management*, **26**, pp 35–9

Tyson, S (1997) 'Human resource strategy: a process for managing the contribution of HRM to organizational performance', *The International Journal of Human Resource Management*, **8** (3), pp 277–90

Tyson, S and Fell, A (1986) *Evaluating the Personnel Function*, Hutchinson, London

Tyson, S and Witcher, M (1994) 'Human resource strategy emerging from the recession', *Personnel Management*, August

Ulrich, D (1998) 'A new mandate for human resources', *Harvard Business Review*, January–February, pp 124–34

Ulrich, D and Lake, D (1990) *Organizational Capability: Competing from the inside out*, John Wiley, New York

US Department of Labor (1993) *High Performance Work Practices and Work Performance*, US Government Printing Office, Washington DC

Walker, J W (1992) *Human Resource Strategy*, McGraw-Hill, New York

Walton, J (1999) *Strategic Human Resource Development*, Financial Times/Prentice Hall, Harlow

Walton, R E (1985) 'From control to commitment in the workplace', *Harvard Business Review*, **63**, pp 76–84

Whipp, R (1992) 'HRM: competition and strategy', in eds P Blyton and P Turnbull, *Reassessing Human Resource Management*, Sage, London

Whittington, R (1993) *What is Strategy and Does it Matter?*, Routledge, London

Wick, C W and Leon, L S (1995) 'Creating a learning organization: from ideas to action', *Human Resource Management*, Summer, pp 299–311

Wickens, P (1987) *The Road to Nissan*, Macmillan, London

Wilkinson, A, Allen, P and Snape, E (1991) 'TQM and the management of labour', *Employee Relations*, **13** (1), pp 24–31

Willmott H (1993) 'Strength is ignorance, slavery is freedom: managing culture in modern organizations', *Journal of Management Studies*, **29** (6), pp 515–52

Wood, S (1995) 'The four pillars of human resource management: are they connected?', *Human Resource Management Journal*, **5** (5), pp 49–59

Wood, S (1996) 'High commitment management and organization in the UK', *The International Journal of Human Resource Management*, February, pp 41–58

Wood, S and Albanese, M (1995) 'Can we speak of a high commitment management on the shop floor?', *Journal of Management Studies*, March, pp 215–47

Woodward, J (1968) 'Resistance to change', *Management International Review*, **8**, pp 231–46

Wooldridge, B and Floyd, S W (1990) 'The strategy process, middle management involvement and organizational performance', *Strategic Management Journal*, **11**, pp 231–41

Wright, L (1998) 'HR Strategy in Practice', presentation at IPD National Conference, October

Wright, P M and McMahan, G C (1992) 'Theoretical perspectives for SHRM', *Journal of Management*, **18** (2), pp 295–320

Wright, P M and Snell, S A (1991) 'Towards an integrative view of strategic human resource management', *Human Resource Management Review*, **1** (3), pp 203–25

Wright, P M and Snell, S A (1998) 'Towards a unifying framework for exploring fit and flexibility in strategic human resource management', *Academy of Management Review*, **23** (4), pp 756–72

Youndt, M, Snell, S, Dean, J and Lepak, D (1996) 'Human resource management, manufacturing strategy and firm performance', *Academy of Management Journal*, **39** (4), pp 836–66

Names index

Subject index

Visit Kogan Page on-line

Comprehensive information on
Kogan Page titles

Features include

- complete catalogue listings,
  including book reviews and
  descriptions

- on-line discounts on a variety
  of titles

- special monthly promotions

- information and discounts on
  NEW titles and BESTSELLING titles

- a secure shopping basket facility
  for on-line ordering

- infoZones, with links and
  information on specific areas of
  interest

PLUS everything you need to know
about KOGAN PAGE

http://www.kogan-page.co.uk